Tea

HISTORY TERROIRS **VARIETIES**

SECOND EDITION

A FIREFLY BOOK

Published by Firefly Books Ltd. 2014

First printing

Publisher Cataloging-in-Publication Data (U.S.)

A CIP record for this title is available from the Library of Congress

Library and Archives Canada Cataloguing in Publication

A CIP record for this title is available from Library and Archives Canada

Published in the United States by
Firefly Books (U.S.) Inc.
P.O. Box 1338, Ellicott Station
Buffalo, New York 14205

Published in Canada by
Firefly Books Ltd.
50 Staples Avenue, Unit 1
Richmond Hill, Ontario L4B 0A7

We gratefully acknowledge the financial support of Québec's Société de développement des enterprises culturelles (SODEC) for the translation of this book.

The publisher gratefully acknowledges the financial support for our publishing program by the Government of Canada through the Canada Book Fund as administered by the Department of Canadian Heritage.

Printed in China

Tea

HISTORY TERROIRS VARIETIES

SECOND EDITION

THE CAMELLIA SINENSIS TEA HOUSE

Kevin Gascoyne, François Marchand, Jasmin Desharnais
and Hugo Américi

FIREFLY BOOKS

Table of Contents

FOREWORD

Tea is the ultimate universal beverage. Whether in a Mongolian yurt, a Berber encampment in the middle of the Sahara, a house in Azerbaijan, admiring a verdant Irish landscape or in the heart of the mountains of New Zealand, it is tea that warms us when we are cold and cools us when we are hot. It welcomes the arriving guest and is a promise from the departing guest to return. From China, where it originated, tea has crossed all the borders of the world. It is known and respected for its virtues and appreciated for its taste.

Celebrated by poets and adored by emperors, tea is the most widely consumed beverage in the world today and forms an integral part of the diet of millions at all levels of society. With its history that spans several millennia, a wealth of cultures that have influenced it and traditions that have raised it to its noble stature, the world of tea is so vast that it can never be completely known.

Whether it comes from the precious first harvests of spring, the sacred mountains of China or the highest gardens of Darjeeling, every cup of tea tells a story, reveals knowledge and conjures up a landscape. If we add in the expertise of master craftspeople who have passed on these traditions over several centuries we have a vast diversity of unique and exotic products.

For many years now, our approach as tasters and importers has led us to discover the terroirs of tea, the way in which it is grown and processed, the role each plays within its own culture and the economy of the country where it is produced, the evolution of the rituals that accompany its serving, and the reasons it came to be considered such a noble beverage. These discoveries have enriched our enjoyment of tea as well as our knowledge of it. This book reflects a progression that we hope will accompany you on your future taste travels.

What we offer you here is naturally a Western approach to tea, but we attribute as much importance to the plant and the places where it grows as to the master producers who devote their lives to its cultivation. For we must not forget that, just like wine, tea represents one of humanity's most fabulous achievements, using precious knowledge inherited over generations and taking advantage of the most distinct properties of its specific growing environment.

Hugo, Jasmin, François, Kevin
and the team at Camellia Sinensis Tea House

Garden in Thiashola, Nilgiri, India.

"The philosophy of tea is not a simple aesthetic in the ordinary meaning of the term, for it allows us to express, together with ethics and religion, our entire concept of man and nature. It is a form of hygiene because it requires us to be clean; it is an economy, for it shows that well-being lies in simplicity rather than in complexity and expenditure; it is a moral geometry, for it defines our size in relation to the universe. Finally, it represents the true democratic spirit of the Far East in that it transforms all its enthusiasts into aristocrats of taste."

Okakura Kakuzô, *The Book of Tea*

PREFACE

My first real contact with the diverse world of tea occurred in the early 1990s, during the hazy but exhilarating days when I was immersed in studies to prepare for worldwide competitive examinations for the title of sommelier, particularly those held in Paris in December 1994 and in Tokyo in June 1995. To become a sommelier one must acquire an in-depth knowledge of wine. What is less well known, however, is that it also requires complete mastery of world cuisine and other alcoholic beverages as well as water, coffee and, of course, tea.

The first stone in the foundation of my interest in tea was laid during my trips to Japan in 1995 and 1997, when I was totally captivated by the aniseed-infused aromas of chervil, fennel, freshly cut grass and chicken stock that emanated from some of the great Japanese Sencha and Gyokuro teas. And that was before I understood the power of their harmony with food. Since that day, tea has replaced coffee in my daily routine when it is … tea time!

The second stone in the foundation of my passion for tea was laid accidentally in 2001 when, following some health issues, I began to look into the healing power of food in order to restore the homeostasis of my body. All the scientific studies undertaken to this day arrive at the same conclusion: the active ingredients of tea — including the same catechins that are present in red wine, cocoa beans, cinnamon, blueberries, cranberries, strawberries, raspberries and blackberries, which are all complementary foods to serve with tea — have beneficial effects on both physical and mental health because they stimulate, among other things, the production of the alpha rhythm, whose relaxing waves have a calming effect on the brain.

Finally, the last but not least important stone in the foundation of my daily savoring of infusions of this ancient plant was my discovery of the tea boutiques of Camellia Sinensis. My contact with the members of the team and the highly original professionals who work there increased my knowledge and my passion a hundredfold — even a thousandfold, as this universe is almost infinite.

However, that foundation still needed to be fully described as a finished "structure" in a way that would do it justice. That has now been done with this monument to the glory of tea. For that is what the taster-importers of Camellia Sinensis offer here, in this new cathedral of tea, whose magnificent architecture is the fruit of their extensive travels through the greatest gardens of the world and of their encyclopedic knowledge.

As you peruse this reference work, which will no doubt resonate throughout many countries, you will finally be able to drink in the world of tea as no other work has allowed you to do before.

You will find out about the history and the various families of tea, the countries where tea is produced, its terroirs and its complex development. You will also learn how to prepare it, how to savor it, the words to describe it, the unlimited possibilities of pairing it with food and, of course, its multiple health benefits. As an added delight, you will find several recipes for cooking with tea.

Finally, this book represents essential nourishment for the body and mind not only of the tea drinker, but also of those who have yet to discover its delights. It is an open door into a world of culture and civilization. Step in and be carried away by its charms …

François Chartier, C. Q.
Sommelier and wine and food
correspondent for *La Presse*

INTRODUCTION

Different Ways of Drinking Tea

Consumed by millions of enthusiasts around the world, tea has, of course, been adapted to different cultures. Long before Westerners regarded it as an aristocratic beverage reserved for the elite, the Chinese consumed tea primarily for its medicinal properties. It was used as a flavoring, in soups or mixed with other ingredients, and it allowed many nomadic peoples to balance diets that were low in vitamins but rich in fat. In the first century BCE, Shen Nong's *Herbal Classic*, the first work on medicine, advised that the stimulating properties of tea "give joy to the body and sparkle to the eyes."

Over the centuries and through successive dynasties, the processing of tea leaves as well as the different ways of preparing tea evolved considerably. In China, the way of drinking tea can be classified under three main periods that correspond to three important dynasties (Tang, Song and Ming). It was successively boiled, beaten then brewed. In the second century CE, tea began to be seen as a beverage in its own right, but it was reserved for emperors and other high officials. It was only later, toward the seventh century, that tea began to be consumed by the common people. Under the Tang dynasty (618–907), Lu Yu, recognized as the first master of Chinese tea, wrote the first book devoted to tea, describing its cultivation and preparation. He raised the preparation of tea to an art. This is what he says in the *Cha Jing*, or *The Classic of Tea*:

> Tea has a thousand and one faces. If we just consider the broad categories, some tea cakes have the tanned look of boot leather, others are rounded like a zebu's chest or curled into wreaths like the clouds floating over the mountain. Still others look like waves caressed by the breeze, or fine silver tiles, transformed into a thick, creamy elixir by pouring a little water over them.

Tea has long been a part of commercial exchange. People began to trade using tea at the end of the sixth century, first between neighboring countries then farther afield, throughout the Tang dynasty. At the time, pounds of tea were exchanged for skins and horses. In the seventh century, as the Chinese were gradually making it their national drink, great harvests from Yunnan and Sichuan Provinces were transported as far north as Lhasa in Tibet, following what would later become the Tea Road: a 930-mile (1,500 km) route fraught with dangers over which a return trip took an entire year. On this legendary journey, encountering nomadic tribes from the west of China as well as Mongols, Turks and Tibetans, tea was adopted by even more enthusiasts.

In Tibet, where tea was endowed with significant spiritual value, it was enhanced with salt, yak butter and

FIRST REFERENCE Although various ancient Chinese texts mention a grass called *tu*, referring to a bitter plant that was served during ancestor worship ceremonies, the consumption of tea is documented for the first time in the *Shijing* (*The Book of Songs*, dating from the seventh century BCE).

The Tea Road in 2007.

A samovar.

goat's milk. This salty beverage prepared by brewing is a symbol of hospitality and is still served today, as it was then, in wooden bowls.

Introduced by Buddhist monks who brought it back from their pilgrimage to China, tea was first tasted in Japan in the ninth century. The Japanese transformed the daily pleasure of drinking tea into a refined, ritualized and highly spiritual practice. They invented the "Way of Tea" (*chado*), a complete art of living that incorporates the basic principles of Japanese culture. This ritual is based on the fundamental concepts of harmony, respect, purity and serenity.

As more and more trade routes were established, tea could be more easily exported. The construction of several ports, especially in Canton during the Song dynasty (960–1279), led to the organization of a maritime trade route linking China to Korea and Japan. In the 17th century, thanks to the trading caravans, Chinese tea began to arrive in Russia, Iran, Turkey and Egypt.

In Russia, the custom of drinking tea spread throughout the 18th century, after the invention of the samovar. In its traditional form, this device uses charcoal to heat a central cavity filled with water over which is placed a small teapot containing a highly concentrated infusion. Each guest can then prepare his or her tea according to taste by diluting concentrated tea with the hot water. Iran, Turkey and Afghanistan all adopted the samovar.

THE ROOTS OF THE WORD "TEA" The various words used to refer to tea were developed with the trade routes. The countries to which tea was brought by a sea route use words that begin with the letter T — "tea" in English, "Tee" in German, "thé" in French, "te" in Italian — that are all variations of the term "t'e," borrowed from *min nan hua*, a Chinese dialect from Fujian Province. On the other hand, countries to which tea was brought by an overland route (Tibet, India, Iran, Russia) use words beginning with the syllable "tch" or "ch," borrowed from the Mandarin "cha."

In Europe, the first shipment of tea was brought ashore from a Dutch trading ship in the port of Amsterdam in 1610. The Dutch subsequently shipped tea to Italy, Germany and Portugal.

In 1645, the first cases of tea from China reached the port of London. Immediately adopted by Catherine of Braganza, the wife of the English king, the habit of drinking tea spread quickly throughout the court and the upper echelons of English society. But it was only after the introduction of "five o'clock tea" by Anne, Duchess of Bedford (1783–1857), that drinking tea became part of the daily routine of the working class. Thanks to the Industrial Revolution, working hours were changing, and the evening meal was being served a few hours later than before, which left time for a pause to drink tea. In some ways, it was this pause that helped introduce tea to the lower classes.

High tea is a special moment, a break in the rhythm of daily life and a symbol of sharing. Traditional high tea is served with milk and sugar and accompanied by sandwiches, scones, biscuits or cakes.

In India, during the 19th century, when China still held a monopoly over the tea trade, the British began to cultivate it themselves in order to avoid the Chinese middlemen. Today, tea continues to play an essential role in the Indian economy as well as in the lives of the people. The preference is for strong tea mixed with several spices and boiled in milk (chai). This beverage, usually bought from street vendors, is served in a disposable earthenware bowl that is traditionally thrown on the ground after use.

In Morocco, the custom of drinking mint tea was popularized in the 19th century and survives today as an important rite of hospitality and conviviality. Tea is the national drink, consumed at all levels of society and at all hours of the day and night. It is prepared in different ways according to the region, but generally the tea is boiled in a metal teapot to which mint and sugar (sometimes even verbena or absinthe) are added. The mint tea is then poured into glasses, always from a great height to cool the tea and create a frothy beverage.

A Tuareg serves mint tea in the Sahara desert, Algeria.

13

Some Historical Milestones

2737 BCE	Founding myth of the discovery of tea by the divine Emperor Shen Nong.
1122 BCE	The *Shijing*, or *Book of Songs*, describes for the first time the use of tea leaves.
618 – 907	The Tang dynasty and the first age of tea: boiled tea.
Circa 700	Tea is distinguished from other bitter plants by the ideogram *cha*.
Circa 780	Lu Yu writes the first book devoted to tea, the *Cha Jing*, or *Classic of Tea*.
Circa 805	Buddhist monks introduce tea in Japan.
960 – 1279	The Song dynasty and the second important period in the history of Chinese tea: the age of beaten tea.
1191	A monk named Eisai (1141–1215) brings the first tea seeds to Japan. Eisai wrote a treatise on the medicinal virtues of tea in 1214.
1368 – 1644	The Ming dynasty and the beginning of the age of infused tea, as we know tea today.
1582	Sen No Rikyu codifies the Japanese tea ceremony, basing it on the principles of harmony, respect, purity and serenity, which are characteristic of the Buddhist movement.
1599	Queen Elizabeth I founds the East India Company, which held an almost total monopoly over the tea trade in the British Empire until 1834.
1610	The first importation of tea into European territory (Amsterdam), by the Dutch, is recorded.
1641 – 1853	Japan is closed to all foreign trade.
1645	Delivery of the first chests of tea at the port of London.
1712	First botanical description of the tea plant *Thea japonense* by Kaempfer.
1773	The Boston Tea Party, which was an act of rebellion against the high taxes levied on tea by the East India Company (which monopolized tea sales in the British colonies). Shipments of tea from three ships were thrown into the harbor, marking the start of the American Revolution.

Trade relations between England and China sour. The British introduce opium trafficking to China to create a dependency among the Chinese and to get them to exchange it for tea.	**Late 1700s to early 1800s**
Robert Bruce discovers wild tea plants in the jungle in Assam, India.	**1823**
The Tea Exchange opens in London.	**1834**
China's emperor orders the port of Canton closed to prevent opium trafficking. The first Opium War, between England and China, ends in the Treaty of Nanjing, in favor of the English.	**1839 – 1842**
The British Empire sends a spy, Robert Fortune, to discover China's tea-growing secrets.	**1848**
The second Opium War in China, which ends with the Treaty of Tianjin.	**1856 – 1860**
The start of the tea industry in Darjeeling, India.	**1859**
A famous clipper race from Fuzhou in China to the port of London in England takes place between the *Ariel* and the *Teaping*.	**1866**
The parasite *Hernileia vastatrix* wipes out the coffee plantations of Sri Lanka. The country switches to tea growing a few years later.	**1869**
Thomas Sullivan invents the tea bag.	**Circa 1910**
The invention of the CTC (crushing, tearing, curling) process allows for large-scale tea production.	**Circa 1930**
The introduction of a new fermentation process for Pu er teas speeds up their aging.	**Circa 1970**
Start of the Luku tea contests in Taiwan.	**1976**
Selection of 22 tea cultivars and varieties considered the best for growing tea in China.	**1987**
The Pu er speculation bubble bursts.	**2007**

PART ONE

FROM GARDEN
TO CUP

The Cultivation of Tea

THE TEA PLANT IS AN EVERGREEN TREE OF THE GENUS *CAMELLIA*, ONE OF 30 MEMBERS OF THE THEACEAE FAMILY. IN ITS WILD STATE, THE TEA TREE CAN REACH A HEIGHT OF 98 FEET (30 M), AND, ALTHOUGH IT ALSO BEARS FLOWERS AND FRUIT, ONLY THE LEAF IS USED TO PRODUCE TEA. DARK GREEN IN COLOR AND ELLIPTICAL IN SHAPE, TEA LEAVES HAVE CRENELLATED EDGES AND CAN MEASURE FROM 1/4 INCH TO 10 INCHES (5 MM TO 25 CM) IN LENGTH. ALTHOUGH IT IS INDISPUTABLE THAT THE TEA TREE ORIGINATED IN XISHUANGBANNA, IN THE CHINESE PROVINCE OF YUNNAN, WHERE IT STILL GROWS IN GREAT ABUNDANCE IN THE WILD, IT IS NOW CULTIVATED ON ALL FIVE CONTINENTS BETWEEN THE 43RD PARALLEL IN THE NORTHERN HEMISPHERE (GEORGIA, IN EASTERN EUROPE) AND THE 27TH PARALLEL IN THE SOUTHERN HEMISPHERE (THE CORRIENTES REGION OF ARGENTINA).

Tea tree varieties

Among the 200 species of *Camellia theaceae* registered today, only one, *Camellia sinensis,* is used to produce tea. This species includes three main varieties: *sinensis, assamica* and *cambodiensis.*

CAMELLIA SINENSIS VAR. SINENSIS

"Sinensis" means "from China," the country where tea was first discovered. This variety is thought to be the most ancient variety used in the cultivation of tea.

In its natural state, the *Camellia sinensis* var. *sinensis* tree can grow to a height of 20 feet (6 m). Its small, dark leaves are light in body. It is a sturdy plant that has greater resistance to cold and drought than other varieties, so it is often grown at high altitudes as well as in regions with difficult climatic conditions, such as parts of China, Japan, Iran and Turkey.

Its productive life is relatively long and in some conditions can last well over 100 years.

CAMELLIA SINENSIS VAR. ASSAMICA

Discovered by Scottish Major Robert Bruce in the region of Assam, India, in the first half of the 19th century, *Camellia sinensis* var. *assamica* is grown extensively in India, Africa and Sri Lanka. Highly suited to a tropical climate, it is grown mainly on plains and in regions that enjoy abundant rainfall.

Less aromatic than *C. s.* var. *sinensis* leaves, its large, thick leaves produce a liquor that is quite robust and very dark when oxidized. *C. s.* var. *assamica* is the tallest of the *C. sinensis* varieties. In the wild, some trees can grow to a height of 98 feet (30 m) and live several centuries. Under plantation conditions, however, the productive life of *C. s.* var. *assamica* lasts no longer than 30 to 50 years.

CAMELLIA SINENSIS VAR. CAMBODIENSIS

Large and flexible, the leaves of *Camellia sinensis* var. *cambodiensis* can grow to a length of 8 inches (20 cm). Its sensorial properties are less appreciated than those of the *C. s.* var. *sinensis* and *C. s.* var. *assamica*, therefore, *C. s.* var. *cambodiensis* is rarely used for tea cultivation. However, thanks to its excellent capacity for natural hybridization with the other two varieties, it is occasionally used to create new cultivars.

The Cultivar

The term "cultivar," a contraction of the expression "cultivated variety," is used to define a plant species that was created through hybridization or mutation and selected for its specific characteristics. As these characteristics are not necessarily transferable by seeding, the cultivar must be reproduced through cuttings in order to retain the same genetic profile.

Camellia sinensis var. *sinensis* is in the background, and in front of it is *C. s.* var. *assamica*, in Jaipur Estate, Assam, India.

As we will see a little farther on, there is a wealth of cultivars that are hardly mentioned in Western botanical registers but are officially recognized in Eastern botanical lore. For, as well as being highly capable of natural hybridization, the tea tree has been frequently crossbred to make it better adapted to its environment and more resistant to disease, as well as to develop unique aromas.

The Terroir

In addition to the choice of plant material, growing season and quality of the picking, the characteristics of a plantation — its soil, climate, altitude, latitude — are important factors that greatly influence the quality of a tea. Each region has specific agricultural properties, so the same tea tree will produce different-tasting teas depending on the conditions in which it is grown. The plant will constantly adapt to its environment, producing substances that, notably, can create interesting flavors. The notion of a "terroir" helps define the specific characteristics of a particular region or expanse of land, by examining its soil, climate, altitude and latitude in combination with the expertise of the local growers.

SOIL

The quality of the soil and the subsoil, which is an essential element in the cultivation of the tea tree, varies enormously from one region to another. Fortunately, the tea tree is endowed with a formidable ability to adapt, and it will thrive just as well in sedimentary as in volcanic soil. However, for optimum growth, it needs an acidic soil (pH 4.5 to 5.5) because acidity will help it absorb nutrients. Ideally, it should also have a soil that is rich in minerals (nitrogen, potassium, magnesium, etc.) and covered with a deep layer of humus. In addition, its central root needs to get a solid grip at a depth of up to 6 feet (1.8 m), so the soil must be loose, not limestone or clay. As tea trees need a lot of rain, the most favorable soil will be permeable and drain well but still have good moisture retention. A mountainous terrain is often ideal.

The ferruginous soil of Anxi, China, where the wulong tea Tie Guan Yin is grown.

CLIMATE

The tea tree grows best in a tropical or subtropical region. It needs plenty of rain, a minimum of about 60 inches (1,500 mm) a year, and a dry season that lasts no longer than three months. The ideal average temperature is around 65 to 68°F (18 to 20°C), with a minimum of five hours of sunshine a day and a relative humidity of 70 percent to 90 percent.

Tea trees are not very resistant to frost and wintery conditions. With the exception of some cultivars, especially those developed to resist the cold, a tea tree is likely to be killed by temperatures below 23°F (−5 °C). Moreover, if the temperature is too low over the course of the year, its growth will slow considerably.

Tea trees do, however, benefit from climatic variations, which can help develop flavors. The stress caused by weather changes disturbs the chloroplasts in the leaves and triggers a reaction from the plant, which strives to retain chlorophyll in its leaves, improving the flavor of the tea. Even the presence of certain insects may improve the flavor.

ALTITUDE

It is not unusual to see tea plantations on the steep slopes of high mountain ranges in Asia for a very good reason: these terrains produce tea of unrivaled quality. While the difficult climatic conditions found at these altitudes can stunt the growth of a tea tree, they are excellent for the development of aromas. Warm days give way to cold nights, and sun exposure is often reduced to a couple of hours a day because of the constant mist during certain seasons. Under these conditions the tea tree's growth is slowed, but the new shoots it produces carry a higher concentration of the aromatic oils that create richer flavors. At an ideal altitude of around 3,300 to 5,000 feet (1,000 to 1,500 m), mist can even be an advantage for a tea tree as, even in the dry season, the new shoots will have the moisture they need to grow. In Taiwan, as in Darjeeling, some of the best harvests are found above 6,500 feet (2,000 m).

LATITUDE

Latitude also has a major impact on the growth of tea trees. It can even be said to determine, to a certain degree, the life rhythm of the tree.

Tea is a perennial plant and, in certain regions close to the equator, its leaves can be harvested all year round. But in regions located beyond 16 degrees north or south, where daily sunlight is less than 11 hours for a period longer than five weeks, the tea tree's growth will slow down, and it will become dormant. The harvest is then postponed until the following season. This period of dormancy is highly favorable for the production of good-quality tea. When the plant awakens in the spring, the aromatic ingredients it secretes are more concentrated and often confer an exquisite taste to the tea from the first harvests of the year.

CAMELLIA SINENSIS (L.) O. KUNTZE   The tea tree has been known to the Chinese since time immemorial, but in the West the first scientific description of it was written in 1712, by Dr. Kaempfer, a physician with the Dutch East India Company, who called it *Thea japonense*. Some 40 years later, in his masterwork *Species Plantarum*, which lists all the plants then known to man, Carl von Linnaeus renamed it *Thea sinensis*. At a later date he distinguished between two different varieties: *Camellia japonica* and *Camellia sassanqua*. Note that, at the time, there were two accepted terms to define the plant: *Thea* and *Camellia*. It was not until 1959, after numerous debates among botanists, that the name *Camellia* was officially adopted by the International Code of Botanical Nomenclature. The term *Camellia* is an homage to a Moravian Jesuit called Georg Joseph Kamel (1661–1706), who studied botany in Asia at the end of the 17th century. The adjective *sinensis* was added by Linnaeus. The letter "L" also refers to the initial of Linnaeus, while "O. Kuntze" is the name of the botanist who, in 1881, combined them all to create the scientific name.

The Gardens

The domestic cultivation of tea began in the fourth century, and the first plantations probably appeared in Sichuan Province in China. Previously, tea was harvested in the forest from ancient trees growing in the wild. There are still ancient tea trees in the forests of Yunnan Province, whose leaves are used to produce rare or unique vintage teas, but today, as a general rule, tea is grown on plantations that are called "gardens" or "estates."

The size of these plantations varies enormously. Some cover less than a couple of acres, others spread over thousands of acres. Either terraced or simply covered in scattered plants, each couple of acres (1 ha) usually holds 5,000 to 15,000 tea trees. In China, the smaller gardens may belong to independent growers who carry out all the different stages of production themselves, but the several-hundred-acre estates are usually the property of large corporations that own many other estates and employ thousands of workers.

Most larger tea gardens have a name, as in Darjeeling, but this is not always the case. Elsewhere in India, such as the Nilgiri Hills, and Sri Lanka, many small-scale growers will bring their fresh leaf and sell it to a local manufacturer. These harvests are less specific and often produce lower-grade teas. These teas will often be named after the region or factory that transforms the leaf.

The largest plantations are found on the plains of Assam, Kenya and the other more industrial regions of Argentina. The smallest gardens are usually spread over the hillsides of very steep mountains at altitudes of up to 8,500 feet (2,600 m).

TAKING CUTTINGS Today, the most common method of producing new tea plants is by taking cuttings. This technique for the propagation of plant species consists of cutting a leaf-bearing stem from a mother plant, then planting it directly into the soil in order to obtain a new plant endowed with the same genetic characteristics. This technique ensures a more homogeneous output with the same sensorial properties and higher yields. However, this method of production can be problematic, as all the plants obtained are clones of a mother plant that has both strengths and weaknesses. If a tree contracts a disease, for example, it may quickly spread throughout the plantation. It is to circumvent this risk that the propagation of tea trees is usually performed using a combination of the two methods of reproduction: seeding and taking cuttings.

Workers manually picking tea leaves in the rain at the Hunwal Estate plantation in Assam, India.

The Coonoor Garden in the Nilgiri Hills, India.

A Bai Ye tea tree nursery for the production of Anji Bai Cha.

Straw is strewn between rows of tea trees, Japan.

PLANTATION MAINTENANCE

The cultivation of tea requires a lot of work and skill. This is why, in most tea-producing countries, there are research centers devoted to the study and creation of new, more resistant cultivars that are capable of adapting to a given climate and offer more interesting sensory characteristics. This work has led to the development of a new growing technique that makes it easier to hybridize and clone the best cultivars. Previously, seeding techniques were quite risky and did not allow the production of uniform crops, especially since the tea tree's prolific natural capacity for hybridization generated new strains that were vastly different from one another.

As well as the constant work of clearing, draining, plowing and weeding that is essential to all agricultural endeavors, tea growers must wait at least three to five years before they see any return on a young tea tree. During this time, the young plant is cared for so that it will become a strong tree. Since, in its natural form, a tea tree can grow to a maximum height of 20–100 feet (6 m to 30 m) depending on the variety, it is regularly pruned so that it grows no higher than about 3 feet (1 m), thus making it easier to harvest the leaves. In addition to stimulating the growth of new shoots, this pruning, which is called "shaping," forces the plant to branch out and develop along a horizontal plane, forming a so-called "picking table."

Throughout its average life span of 30 to 50 years, a tea tree will undergo regular pruning to help maintain a healthy yield. In addition to the frequent shaping, the tree will be more heavily pruned every five years to stimulate regeneration, strengthening the plant's structure and increasing its growth.

In order to filter the sunshine and introduce essential nitrogen into the soil, "shade trees" of other species are used. Pruning waste and straw are strewn between the plants to protect and develop the topsoil.

Tea Harvests

PICKING TEA LEAVES IS A SIMPLE YET CRITICAL ACTIVITY THAT INVOLVES DETACHING THE YOUNG SHOOTS FROM THE PLANTS. IN ALMOST ALL COUNTRIES, THIS TASK IS ENTRUSTED TO THE DELICATE HANDS OF WOMEN. THE PICKERS MUST PINCH THE DELICATE SHOOTS BETWEEN THEIR THUMB AND FOREFINGER, ACCORDING TO THE TYPE OF PICKING DESIRED, AND THEN PLACE THE LEAVES IN A BAMBOO BASKET OR BAG THAT THEY CARRY BEHIND THEM. IT IS A CRITICAL OPERATION BECAUSE THE QUANTITY OF AROMATIC SUBSTANCES FOUND IN THE LEAVES VARIES ACCORDING TO THEIR DEGREE OF MATURITY. THE YOUNGER THE LEAF, THE HIGHER THE CONCENTRATION OF DESIRABLE AROMATIC COMPOUNDS; HOWEVER, THE YOUNGER THE LEAF, THE SMALLER IT IS AND THE SMALLER THE HARVEST WILL BE. THEREFORE, THE YIELD OF A GARDEN AND THE TASTE QUALITY OF THE TEA WILL DEPEND TO A VERY LARGE DEGREE ON THE MOMENT CHOSEN TO HARVEST THE LEAVES.

The garden where Huang Shan Mao Feng tea is grown, Anhui Province, China.

A bud and two leaves.

Picking Lu An Gua Pian green tea.

In tropical regions where the climatic conditions are favorable, tea trees grow continuously. Therefore, the leaves can be harvested all year round, at intervals of 4 to15 days. In more temperate or mountainous regions, picking follows the rhythm of the seasons and weather and usually takes place from April to November. However, certain times of year are more favorable for the blossoming of aromas. For example, because the delicate and tender leaves from the first harvest of the year contain more concentrated aromatic oils, they are the most highly prized.

The Three Traditional Tea-Picking Styles

The term "pekoe" is used for the young shoot located at the end of each stem (also called the terminal bud). As this bud has not yet unfurled, it is usually covered with a fine down. In fact, "pekoe," from the Chinese

pak-ho, is often used to describe the fine down on a newborn's skin. This pekoe serves as a reference for the three types of tea-leaf picking: imperial picking, fine picking and medium picking.

As it includes only the bud and the first leaf below it, imperial or "super-fine" picking is the most prestigious. It is, in fact, for this reason that in the China of ancient times it was reserved for the use of emperors and high officials, hence the name. It is usually harvested once per year, in the spring. Also of very high quality, fine picking harvests the bud and the first two leaves. Medium picking harvests the bud and the following three leaves.

Today, there are many machines for harvesting tea, but they are less practical on sloped terrain and cannot carry out the delicate picking achieved by the hands of an expert. This is why, to obtain the best harvest in the small gardens on high, steep slopes or in countries where labor costs remain low, manual picking is still prevalent.

It takes 10 pounds (5 kg) of fresh leaves, about 12,000 shoots, to produce 2 pounds (1 kg) of tea. In India, a tea picker will harvest on average 65 to 110 pounds (30 to 50 kg) of leaves per day.

The Tea Families

Before Robert Fortune discovered the "secrets" of tea in the mid-19th century (see page 156), Europeans believed that green teas and black teas came from different plants. We know today that it is the phenomenon of oxidation that modifies the natural state of the leaves, changing the color and taste.

Oxidation is produced by oxidase, enzymes that reacts when the cells of a tea leaf are broken. Reacting with oxygen, these enzymes trigger the oxidation of the leaf, so it is possible to change freshly harvested leaves into any type of tea.

If how the leaves are picked is one of the determining factors regarding the quality of a tea, mastering the process of transforming those leaves, often done through traditional knowledge, is the decisive factor regarding a tea's final taste. First, oxidation must take place shortly after harvesting, which is why most plantations have their own processing plant (a factory) to process the leaves as soon as they arrive from the garden. Smaller growers who do not have their own factory often join together to send their harvest to a larger producer who can process the leaves.

Each family of teas comes from a particular method of processing the leaves, which we will review in greater detail in relation to each country. For example, to obtain a green tea, the leaves must be "fired" or steamed to disable the enzymes that causes oxidation. A light and controlled oxidation is permitted in the case of wulongs. Whereas with black teas, oxidation is often fully encouraged, with leaves exposed to humidity (80 percent to 90 percent) and to an ambient temperature of 71 to 74°F (22 to 23°C).

There are six main categories or families of tea: white, green, yellow, wulong (or oolong), black and Pu er (or sometimes Pu-erh).

WHITE TEAS

The best white teas come from prized harvests consisting entirely of buds. White teas also undergo the least handling. The leaves are dried naturally or with the help of fans to eliminate some of their moisture. The liquid they yield is delicate, extremely refreshing and less likely to contain much caffeine.

A few examples of the vast array of tea infusions and tea leaves.

Chai, which is a blend of tea and spices.

A green tea scented with flowers.

GREEN TEAS

Produced mainly in China and Japan, where over 1,500 varieties can be found, green teas are the preferred beverages of these countries. The fresh leaves are dehydrated to prevent any possibility of oxidation, which increases the "green," plant characteristics of the beverage.

YELLOW TEAS

The rare yellow teas undergo slight post-oxidation by steaming under a damp cloth while the leaves are still warm from being dehydrated. This produces a slight enzymic oxidation, giving the leaves and the liquid obtained from them a yellowish hue.

WULONG TEAS

Wulong teas (often referred to as "oolong" in English; "wulong" is the official Mandarin translation), processed according to a three-century-old tradition, are teas that undergo partial oxidation before being twisted or rolled. The Chinese and Taiwanese produce

two main types: teas that undergo 10 percent to 30 percent oxidation and whose slightly sweet floral aromas are similar to those of green tea, and those that undergo 40 percent to 70 percent oxidation, which gives them woody, fruity and sometimes caramelized notes. "Wulong" means "black dragon" and refers to the black snakes that coil around the branches of the tea trees. To reassure the children who were scared of them, adults told them they were really little black dragons.

BLACK TEAS

Black teas undergo a more rigorous oxidation. Referring to the copper color of the infusion they produce, the Chinese call them red teas.

PU ER STYLE TEAS

Pu er (also Pu-erh) teas, which originated in Yunnan Province (in the south of China), where tea was harvested from ancient trees growing in the wild before being compressed for transportation, remain a Chinese specialty. Chinese medicine practitioners have used them for centuries for their digestive properties and cleansing action.

Flavored or Scented Teas

In addition to the six families of "natural" teas, it is possible to buy teas to which flower, fruit or spice-based flavors have been added in order to create a new type of tea. Although this is a totally different approach, it is undeniable that the flavoring of tea is an art in its own right and must be taken into account as another facet of this fascinating world.

Scented teas are created by adding flowers or blended spices to the leaves, whereas flavored teas are produced by spraying the leaves with the essential oils of fruits or with synthetic flavorings.

The preparation of a flower-scented tea traditionally involves the use of a layered dryer in which rows of flowers are alternated with rows of tea leaves. In this process, the quality of the flowers is more important than the quality of the tea, but a lot of care must be taken to achieve the right balance between the slight bitterness of the tea and the fragrance of the flowers. Heated to a temperature of 104°F (40°C) for a period of about 12 hours, the leaves absorb the perfume of the flowers with which they are dried. Depending on the intensity of the aroma desired, the tea leaves will be treated four to eight times, with the flowers being changed every 12 hours.

Smoked Teas

Produced from coarsely harvested teas called *su-chong*, smoked teas are dried over burning spruce, which gives them a specific flavor. This process was probably discovered by accident in Fujian Province in the early 19th century.

Legend has it that a tea grower — forced by the government to give up his warehouse but not wanting to lose his latest crop, which was still moist — had the idea of placing the leaves over some spruce that was burning nearby. The leaves dried quickly and, in the process, acquired a smoky aroma. Although he was proud of his discovery, the grower had difficulty finding someone to buy his tea. Finally, a foreign merchant, enchanted by the smoky character of the tea, brought it back with him to Europe, where it became very popular.

33

PART TWO

FROM ONE TERROIR TO ANOTHER

CONSIDERING THE HIGH GLOBAL DEMAND FOR TEA, IT IS NOT SURPRISING THAT THE MAJORITY OF TEAS THAT ARE EXPORTED TO THE WEST OR ELSEWHERE ARE INDUSTRIALLY PRODUCED. THIS LARGE-SCALE PRODUCTION TENDS TO BE MORE CONCERNED WITH PRODUCTIVITY. THEREFORE, IN ORDER TO CONCENTRATE MORE ON QUALITY, WE HAVE CHOSEN TO LOOK AT THE MOST UNUSUAL TERROIRS, THOSE THAT REVEAL THE PARTICULAR CHARACTER OF A REGION OR A PARTICULAR EXPERTISE.

China

WITH A RICH CULTURAL HISTORY GOING BACK THOU-SANDS OF YEARS, CHINA — WHERE GUNPOWDER, PRINTING AND THE COMPASS WERE INVENTED — IS THE CRADLE OF NUMEROUS DISCOVERIES THAT HAVE TRANSFORMED CIVILIZATIONS THE WORLD OVER. THE DISCOVERY OF TEA IS JUST ONE ELEMENT OF THIS CULTURAL HERITAGE, TAKING ROOT IN CHINA BEFORE CONQUERING THE OTHER CON-TINENTS. OVER THE CENTURIES, TEA HAS NATURALLY EMER-GED AS AN ESSENTIAL PRODUCT, ADOPTED FOR ITS MEDICINAL BENEFITS BEFORE BECOMING PART OF THE EVERYDAY LIFE OF CHINESE SOCIETY. TODAY, CHINA IS REMARKABLE FOR THE WIDE VARIETY OF TEAS IT PRODUCES, THE DIVERSITY OF ITS TERROIRS AND ITS INCOMPARABLE EXPERTISE, WHICH HAS BEEN HANDED DOWN THROUGH A CULTURE THAT HAS MADE TEA A WAY OF LIFE.

A wild tea tree at Nannuo Shan, in Yunnan Province, China.

History

China is where tea was born. Chinese legends that speak of its discovery are so ancient it would be easy to believe that tea has always existed there. But if tea has been known in China since time immemorial, it has not always been in its current form. Indeed, different ways of growing and drinking it have evolved over time and according to changing customs.

SHEN NONG — THE FOUNDING MYTH

Among the Chinese legends that recount the discovery of tea, the oldest dates from 2737 BCE. It involves the mythic Emperor Shen Nong (known as the "Divine Emperor"), who, it is said, habitually tried new plants to discover their curative properties. Suffering from an unusual malady, he sat under a tree, put some water on to boil to purify it and then fell asleep from exhaustion. When he awoke, he noticed that some leaves had fallen into the water. Intrigued, he tasted the infusion and realized that, in spite of its bitter taste, it was able to both detoxify and stimulate him.

Taking this legend into account, it is possible to say that tea has been used in the Chinese pharmacopoeia for over 4,000 years. According to Lu Yu, author of the first work devoted to tea, it was in the time of the Zhou dynasty (1121–256 BCE) that tea became a popular drink. Until then tea had been used medicinally or as a food, mixed into soup or with other foods. It was not until the Han dynasty (206 BCE–220 CE) that tea was considered a beverage in its own right.

THREE DYNASTIES, THREE AGES OF TEA

Chinese feudal society was at its peak in the pros-perous days of the Tang dynasty (618–907). During this era, the art of tea was developing along with the arts of painting, calligraphy and poetry. Strong economic growth, a rich social life and the abundance of cultural exchanges combined to create the conditions necessary for the spread of a culture centered on tea. More and more plantations appeared, the art of tea growing progressed and more specialized techniques for the processing of tea were developed.

It is also during this dynasty that tea was democratized. Whereas courtiers, nobles, intellectuals and monks had always been accustomed to receiving their visitors over a serene cup of tea, this privilege now became a popular pastime. The custom quickly spread through every level of society. Tea became the beverage of choice for poets, artists and philosophers, as it was cheaper and more stimulating than alcohol. In addition, tea became an essential element of nomadic peoples' diets, which was very poor in vitamins. This growing popularity triggered, among other things, the founding of the first teahouses. Poetry, ceramics and painting also contributed to the burgeoning of tea culture as a true art.

During the Tang dynasty, tea was not prepared in the same way it is today. At that time, tea was compressed into bricks that were then softened so they could be crumbled with a mortar and pestle. The resulting powder was mixed with salt water and sometimes with ginger, onion, orange zest and rice before being boiled. The broth was drunk from small wooden bowls and was more like a soup than an infusion. For Lu Yu, who was largely responsible for spreading the idea that tea should be consumed without the addition of any other ingredients, "These drinks were no better than the rinsing water of gutters." Tea was also shaped into bricks to make it easier to transport because, from the south of China to the north of Tibet, tea traveled more than 900 miles (1,500 km). It would have been extremely bulky to carry several pounds of loose-leaf tea on the back of a donkey.

During this time, the popularity of tea was expanding beyond China. Entranced with the taste and the benefits of tea, neighboring countries, such as Korea and Mongolia, and many nomadic tribes

39

became major consumers. Recognizing that trading in tea bricks could increase court revenues, tea became a valuable exchange currency. Under the Tang dynasty, the Ministry of Horses and Tea was set up so that the Chinese could exchange their tea bricks for Mongolian horses, a trade that allowed them, among other things, to create their cavalry regiment.

During the Song dynasty (960–1279), important changes occurred in the way tea was manufactured and consumed: it was the age of beaten tea. The dried leaves were ground with a millstone to obtain a fine powder that was then beaten in a bowl with a bamboo whip until "jade foam" appeared. The Japanese, who were introduced to tea during this period by Buddhist monks, still use this process during the *chanoyu*, the tea ceremony.

Among the general population, using and drinking tea was becoming an easier process. It grew in popularity as its processing time was reduced and its preparation was simplified. The custom of "precious" harvests began, when only the bud and the first leaf of the first spring harvest were picked. These were called imperial harvests, and the crop was reserved for the emperors. More luxurious accessories also appeared. Finished with a dark glaze that enhanced the jade green hue of the tea, wide and flat ceramic bowls gradually replaced wooden bowls.

Unfortunately, the end of the 13th century was marked in China by the invasion of Mongol hordes, which slowed down the diffusion of tea. It was not until the cultural renaissance of the Ming dynasty (1368–1644), almost a century later, that tea culture was reborn. It was at this time that tea began to be prepared as we do it today, by pouring simmering water over dried leaves, marking the beginning of the age of brewed tea. Most of the instruments that serve to brew tea today (kettles, teapots, *gaiwans*, cups without handles, etc.) were invented during this period.

The Qing dynasty (1644–1914) was another important period in the history of tea in China. Indeed, several prestigious teas were named during the Qing dynasty. The famous Bi Luo Chun and Long Jing were named by the Emperor Qianlong. During this time the Chinese also lost their monopoly over the tea trade. High demand in Europe encouraged the cultivation of tea in other parts of Eastern Asia and in India, Africa and Sri Lanka. Having discovered the secrets of tea (see page 156), the British no longer needed to rely on China to satisfy their thirst for it.

Throughout the 20th century — with the demise of the imperial era, the Japanese invasion of China and the civil war followed by the communist revolution of 1949 — China underwent fundamental changes in its society and customs. The Cultural Revolution

THE STORY OF LU YU   Abandoned on the banks of a river, Lu Yu was adopted by a Zen monk from the Dragon Cloud monastery. Despite the influence of the environment in which he was raised, Lu Yu remained indifferent to Zen teachings and quickly discovered other interests. According to the story, he took advantage of a traveling theater troupe to flee the monastery and join the actors as they traveled throughout China. Lu Yu became famous for his talents as a teataster, his mastery of the method to prepare tea and for having written *Cha Jing*, the first book devoted to tea. The book was published around 780 and different versions, translated into several languages, are still available today. This was a unique moment in the history of tea.

Tea, the elixir of life.

(1966–1976) in particular, with its slogans like "we must forget the past and march toward the future," was especially detrimental to tea culture. Most teahouses closed. Tea growers, most of them the bearers of a long family tradition, were set to other tasks, often in distant provinces. During this century, the use of intensive production and industrial processing techniques for tea were greatly expanded. Tea bags and iced tea in cans also appeared on the Chinese market.

With the softening of the regime since the late 1980s, we have seen a renewed vigor in the tea industry in China. Several prestigious teahouses have reappeared. Universities and agricultural schools are specializing in the study of tea. In order to develop the culture of tea on a more scientific basis, the Institute for Research into the Culture of Tea in China was founded in 1993 in Hangzhou. Museums devoted to tea and teapots are also being opened. Cultural associations, festivals and various activities are organized in order to emphasize the importance of the cultivation of tea in Chinese culture and to further stimulate the industry.

Today, with the emergence of a newly affluent level of society in China, lifestyles are changing and the demands of the nouveau riche in regard to tea are encouraging the growth of an increasingly refined market.

Chinese Terroirs

China covers a vast territory, and tea growing spreads over thousands of miles. More than 3.7 million acres (1.5 million ha) are devoted to tea plantations. The best estates are concentrated in the southeastern part of China, particularly Fujian, Zhejiang and Anhui Provinces. The coastal provinces, with their mild, misty climate and numerous mountain ranges, are also favored terrain. Further south, Yunnan Province, where the tea tree originated, is famous for its tea production.

The remarkable variety of the weather and geological conditions of each of these regions gives the tea leaves produced there a unique character. In fact, these teas are often named after the region where they are grown.

We can divide China into four regions: the southwest region, the southeast region and the regions located to the south and the north of the Yangzi Jiang River. We present here the most important tea-producing provinces in each of these regions.

The village of Yiban in Yunnan Province.

THE SOUTHWEST REGION

The southwest region includes the provinces of Yunnan, Sichuan and Guizhou. In spite of its irregular terrain, the overall climate is generally mild and humid (subtropical) but punctuated by a season of heavy rains. The high mountains offer very diverse climatic conditions in relation to the elevation.

YUNNAN PROVINCE

Considered to be the birthplace of tea, Yunnan Province is undoubtedly one of the most ancient tea-growing regions. Wild tea trees, one of which is reputed to be 1,700 years old, can still be found in the tropical forests of Xishuangbanna. Its extremely varied terrain includes mountains with peaks soaring to over 6,500 feet (2,000 m). Yunnan has a temperate, moist climate that alternates between hot summers and mild winters. The region has an average annual rainfall of between 40 and 80 inches (1,000 to 2,000 mm). Yunnan Province is also blessed with a rich red soil that abounds in organic materials. This region has always offered ideal conditions for the cultivation of tea.

True to the tradition preserved over thousands of years, Yunnan still produces bricks of Pu er tea. In fact, black teas and Pu er teas represent the two major specialties of the region. The town of Pu er,

43

which for a long time was the starting point of the Tea Road, is still an important trading center. Indeed, the recent enthusiasm for this type of tea has convinced several growers to follow the market trend and give up the cultivation of green or black teas in favor of the Pu er style. However, Yunnan Province remains one of the major producers of black teas, including the famous Yunnan Hong Gong Fu.

THE SOUTHEAST REGION

The southeast region includes the provinces of Guangdong, Guangxi and Fujian as well as the island province of Hainan. It produces many famous teas belonging to the six families, including Anxi Tie Guan Yin, Bai Hao Yin Zhen, Bai Mu Dan, Zhenghe Hong Gong Fu, Da Hong Pao, Rou Gui, Zhi Lan Xiang, Qi Lan Xiang, Huang Zhi Xiang and Mi Lan.

The most common soil type is old clay soil that contains both red and yellow clay.

Except in the north of Fujian, the temperature is warm, with an annual average of 66 to 72°F (19 to 22°C), the rainfall is abundant, with 45 to 80 inches (1,200 to 2,000 mm) annually, and the picking season extends over a period of 10 months.

FUJIAN PROVINCE

Fujian Province, a region with a subtropical climate (meaning hot, humid summers and mild winters) is renowned for the variety of teas it produces. The mountainous massif of the Wuyi is famous for its wulong teas, and the Anxi district produces excellent Tie Guan Yin varieties. The plentiful organic matter contained in the rich, deep soil of this region is ideal for growing the best white teas, which can be found mainly in the Tai Mu mountains and near the towns of Zhenghe and Jianyang. Fujian is also said to be the birthplace of black teas and wulong teas.

THE REGION SOUTH OF THE YANGZI JIANG RIVER

The provinces of the region south of the Yangzi Jiang River are Zhejiang, Hunan, Jiangxi and the southern parts of the provinces of Anhui, Jiangsu and Hubei. Two-thirds of the tea produced in China, including several famous teas, come from this region. Most plantations are located on hillsides, and some of them are at very high altitudes. The mountainous terrain is extremely favorable for the production of high-quality teas, as the plantations enjoy excellent soil drainage and plentiful sunlight.

The annual temperature varies from 59 to 65°F (15 to 18°C), and rainfall, which is concentrated in the spring and summer, can be up to 55 to 63 inches (1,400 to 1,600 mm) annually. The soil is red with yellow and yellowish-brown patches, and it can be alluvial in places. The soil quality is also excellent for pottery and is used, in particular, in the production of the famous Yixing teapots (see page 202).

ZHEJIANG PROVINCE

Zhejiang, a rich coastal province, produces mainly green teas. These plantations enjoy a moist, subtropical climate and alluvial soil that is rich in minerals. Production includes high-quality vintages made according to traditional methods, such as Long Jing, Anji Bai Cha and Huiming, as well as lesser-quality teas industrially manufactured for export, such as the Gunpowder brand. This diversity is due to the fact that some plantations are in the mountains, where the best teas are cultivated, and others are on the plains, where industrial teas are grown.

ANHUI PROVINCE

Renowned for the beauty of its landscape, Anhui Province produces teas of exceptional quality. In the mountainous massif of Huang Shan ("yellow mountain"), where the highest peaks soar to 5,900 feet (1,800 m), Huang Shan Mao Feng ("downy point of the yellow mountain"), one of the best-quality Mao Feng teas, is produced at altitudes between 1000 and 2,600 feet (300 to 800 m). A temperate climate combined with a mainly red soil, rich in humus and iron, allows the growers in Anhui to maintain a high standard of production.

Tea harvest near Zhenghe, in Fujian Province.

The most famous black teas are grown in the southwest of the province, in the county of Qimen, located in the extension of the Huang Shan massif. With an annual mean temperature of about 60°F (15°C) and an annual rainfall of almost 67 inches (1,700 mm), the region is blessed with highly favorable growing conditions. Famous teas, such as Tai Ping Hou Kui and Qimen, are cultivated here.

THE REGION NORTH OF THE YANGZI JIANG RIVER

The provinces of Henan, Shaanxi, Gansu and Shandong, as well as the northern parts of the provinces of Anhui, Jiangsu and Hubei, make up the major growing region that lies north of the Yangzi Jiang River.

These regions are newcomers to the history of tea growing in China, and they have the coldest climate of all the Chinese tea-growing provinces. The average temperature is around 55°F (12°C), and it can drop several degrees below freezing in the winter months. Precipitation is low and rarely exceeds 40 inches (1,000 mm) a year, with an average between 28 and 40 inches (700 to 1,000 mm). The yellow to yellowish-brown soil, which is very poor in some areas, resembles the desert terrain of northern China. However, there are several mountainous regions with interesting climatic conditions that can produce good-quality teas, such as Lu An Gua Pian and Huo Shan Huang Ya. The most famous tea cultivated in the region, Xin Yang Mao Jian, is grown in Henan Province.

The famous massif of Huang Shan, Yellow Mountain in Anhui Province.

The Chinese Tea Industry

In China, annual tea production now exceeds a million tons (according to 2008 data from the Food and Agriculture Organization of the United Nations), and government initiatives designed to promote trade are beginning to have a significant impact on this industrial sector. Annual tea exports from China are close to 330,700 tons (300,000 t), and most of this is green tea, which represents more than 75 percent of the total product exported. The industry is extremely diverse and includes numerous small traditional harvests from artisans alongside huge industrial corporations producing vast quantities of tea.

INDEPENDENT GROWING AND INDUSTRIAL GROWING

Tea growing in China is predominantly the domain of peasants who cultivate small-scale plantations. This explains, in part, the low yield of tea per acre compared to India, for example. In all tea-growing regions we find independent producers who grow and process tea according to traditional, ancestral methods. Manual picking and processing is still common practice among artisans. In addition, a very large part of the tea produced by these traditional methods is distributed for local consumption. Except in large towns, it is rare to see certain types of teas outside the region in which they are produced.

Industrial growing, on the other hand, is a relatively recent development in the history of tea in China, even more recent than industrial growing in India or Japan. Although large-scale tea production first appeared in the 1950s, it was not until the 1980s that the industry began to organize and diversify. To satisfy the needs of this industry, and in spite of the fact that cheap labor is still frequently employed, harvesting and processing methods have become increasingly mechanized. Unfortunately, this massive industrialization has created many undesirable side effects, and today it is not unusual to find industrial copies of famous independently grown teas.

THE SPECIALTY TEA MARKET

The tea market in China has changed considerably in recent years. Whereas production was originally destined for local consumption only, today it responds to an increasingly diversified market, one in which the quest for quality is the principal challenge. While quality tea is still a luxury product beyond the reach of Chinese lower classes, demand has increased substantially since the end of the 1990s, with the rise in average incomes.

The demand for rare and unique products has put pressure on the artisans, leading them to specialize in certain types of cultivation and the production of several types of tea that only China can boast of offering. That is the case with the oldest

A BRIEF SUMMARY OF THE CHINESE TEA TRADE

Total annual production: about 1,257,000 tons (1,140,000 t)
Percentage of production by type of tea: green tea, 73.7%; black tea, 5.6%; wulong: 10.5%; other, 11.2%
Average production yield: about 665 pounds per acre (745 kg/ha)
Annual exports: about 315,000 tons (286,000 t); Zhejiang Province exports the most
Principal purchasing countries: Morocco, 62,600 tons (56,800 t); Japan, 30,500 tons (27,700 t); Uzbekistan,
    21,000 tons (19,000 t); United States, 20,700 tons (18,800 t); Russian Federation, 18,300 tons (16,600 t)

Source: 2008 data from the Food and Agriculture Organization of the United Nations.
(Values in imperial units of measure supplied by publisher.)

BEAUTIFUL TEAS   Over the past several years, a new aspect of tea appreciation has appeared in China: visual appreciation. Strangely, many new tea enthusiasts are more interested in the aesthetic appearance of a tea than in its taste. And so, some teas are analyzed in relation to the beauty of their leaves and the way they move in a glass. If the leaves have an attractive shape and color and remain parallel to the sides of a glass during infusion, they will be considered highly valuable, regardless of their taste. The reverse is also often true. As such, if a tea does not look attractive, it will be sold for a cheaper price even if it tastes very good. In conjunction with this fashion for beautiful teas, tea producers have also made great strides with their packaging in the past few years. Utilitarian bags have been replaced with more luxurious containers, such as metal boxes and cardboard packaging.

Tasting Tie Guan Yin at the tea market in Anxi, Fujian Province.

known family of teas: Pu er teas have been captivating the attention and the taste of a large number of tea collectors. The same is true of the famous green teas — such as Long Jing, Bi Luo Chun and Anji Bai Cha, which are now available in most large Chinese cities — whose first harvests are fought over by enthusiasts.

PROVINCIAL EXPORT COMPANIES

Like the history of Chinese tea, the trading of tea in China has a rich tradition. Once used as a form of currency, tea remains vital to the economy of many regions throughout the country.

As far as exports are concerned, China is an exception: it is one of the few tea-producing countries that does not sell its product under the auction system. Until very recently, the export system was managed by government agencies grouped by province, which handled most of the teas on the market. Any tea destined for export had to go through the regional offices under government control, which proposed a standardized product typical of each region. To purchase tea, a foreign importer had no alternative but to deal with the representative responsible for the region in which he or she was interested. This representative exercised tight control over what product could be exported. For example, a buyer could not obtain a tea from any estate that did not fall under the jurisdiction of the government specialists.

Today, in spite of a certain liberalization of the market system, large-scale exportation is still mostly organized through regional wholesalers. There are a number of wholesalers and exporters in the capital cities of every tea-producing region, and they offer different harvests according to the growing region to both Chinese and foreign buyers.

THE APPELLATION SYSTEM

In China, many elements are involved in the choice of a name for a tea. Some are named for the cultivars from which they were derived or for the region in which they are grown. In a more poetic vein, the name is sometimes inspired by a legend (for example, Tie Guan Yin and Long Jing). In some cases, the tea was named by an "interested" emperor, as is the case with Bi Luo Chun.

Unfortunately, in the absence of a functioning system of controlled appellation, disreputable growers can usurp the name of a celebrated tea and use it to designate products from another terroir or made using a different method. One of the best examples of this is the case of Long Jing, the most famous green tea in China.

Long Jing is the name of a little village close to the town of Hangzhou in Zhejiang Province. The region has been famous for the tea it produces for many centuries. Picked by hand, it is processed almost exclusively in the traditional way, thanks to the expertise of the local growers. As the tea trade has grown in China and the world, certain producers have tried to copy this type of tea in order to increase their sales based on their competitor's famous name.

Today, most Long Jing teas sold exclusively for export on the international. market are in fact teas that come from Sichuan, Taiwan or, in the case of organic teas, Jiangxi Province. Some traders will even buy tea leaves from the south of Zhejiang and sell them to producers who live close to Long Jing so they can be processed there. They then sell the teas produced as genuine Long Jing teas. It must be said, however, that this type of deception does not only happen in China. This problem is also a challenge for some of the other major tea-producing countries, such as Japan, India and Taiwan.

THE WORK OF A SPECIALIZED TASTER-IMPORTER The world market for tea is enormous: 3.5 million tons (3.2 million t) of tea are produced every year. As a rule, distribution is handled by major import-export companies that buy from and sell to wholesalers. These wholesalers then resell the merchandise to other distributors, who are responsible for practically all the tea in circulation on the international market. These corporations are, of course, looking for cheap tea to sell to a mass market rather than high-end teas. The taster-importer, who is looking for a better-quality tea, tries first and foremost to establish contacts with independent traditional growers in order to build a trusting relationship. That is why he or she travels every year to tea-growing countries, visiting plantations and the people who work on them. Once a feeling of trust is established, taster-importers are sometimes invited to taste small, experimental batches of tea that would never find their way to the wholesalers. This is how they make valuable finds. And so, by dealing directly with the growers and avoiding the middlemen, taster-importers can choose teas on the basis of their complexity of taste or their unique characteristics. They can then purchase them for a fair price and import them by air to preserve their freshness.

A Meeting with **Mr. Liu Xu**,

Industry Professional

Mr. Liu Xu is a national tea taster. He has also coauthored eight books on tea.

Mr. Liu Xu, how long have you been working in the world of tea?
I have been working in the world of tea since I was a university student 23 years ago. Today I am a national taster.

What is your background? How does one become a taster of national standing?
I was born in Chengdu in the province of Sichuan. I graduated in July 1991 from the Faculty of Food Products at the Agricultural University of Xinan, where I obtained a bachelor's degree specializing in tea. In July of the same year, I started working at the Institute for Tea Research in the Department of Inspection and Tea Research. In 2003 I obtained my master's degree and then the Certificate of Professional Tea Taster at the national level. Later I was involved in different types of training for tasters of all levels and from various countries. I have also been responsible for numerous evaluations on behalf of the China Tea Association, the Tea Inspection Center of the Ministry of Agriculture, the Huayun Art of Tea School and Shuren University in the province of Zhejiang. I have been invited to speak on many occasions at conferences overseas, in Japan and in Korea.

What are your main responsibilities?
In general, my duty is to evaluate newly created teas and teas from different regions. I regularly participate in several tea contests, inspecting and evaluating teas on a local and national level, and I teach tea-tasting courses to pupils who wish to become professional tasters.

Which aspect of your profession do you like best?
The opportunity to taste exceptional teas and to travel to the different growing regions to meet many people who are passionate about the field.

What major challenges do you think the Chinese tea industry will have to face in the coming years?
It is my opinion that the biggest challenge will be to interest younger generations in the culture of tea. It will also be critical to maintain a steady growth in tea production.

What is your favorite tea?
In each family of teas there are varieties of a superior quality. They are the ones I prefer.

How would you define a good tea?
The tea that you like is a good tea. A good tea is the tea that is at hand when you are thirsty. A good tea brings you all the joy of nature. A good tea lifts your spirits and fills you with enthusiasm.

Gardens and Plants

Spread over 3,781,000 acres (1,530,000 ha), the tea gardens of China are organized in many different ways. Tea trees are arranged in rows about 3 feet (1 m) wide and are usually on a mountainside, according to the relief of the terrain. On the steepest slopes, small stone retaining walls are built to create a stepped effect. The tea trees can be set out as hedges, separated into bushes or cultivated in a terraced pattern.

Although new machinery appears every year in the factories, most of the plantations in China are still cultivated according to traditional customs.

CULTIVARS AND VARIETIES

In the early 1980s, the All-China Commission of Examination and Approval of the Best Genus of Tea was created to record, examine and analyze every cultivar of tea tree growing in China. At that time, some 2,700 species were cataloged. In 1984, the commission recommended 30 teas that were considered the most promising. A few years later, in January 1987, 22 cultivars were selected as the best and therefore most worthy of being cultivated in China. Consequently, these 22 cultivars were given priority over all others. Unfortunately, instead of seeking to protect the naturally rich diversity of the numerous tea trees grown in China, the principal thrust of this kind of research is to increase productivity by standardizing cultivation.

We have chosen to present here four cultivars that are found primarily in China and are outstanding for the production of tea. Each of them belongs to a different tea family. The Fuding Da Bai variety is used for the cultivation of white tea, Long Jing 43 for green tea, Tie Guan Yin for wulong and Zhu Ye for black tea.

FUDING DA BAI

The Fuding Da Bai variety seems to have been discovered in 1857, growing wild on a mountain close to the town of Fuding. The person who discovered it, Chen Huan, is said to have then begun cultivating it. The Fuding Da Bai variety enjoys a long period of vegetative growth from the beginning of March to the end of November. Its buds are white, sturdy and very hairy, which allows them to remain tender longer. Rich in nutrients, the leaves are perfect for the production of white tea, but they can also be used to produce black and green teas. In addition to being highly resistant to drought and cold, Fuding Da Bai has a survival rate of close to 95 percent. Its very high yield has made it one of today's most widely grown teas in China. Some 840,000 acres (340,000 ha) are devoted to the cultivation of Fuding Da Bai.

LONG JING 43

The Long Jing 43 cultivar was developed by the Center for Tea Research at the Agricultural Institute of China in the 1960s. In 1978 it won an award at the Science Conference of China.

Chosen in 1987 as one of the best cultivars, today it is grown in more than a dozen provinces, including Zhejiang, Jiangsu, Anhui, Jiangxi and Henan. Extremely productive and resistant, it bears buds that appear in great abundance in early spring. Its flat, pale-green leaves with brownish edges are very aromatic and thus perfectly adapted to the production of high-quality tea.

TIE GUAN YIN

The Tie Guan Yin variety, which produces a tea of the same name, is widely grown in China, mainly for the production of wulong teas. Legend has it that a certain Mr. Wei discovered it 200 years ago. Renowned for the speed of its growth and the abundance of its harvests, Tie Guan Yin has oval leaves, and its young buds, easily recognizable by their purplish-red hue, are lacy and pointed and have a thick, silky texture.

Compared to other cultivars, Tie Guan Yin contains a larger diversity of organic components, such as polyphenols, catechins and other amino acids. It is also rich in minerals, such as manganese, iron and potassium, which gives it a slightly mineral taste.

THE AGE OF TEA TREES From one garden to another, or even within the same garden, the age of tea trees can vary enormously according to customs and the preference of the grower. Whereas young trees are usually preferred for the production of green teas, you can find ancient trees that may be several hundred years old being used for the production of Pu er and wulong teas in Yunnan and Guangdong Provinces.

ZHU YE

Today, the Zhu Ye cultivar is used for the production of Qimen, one of the most famous black teas of China. Previously intended for the production of green tea, this cultivar seems to have been used to produce Qimen for the first time in 1815, thanks to Hu Yun Long. According to legend, he had cultivated Zhu Ye to produce green tea until he returned from a trip to Fujian, the birthplace of black teas. He decided to convert his production of green tea to the production of black tea using the same trees. When he realized that the black tea he obtained from the Zhu Ye cultivar was better than the green tea, Hu Yun Long gave up the production of green tea to devote himself entirely to the production of Qimen.

55

The Processing of Chinese Teas

Just as the cultivation of the tea tree has a long tradition in China, the processing of the leaves is an art that the Chinese mastered many centuries ago. This experience, acquired over time and through trial and error, has spawned a wide variety of processing methods, so much so that it would be easy to believe that every region now has its own specific process. In fact, that would not be too far from the truth. Chinese tea production is based on the agricultural traditions of each region, and so different methods of processing have been adopted by each region, which has given rise to new types of teas. As well as being recognized as the birthplace of the six great tea families, China has developed methods to produce several hundred different types of teas.

Before the processing methods were refined, the leaves were brewed when freshly picked. However, since they spoiled very quickly, growers decided to first dehydrate them in the sun in order to preserve them for longer. This idea was probably at the root of tea processing, because the heat of the sun on the leaves also created a natural chemical reaction that affected the taste and properties of the tea. Over time, the Chinese have learned to take advantage of this reaction.

As most of the teas produced in the world are marketed in tea bags, the different methods of production, from picking to processing, are almost always industrialized. These techniques are only efficient in the case of high volumes, so large-scale producers need to emphasize quantity over quality. And yet it is still the small-scale traditional methods that are characteristic of Chinese expertise: it is also these methods that are best at bringing out the distinctive characteristics of a tea from a specific terroir.

Factory producing Huo Shan Huang Ya tea in Anhui Province.

56

WHITE TEAS

Renowned for their delicate aroma and their refreshing properties, white teas are a specialty of Fujian Province, which is divided into three main regions: Fuding, Zhenghe and Jianyang. Now, however, several estates in Darjeeling are producing white teas, and this trend seems to be spreading to other countries.

Traditionally produced from precious harvests that last only a very short time (about two weeks) in the spring, white teas were once reserved exclusively for emperors and other high-ranking officials. These teas are the most minimally processed of all.

White teas are usually divided into two types: those made only from downy buds (such as Yin Zhen and silver needles) and those made from a mixture of buds and leaves (such as Bai Mu Dan and Shou Mei). They are processed in two main stages, withering and sorting.

WITHERING

During the withering stage the leaves are simply spread out over bamboo racks. Depending on outside conditions, the leaves will be left to air-dry on the racks for 12 to 24 hours. To speed up the drying process, fans of different intensities are sometimes used to increase air circulation. In larger-scale production settings, a leaf-drying machine is used for the withering stage.

SORTING

This next stage consists of picking out broken leaves and other undesirable residue so only the whole buds and leaves are preserved. Sorting is often carried out using sieves of varying sizes, and branches are removed by hand. Sorting can also be done mechanically.

FIRING

Traditionally, leaves for white teas are not fired. However, certain lower-quality teas of the Mu Dan variety are subjected to oxidation or high-temperature drying, which changes their taste and appearance.

YELLOW TEAS

Although they have been known and appreciated for several centuries, yellow teas are becoming increasingly rare. Only a few remain, such as Jun Shan Yin Zhen. One province, Hunan, still produces limited quantities, ensuring the survival of this prestigious tea. It is called "yellow" because of an unusual characteristic arising from its processing: after being dehydrated, the still-warm leaves are covered with a damp cloth, triggering a slight oxidation through steaming, which gives the leaves a yellowish tinge.

PICKING
Only the bud is picked. In order to obtain a high-quality yellow tea, the bud is picked before it becomes downy.

WITHERING
The withering stage is carried out in the same way as for green tea, on cloths or bamboo racks.

HEATING
Heating is carried out in pans, and the leaves are stirred by hand.

STEAM OXIDATION
The process of steam oxidation involves spreading the leaves directly on the ground and leaving them covered with a damp cloth for a period of four to 10 hours, depending on the weather conditions. Covering the leaves gently warms them, which affects the development of their aroma.

DRYING
The leaves are then dried for 10 to 20 minutes at a temperature of 230 to 250°F (110 to 120°C). At the end of this stage, the leaves should contain no more than 5 percent humidity. The next stage is sorting by means of sieves, if the sorting is done manually.

GREEN TEAS

China overflows with famous green teas, including Long Jing, Bi Luo Chun, Anji Bai Cha and Xin Yang Mao Jian, to name but a few. Numerous traditional methods — handed down through centuries according to the customs of each region — have lead to a profusion of green teas, which today represent more than 70 percent of all Chinese production. The major growing regions are located in the south of the country, especially in provinces like Fujian, Zhejiang, Anhui, Henan, Jiangsu and Jiangxi.

PICKING

Methods of picking vary greatly from one region to another. Usually the leaves are picked when young (the bud plus one or two leaves), but there are exceptions to this rule. For example, more mature leaves are harvested to produce Tai Ping Hou Kui, and in the case of Lu An Gua Pian, only the leaves are picked and the bud is left on the stem.

WITHERING

Immediately after picking, the leaves are transported to the factory, where they will undergo the process of withering. Withering time will vary depending on the prevailing conditions and the water content of the leaves. The traditional method of withering is to spread the leaves on bamboo racks and leave them to dry for one to three hours in order to remove the surplus water. To prevent them from drying too rapidly, they are sometimes spread on cloths in the shade. The mechanical method involves placing the leaves in a cylindrical machine with bamboo walls, so that they "spin dry" for a few minutes while fans blow air through them.

It is important to note that, as soon as the leaves are picked, a natural chemical process causes oxydase, a process by which enzymes contained in the leaves react with oxygen in the air. Handling the leaves during the withering and rolling processes breaks down the leaves' cell structure, releasing the oils they contain, which, on contact with oxygen, trigger a chemical change in the leaves. In order to produce green tea, this natural process of oxidation must be interrupted. This is achieved through dehydration.

GREEN TEAS *(continued)*

HEATING

This is the process of heating the leaves until the enzymes that cause oxidation lose their potency. Methods vary according to the region and the customs of the individual grower. There are many ways to heat leaves. In China it usually involves the use of vats.

Small quantities of leaves are put in pans or vats that are heated with wood, coal or electricity. The leaves are pressed to the bottom of the vat and then constantly stirred so they don't burn. The leaves are processed in small batches. Next, different techniques are used according to the form the leaves are supposed to take. If the leaves are to be flat, as in the Long Jing variety, they are pressed to the bottom of the vat briefly before being stirred in a back-and-forth movement. If the type of tea is curly, like the Bi Luo Chun variety, they are rolled by hand and constantly stirred until they are dry. The heat of the vat can vary. At first the heat is low, but once the process is under way the heat is increased.

When the leaves are mechanically processed, they are heated at least three times in rotating cylinders. In between heating periods they are sometimes spread on cloths to cool. As the leaves are heated, a chemical process is triggered: the sugars and proteins they contain are transformed, giving the tea an aromatic quality that is sometimes reminiscent of grilled nuts. This stage also releases the polyphenols contained in the leaves.

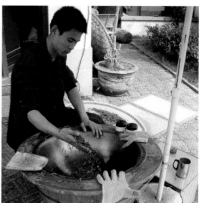

ROLLING

This stage consists of rolling the leaves to break down their cell structure and release the aromatic oils they contain. Rolling, which is partly responsible for the taste and appearance of Chinese green teas, also changes the shape of the finished product, determining whether they will be twisted, flat, needle-shaped or bead-shaped leaves.

When processing is done by hand, rolling and dehydrating are part of a single process, as we have seen. In the case of mechanical processing, various machines are used to obtain curly or flat leaves.

DRYING

During this penultimate stage, the aromatic oils released during rolling become stabilized on the leaves. In addition, any remaining water is eliminated so there is no risk of mold. At the end of this process, only 2 percent to 4 percent moisture remains in the leaves.

SIFTING

Lastly, the leaves are sifted through a fine sieve to remove any that broke during processing. At this stage, the leaves are sorted into sizes by means of bamboo meshes of different sizes placed one on top of the other.

WULONG TEAS

By mastering how to oxidize tea leaves, Chinese craftspeople have, over time, created a new family of teas, called wulong. They are different from black teas in that they are only partially oxidized, and so wulong teas fall between green and black teas. It was in the 17th century that growers developed the method of processing these teas that come from Fujian Province, especially from the Wuyi Mountains and the Anxi district.

Because of the vastness of the Chinese territory, the great variety of cultivars grown there and the different processing methods used, wulong teas come in a wide range of aromas and tastes. However, wulong teas fall into two main categories: teas that may be 10 percent to 45 percent oxidized and are close to green teas, and teas that may be up to 70 percent oxidized and are closer to black teas. As for taste, the wulong teas that are less oxidized (green wulongs) are generally distinguished by their more delicate, floral aromas, whereas the more oxidized wulong teas (black wulongs) have more woody notes and are sometimes fruity or even a bit sweet.

In the following paragraphs we will examine the processing of wulong teas more closely, and we will explore this further in the chapter on Taiwan (see pages 138–142).

PICKING
Black wulong teas are produced from highly mature leaves. The leaves will be larger and more mature than those chosen for the production of green tea, for example. Often three leaves will be picked in addition to the bud.

WITHERING
Withering is usually carried out on cloths outside, but bamboo racks are also often used. The leaves are left for about two hours, depending on the weather conditions.

OXIDATION

Next comes the very important stage of oxidation, which governs the development of the sensorial characteristics of the leaves. When processed manually, the leaves are spread on racks and stirred regularly for 12 to 18 hours in order to break down the cell structure and release the oils, facilitating the oxidation process. During mechanical processing, the leaves are heated at ambient humidity in rotating cylinders at temperatures varying from 77 to 86°F (25 to 30°C), for about eight hours.

HEATING

Next, the leaves are heated to stop the oxidation process. The traditional method uses the same type of vat used to dehydrate green teas. Mechanical processing involves using a rotating cylinder.

ROLLING

To obtain the twisted leaves typical of Chinese black wulong teas, the same machine is used for preparing twisted-leaf green teas or rolling the leaves for black teas. Traditionally, the leaves were rolled manually on a bamboo mat.

DRYING AND FIRING

The leaves are then dried in a rotating cylinder for 10 to 20 minutes at a temperature ranging from 230 to 250°F (110 to 120°C).

Finally, the firing stage is the same as the firing process for Taiwanese wulong teas (see page 141) but at higher temperatures. The leaves are usually fired twice, and temperatures can vary according to the region of production. In the case of mechanical processing, an electric machine is used to heat the leaves to higher temperatures. It must be noted that firing is not necessarily done immediately after drying the leaves. It is possible to wait several months after the initial processing.

BLACK TEAS

Black teas are made from completely oxidized leaves. They are found mainly in the south of China, in the provinces of Yunnan, Anhui (particularly Qimen) and Fujian (particularly Zhenghe). The Chinese often call them "red teas" (not to be confused with the red teas of South Africa), on account of the copper color of the infusion they produce. The method used to process black teas was developed during the 18th century.

Usually, more mature leaves are picked for the production of black teas, except in the case of very high-quality teas and "beautiful" teas (see "Beautiful Teas" on page 49).

WITHERING

Withering is usually carried out either on the ground or on bamboo racks and lasts for five to six hours, long enough for the leaves to soften and to lose 60 percent of their moisture. They must be stirred often at this stage.

In the case of mechanical processing, withering takes place in a controlled environment. The leaves are placed on sieves in brick containers that are usually heated by wood fires, a technique that gives Chinese black teas a slightly smoky aroma. The containers allow air from a turbine to circulate below the leaves. About four hours later the leaves are ready for the next stage.

ROLLING

Once the leaves have been thoroughly softened through withering, they are rolled in order to break down the structure of their cells, releasing the enzymes that trigger oxidation. Depending on the quality of tea desired, this is usually done by a machine that presses the leaves onto plates divided into strips.

OXIDATION

The oxidation period can vary from eight to 12 hours, depending on the ambient conditions. The leaves are spread on the ground and covered with large wet cloths to stimulate the chemical reaction. The temperature must be around 72°F (22°C). This technique takes longer than the method used for Indian black teas. As the oxidation takes place in milder conditions, a less astringent tea is obtained. This method also produces an earthy aroma and a burnt, sweet taste that is typical of Chinese black teas.

Relying on their talent, experience and intuition, independent tea growers may decide to tweak different stages of the process.

DRYING

Any residual moisture in the leaves is eliminated and the oxidation process is stabilized during the drying stage. Drying techniques vary from one region to another. The most common method uses conveyor belts through which warm air is blown to dry the leaves. Sometimes they are transferred to another wood-heated machine.

SORTING AND SIFTING

Whether it is carried out manually or mechanically, sorting and sifting separates the leaves into different grades (the sorting) while eliminating dust, branches and other residue (the sifting). In the case of a large harvest, the process may be mechanized. A bamboo sieve is most commonly used for higher-quality teas. After sorting, the teas are ready for packaging.

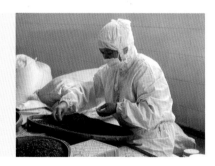

FIRING (OPTIONAL)

In certain cases, another stage is added: firing. This further reduces the moisture content and helps standardize the batch.

PU ER TEAS

Famous for their history and curative properties, Pu er teas are post-fermented teas whose oxidation is not enzyme related. Also known as "aged teas," "post-oxidized teas," "black teas" (by the Chinese) or even "dark teas," they owe their specific properties to their processing method, which gives them the advantage of improving over time. They can be traced back to the Tang dynasty (618–907), when tea was boiled and added to soup as a flavoring.

They derive their name from the town of Pu er in Yunnan Province (in southwestern China), where growers from the neighboring mountains brought their harvests to be sold and sent elsewhere in China or in more far-flung regions, such as Tibet and Mongolia. Because of the high demand for tea and the fact that it was transported on horseback, the local population devised a processing method that consisted of compressing the tea into cakes of different sizes and shapes.

During the Song dynasty, the town of Pu er was a major trading center for tea: all the teas sold there were called "Pu er," whatever their particularities. Today, although Pu er teas are still produced mainly in Yunnan Province, other regions, such as Guangxi, Anhui, Guangdong and northern Vietnam produce them too.

In a bid to prevent others from usurping the appellation, the Bureau of Standard Measurement of Yunnan Province (2003) defined Pu er teas as "fermented green tea products obtained from the large leaves of tea trees harvested in Yunnan Province." Although not all experts agree with this definition, it is justified in part by the variety of tea tree,

SHENG AND SHOU: TWO PARENTS OF THE PU ER TEA FAMILY Sheng ("raw") Pu er, renowned today for its rich taste and medicinal properties, is certainly one of the first teas to have appeared in China. In accordance with the traditional method of processing, the leaves are usually compressed into cakes, thereby slowly oxidizing on contact with the air, which improves their flavor. They are fermented over a very long period of time, from 10 to 50 years. Sheng Pu er teas are not considered fully mature until they have been aged for 30 years. At this stage they are referred to as "vintage."

As with all teas, the plant matter used to create them determines their quality. Therefore, the best Sheng teas come from wild tea trees that are often several centuries old. During the 1970s, because of the growing demand for rare Pu er teas, the Chinese tea industry developed a new type of Pu er that could be brought to market faster: Shou ("cooked") Pu er teas. Shou Pu er teas are processed in the same way as the Sheng variety, but they are exposed to a rapid fermentation over 45 to 60 days

to speed up the aging process. These teas are meant for immediate consumption, and, unlike the Sheng teas, they do not get better if they are preserved over a long period of time. Their flavor improves only slightly with aging. Shou Pu er teas are usually of lower quality, and the leaves used for their production come almost exclusively from plantations. Long considered an industrial product by true enthusiasts, Shou Pu er teas are appreciated today for their distinctive characteristics, including an earthy taste with hints of undergrowth and the animal-like notes triggered by rapid aging.

Two teas from the same year: Shou and Sheng

Da Ye ("large leaves"), grown in Yunnan. The best Pu er teas come from the famous mountains located in Xishuangbanna. Some of these mountains, including the well-known Youle, Banzhang, Manzhuan, Yiwu, Mensong, Banpen and Yiban, are still renowned for their tea production.

Considering it takes several years for the aging process to improve the taste of these teas, aged Pu er teas are becoming ever more rare, and collectors are willing to spend a fortune to obtain a cake of aged Sheng. Rarity created a sudden rise in price that many investors saw as an opportunity. Therefore, at the beginning of 2000, plantations were springing up like mushrooms, as mountainsides were cleared to make way for the cultivation of tea trees dedicated to the production of Pu er teas. However, this furious growth of Sheng Pu er peaked in the fall of 2007, when the speculative bubble burst. Seeing the market collapse due to the inflated prices, the new investors pulled out. Since then the Pu er market has trended toward stabilization. However, the market for aged Pu er teas was not affected by this phenomenon. Because of the rarity of this product, demand and prices remain high.

DIFFERENT SHAPES OF PU ER TEA In addition to the difference between Sheng and Shou, Pu er teas have other distinguishing features. One of the most obvious is indisputably their shape. There, too, the Chinese have shown great inventiveness. While the most common shape is the cake, Pu er teas can be compressed into many other shapes and sizes. The most common shapes are:

- the cake (bing cha), which usually weighs around 12 ounces (355 g);
- the brick (zhuan cha), weighing 9 ounces (250 g);
- the nest (tuo cha), which normally weighs 3½ or 9 ounces (100 or 250 g) but is also found in a ⅙-ounce (5 g) size;
- the pumpkin (jin gua), which comes in several sizes;
- the mushroom, weighing around 8 ounces (240 g);
- the cube, weighing roughly ⅙ ounce (5 g).

Pu er teas are also made into various custom shapes (Buddha, pig and the like) to honor specific events, and they can also be left loose.

THE TRADEMARK, OR *NEI FEI* A cake of Pu er tea is usually marked with a trademark, also called a *nei fei*, which often indicates the place where the tea was processed. The trademark is inscribed on a small piece of paper, which is placed on the leaves just before they are compressed.

PU ER TEAS *(continued)*

To first step in the process to make Pu er tea is to produce what is called *maocha*.

PICKING

As is the case with other teas, the quality of a Pu er tea depends in part on the plant material used. A grading system from one to nine defines the size of the leaves that are used.

WITHERING

Processing Pu er teas begins with withering. To do this, the leaves are spread in the sun for a few hours. In industrial processing, the leaves are spread on racks in a room and heated with hot-water radiant heat.

HEATING

Small-scale heating takes place in pans and lasts for two to three minutes. The batches of leaves are far bigger that those used when producing green teas. The pans are usually heated by means of wood fires.

ROLLING

The leaves are then rolled by hand on a bamboo mat until they form a large ball. In industrial processing, the leaves are rolled in the same type of round roller press as used for black teas or for curly-leaf green teas.

SECOND HEATING

Sometimes the leaves are heated a second time in the pans, also for two to three minutes.

SECOND ROLLING

The same method is used as for the first rolling: by hand on a bamboo mat (the traditional method) or rolled in a round roller press (the industrial method).

DRYING

After the second rolling, the leaves are dried in the sun or in a temperature- and moisture-controlled greenhouse. In industrial processing, the leaves are dried on a conveyor belt that passes through a heating machine.

SORTING

Next, all residue is eliminated from the leaves by means of manual sorting.

After all these stages, the *maocha* is ready. Often, the peasants who produce it sell it to other specialized processors who then compress the leaves into different shapes. Although the highest-quality leaves are usually reserved for the production of Sheng, the *maocha* can be used to produce both types of Pu er teas. However, from this stage onward, the processing methods of Sheng and Shou are different.

SHENG PU ER TEAS

Only two stages remain to finalize the processing of a Sheng Pu er tea: sorting and compression into cakes (or whatever shape is being used).

YUNNAN QI ZI BING CHA   In the world of tea, some methods still represent a tradition or particular way of thinking. Such is the case with the cakes of Pu er tea that are inscribed *Yunnan qi zi bing cha*, which means "tea cake of the seven sons of Yunnan." Why seven sons? Seven is a lucky number for the Chinese, and the use of the plural implies that the family will be able to produce several sons, which will bring it good fortune. Consequently, by buying a cake of Pu er tea, the customer is acquiring not just tea but also the promise of prosperity. In addition, the round shape represents the full moon, which, for the Chinese, symbolizes a gathering of the whole family.

SHENG PU ER TEAS *(continued)*

SORTING AND GROUPING

Sorting — separating the leaves into different grades — is usually done by hand or by means of a machine. The leaves are sorted into nine principal grades, the first containing the smallest leaves and the ninth, the largest. It is at this stage that leaves from different origins may be grouped together.

COMPRESSION

First the leaves are split into groups that correspond to the desired weight of each cake to be formed. Next they are sprayed with steam to hydrate and soften them so they are more malleable. It is at this stage that the paper indicating the trademark of the tea (*nei fei*) is inserted into the leaves. The moist leaves are then placed in a cloth. According to traditional practice they are then pressed under a stone. A hydraulic press is used for mechanical compression.

DRYING

Once the cakes have been compressed, they are laid out to dry in the air, without any cloths over them, so any residual moisture can escape. In industrial processing the cakes are sometimes placed in a room heated by hot water pipes, which speeds up the drying process. The cakes are dried until they return to their original weight, the weight prior to the dampening they received at the compression stage.

PACKAGING

The traditional way of packaging Pu er teas was to wrap each cake in its individual identifying paper, group the cakes in lots of seven (called *tong*) and package each lot in dried bamboo bark. Each *tong* was placed in a bamboo basket as part of a lot of six (called *jin*). If we do the math, six times seven cakes makes 42 cakes. Given that every cake weighs 13 ounces (375 g) and that there are 42 cakes in a *jin*, a *jin* weighs 33 pounds (15.7 kg).

SHOU PU ER TEAS

To produce Shou Pu er teas, the fermentation process is accelerated by exposing the *maocha* leaves to high heat and humidity.

FERMENTATION
First the leaves are placed in a room and covered with a little water and a cloth. Next, they are exposed to high heat and humidity for 45 to 65 days. During this stage they will be turned over several times.

SORTING
Once the accelerated fermentation is over, the leaves are first sorted by machine then by hand in order to eliminate any unfermented leaves.

COMPRESSION
Next, the same compression process as for Sheng Pu er teas is used. However, few Shou Pu er teas are compressed by the traditional method. Hydraulic presses are generally used.

Once all these stages are completed, it is wise to wait at least three months before drinking the teas produced, to allow the fermentation process to stabilize.

AGING PU ER TEAS

The conditions during the aging process can greatly affect the taste a Pu er tea develops. Ideally, the temperature should be maintained between 68 and 86°F (20 to 30°C), although it does not have to be kept constant. At temperatures below 68°F (20°C) the aging process would take much longer. The leaves should also be kept at a constant humidity between 60 percent and 70 percent, and in a dark room, where they will not be exposed to light, that has good air circulation. The leaves should be kept away from any substance that might give off an aroma that they could absorb (such as coffee, spices, etc.). Ideally, Sheng Pu er and Shou Pu er varieties should be kept separate. In Hong Kong, several techniques have been developed with a view to aging Sheng Pu er teas more quickly. One of them, wet storage, involves creating a hot environment between 68 and 95°F (30 to 35°C) with a very high relative humidity (90 percent). These conditions greatly accelerate the aging of the leaves.

Local Customs for the Preparation of Tea

Tea is an essential element of daily life in China, and, in a territory that includes almost 2.5 million acres (1 million ha) of cultivated land, it is not surprising to find that the methods to prepare tea vary from region to region. Several provinces in western China follow different customs. In Yunnan Province, for example, the Dai, Hani and Jingpo peoples ferment their tea in pieces of bamboo and then add it to vegetables. Others chew it as a snack. The Muslims of Xinjang, in northwestern China, drink their tea from a *gaiwan* and infuse it with walnuts and sugar.

China is the only country to produce all six families of tea. As the consumption of tea is based on local culture, Chinese tastes vary according to region and custom. Near Anxi, for example, in the south of the country, it is almost impossible to find anything other than Tie Guan Yin. Amazingly, even growers who have developed prestigious harvests usually show little interest in sipping anything other than the specialty of their region.

In general, the Chinese prefer to drink green tea, and they drink it unceremoniously from a tea glass or bottle. They usually pour boiling water over the leaves — even a very high-quality vintage — then dilute the infusion when they have drunk about a quarter of the glass. Although it does nothing to develop or enhance the taste, this is by far the most prevalent practice. However, there is another way of drinking tea in China that, by paying more attention to the tea, gives far better results: preparing tea in a *gaiwan*. (The words *zhong* and *gaiwan* refer to the same object; the first is the Cantonese term and the second the Mandarin.)

THE EVERYDAY TEA BOTTLE   In China, the main utensil used for the infusion of tea leaves is the tea bottle. It can be found everywhere. Made of glass, plastic or stainless steel, it comes with a lid and sometimes a filter to keep the leaves in the bottom, so that several infusions can be made from the same leaves. And so, throughout the day, whether they are in a train, a workshop, an office or a bus, the Chinese can drink their tea at will.

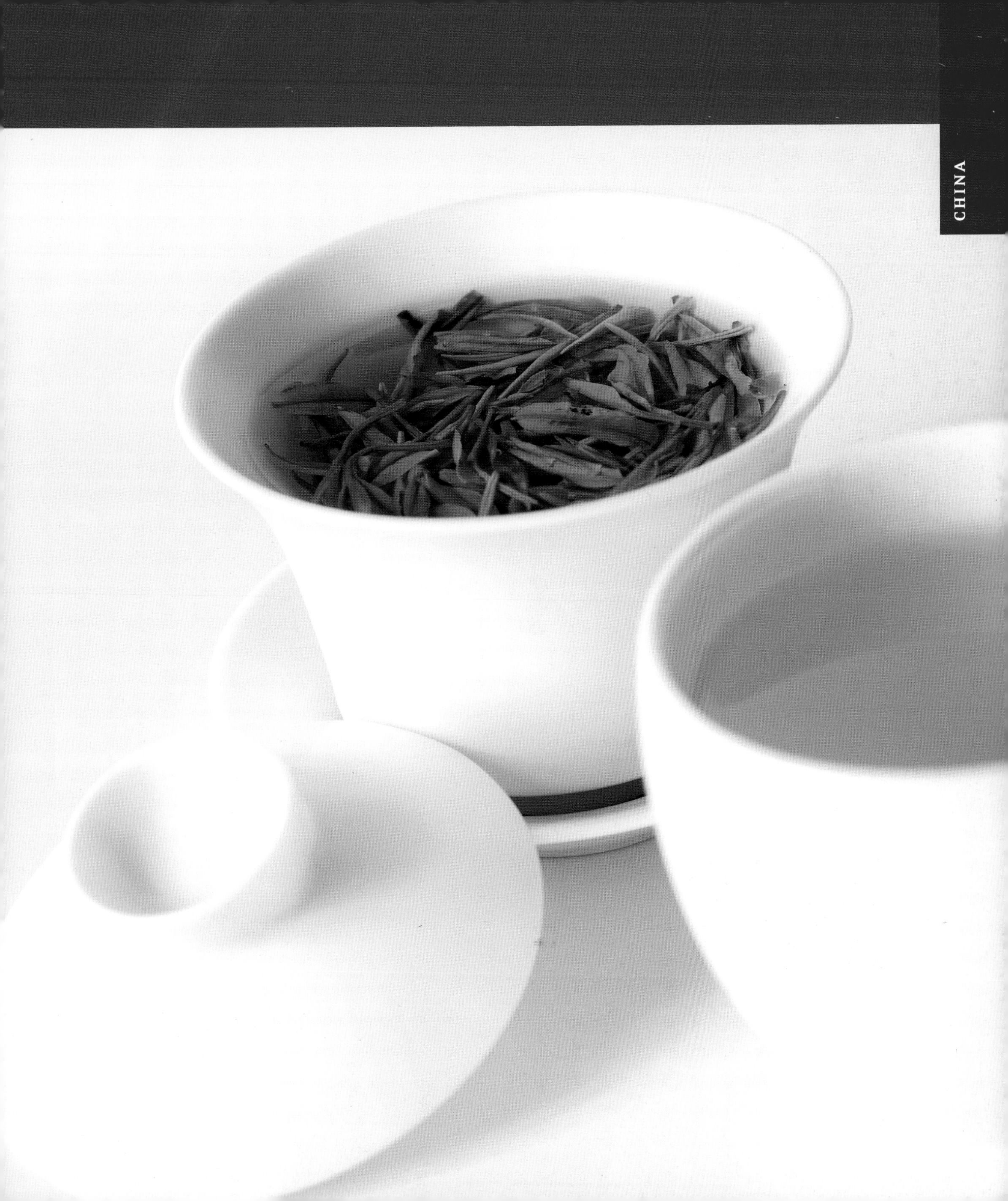

The *gaiwan*

Made up of a simple saucer, bowl and lid, whose under-side is used for inhaling aromas, the *gaiwan* is a Chinese container in which tea leaves can be infused in a small amount of water in order to concentrate the flavors. This method of infusion, introduced in China during the Ming dynasty (1368–1644) is still used today by the general public as well as by tea enthusiasts. In addition to concentrating the flavors, it allows the same leaves to be infused several times so that slight differences of flavor are revealed with each infusion.

Although the *gaiwan* can be used with all kinds of tea, it bring out the aromas of more delicate teas, such as white or green teas, particularly well. (It is also very effective for wulong and Pu er teas.) Traditionally, the liquid is drunk directly from the *gaiwan*, and the lid is used to hold back the leaves. However, to control the infusion better, it is preferable to use a *cha hai,* or reserve container, into which the liquid is transferred when it is ready.

Here are the main steps of the tasting process using a *gaiwan* :

- Heat the *gaiwan* using hot water. Although this step is not absolutely necessary, it prepares the *gaiwan* for the infusion stage and, symbolically, as in many rituals related to tea, it is part of the purification of the utensils.
- Place approximately 1 heaping teaspoon (5 ml) of tea in the *gaiwan*. The quantity of leaves used can vary from ½ to 2 teaspoons (2 to 10 ml), depending on the type of tea and the strength desired. As a general rule, the more leaves used, the shorter the infusion should be **1**.

- Pour water at the required temperature over the leaves **2**. Make sure that all the leaves are fully soaked with water by stirring gently with the lid **3**.

- Leave the tea to infuse as long as necessary. Because of the large amount of leaves used in

1

2

relation to the volume of water, the first infusion should be short (15 to 45 seconds). If you would like to check the progress of the infusion, pour a small quantity of the liquid into a bowl and taste it.

• When the infusion is ready, transfer the liquid into a separate cup or pot, holding back the leaves with the lid. Tilt the lid to keep all the leaves in the *gaiwan*, then pour off the liquid completely to prevent any leftovers from affecting subsequent infusions. Use the saucer to get a better grip on the *gaiwan* **4**.

• Inhale the aromas that emanate from the infused leaves and from the inside of the lid. Some of the subtlest aromas released by the freshly infused leaves are very volatile and can only be detected as they evaporate.

• Taste.

For the subsequent infusions, repeat the same steps, lengthening the infusion period each time. There are several methods for preparing an infusion in a *gaiwan*. Some recommend several short infusions, while others stop after two.

If you are having difficulty getting the water to the right temperature for green or white teas, use a small amount of cold water (about a quarter of the *gaiwan*) and top up with water at just under the boiling point.

A Meeting with Mr. He, Tea Grower

Mr. He works for the Office of Agricultural Research, where he develops new teas. He has also been a tea grower since 1991.

How did you get to where you
are today in the world of tea?

My family has been producing tea for several generations, I forget how many exactly, but we grew it only for our own use. When we had too much we gave it away. Tea is part of my family heritage.

From 1987 to 1991, I studied tea at the Agricultural University of Zhejiang, and since then I have always worked in this field. At first I worked for the Department of Agriculture, whose main function was to teach farmers how to cultivate tea trees and the techniques for processing the leaves. Now I work for the Office of Agricultural Research on the development of new teas. At the same time, I own a tea garden where I have been producing my own tea since 1991.

How big is your tea garden?

My garden covers approximately 2 mous [1 mou = ¹/₆ acre or ¹/₁₅ ha]. I also rent a tea garden covering 580 mous.

How much tea do you produce every year?
Do you have employees?

I produce more than 1,500 kilos [3,300 pounds] of high-quality tea every year. About 20 people work with me on the plantations and in the factory. In addition, in harvest season, I employ roughly 300 pickers.

Do you have a store where you sell your tea?

I am both a producer and a trader. I own two tea stores, and eight others help me sell my tea.

To whom do you sell your tea?
The local or international market?

I produce mainly for the local market.

What kind of tea do you produce?

When I started out, purchasing power was low in China, so I produced low-grade teas using machinery for picking. Now that purchasing power has increased, I produce high-quality teas from handpicked leaves. I produce less tea now than I did when I started. Even if production costs have risen considerably because of the increase in salaries, I want to continue to produce high-quality teas.

Have you noticed changes in the industry
and in your clientele since you started?

At the moment, the Chinese appreciate tea for the way it looks, and that limits the development of the industry. I try to educate consumers so they will learn to better appreciate the taste and the nutritive values of tea and not just the way it looks.

On the boat going to the garden of Tai Ping Hou Kui, which is inaccessible by car.

"One life is not enough to learn the names of all the teas in China."
— CHINESE PROVERB

Tai Ping Hou Kui:
Green Tea from Anhui Province

A very long time ago, there lived in the magnificent mountains of Huang Shan a monkey couple and their baby. One day, the intrepid little monkey went out to explore the surrounding area but, caught in a thick fog, lost his way. Worried, his father set out to find him. Alas, after searching for several days in vain, the old monkey dropped from exhaustion into a ditch close to Taiping County.

An old man who used to gather wild tea in the area came across the monkey's body. Saddened by this gruesome find, he buried the monkey at the foot of the mountain and, to honor him, planted a few tea trees and other flowering plants. As he was leaving the place he heard a voice say, "Sir, I will repay you for what you have done." The man turned around but saw no one.

The following spring, the man returned to the mountain to harvest the leaves of the tea trees he had planted there and, to his great surprise, saw that the mountain was covered in them. That was when he heard the voice again, "I give you these tea trees so that you may live well by cultivating them." Frightened at first by the strange voice, the man then remembered the monkey he had buried at this very spot, and he understood that it was his spirit he had heard. To commemorate this unexpected gift, he named the hill Hou Gang ("monkey hill") and the tea Hou Cha ("monkey tea"). And as the tea was of exceptional quality, the name became Hou Kui (kui meaning "the first" or "the best").

On a more historic note, Tai Ping Hou Kui has been cultivated in the region of Taiping (Anhui Province) since the Ming dynasty. Harvested exclusively for emperors under the Qing dynasty, Tai Ping Hou Kui tea was awarded the title "King of Tea" at the 2004 China Tea Exhibition.

The garden in which Tai Ping Hou Kui is grown.

Chinese Teas

Bai Hao Yin Zhen | white tea |
Translation: Silver needles. The words *bai hao*, ("white down") indicate the superior grade of Yin Zhen.
Alternative names: Yin Zhen, Silver Needles
Region: Fujian Province (Fuding, Zhenghe, Jianyang)
Harvest season: Late March to early April
Cultivar: Da Bai or Da Hao

The production of this tea, as we know it today, dates from the early Jia Qing period of the Qing dynasty (1796). This tea was grown exclusively as a tribute paid to the emperor. At the time, wild tea buds were picked in the Fuding region. After 1885, these were replaced by the buds of the Da Bai tea tree. Considered a great delicacy, this tea is made from a harvest of fine picking in which only the buds are taken.

Tasting notes: The smell of fresh-cut hay and fields of flowers bathed in dew emanates from the steeped buds. The liquid, which tastes both sweet and vegetal, releases delicate notes of flowering clover and wheatgrass. Smooth and fluid, it leaves graceful aromas, in which apricot and artichoke combine, in the mouth. Its long finish, honeyed and thirst quenching, is soothing to the palate.

Recommended infusion accessory: A *gaiwan* or small teapot.

Jun Shan Yin Zhen | yellow tea |
Translation: Silver needles from the emperor's mountain
Alternative name: Mountain Silver Needles
Region: Hunan Province
Harvest Season: April
Cultivar: Jun Shan Qun Ti Zhong.

This tea is extremely rare. Produced in very small quantities, it is grown on a tiny island in the middle of Lake Dongting. Although it is processed in a similar way to green tea, it is characterized by low oxidation through steaming. This process gives the leaves a yellowish tinge.

Tasting notes: The fine bud is encased in the exquisite down of the green needles. The steeped leaves release a rich but subtle aroma of plantain, roasted peanuts, green vegetables and papaya. Beneath this fruit and vegetable mixture, fine notes of vanilla and white pepper can be detected. The straw-colored liquid is made hazy by fine down particles in suspension. The liquid, round in flavor, is remarkably thick and coats the tongue. The sweet taste is counterbalanced by a touch of acidity. The lasting, slightly pungent aroma of artichoke is enriched by notes of green wood and peanut. The long vegetal and vanilla finish is very gentle.

Recommended infusion accessory: A *Gaiwan* or small teapot.

Long Jing Shi Feng | green tea |
Translation: Dragon's well
Alternative name: Dragon's Well, Lung Ching
Region: Zhejiang Province (Shi Feng, Meijiawu)
Harvest season: Late March to early April
Cultivar: Long Jing 43

This tea, which is the most prestigious tea in China, is cultivated near Hangzhou, capital of Zhejiang Province and renowned for its magnificent Lake of the West (Xi Hu). Today, because of its enormous popularity, the Long Jing appellation is overused. It is therefore important to differentiate between Xi Hu Long Jing and Zhejiang Long Jing. Grown in the region of origin, Xi Hu Long Jing teas are processed entirely by hand, from picking to final sifting. Zhejiang Long Jing teas are harvested throughout the province and are, for the most part, picked by hand and processed mechanically. As this tea is the most frequently copied tea in China, it must be noted that the majority of Long Jing teas on the market are produced outside the region of origin and often even in other provinces. They are also usually just poor imitations.

Most Xi Hu Long Jing teas are grown on two facing mountain slopes, the famous Shi Feng ("Lion's Peak"), actual site of the village of Long Jing, and Meijiawu, the neighboring village. The spring harvest is divided into two categories. The most prestigious is the imperial picking, known as *ming qian*, which takes place before the feast of Qingming, around March 20. Two weeks later it is the *yu qian* picking, which is also a high-quality harvest.

According to legend, around the year 250, a Taoist monk came across a dragon hiding in a well not far from Hangzhou. The peasants were praying night and day for the rains to return because a terrible drought was devastating the region. The monk told the villagers of his discovery, and they implored the dragon in the well to come to their aid. As soon as they started praying, clouds began to gather and it began to pour with rain. To commemorate the event, the tea and an ancient temple nearby were given the name "Dragon's Well."

Tasting notes: The tender green leaves harvested on the slopes of Shi Feng are of a classic long, flat shape. Fine notes of seaweed and raw scallops emanate from the steeped leaves. The jade-green liquid releases a gentle vegetal aroma. In the mouth, the herbaceous attack is fresh and slightly sweet. The vegetal opening is full and followed by notes of green bean, cooked fennel and arugula in a gently unctuous stream. The finish is long in the mouth and mildly astringent, with a remarkable balance between sweetness and strength.

Recommended infusion accessory: A *gaiwan* or small teapot.

Huang Shan Mao Feng | green tea |
Translation: Downy point of the yellow mountain
Region: The massif of Huang Shan, the Yellow Mountain, in Anhui Province
Harvest season: April
Cultivar: Huang Shan Da Ye Zhong

It is said that long ago a man and a woman, madly in love with each other, saw their happiness destroyed by a lord who took the woman as a concubine. Driven half mad by this separation, the woman ran away to rejoin her lover only to find that the lord had had him killed. When she found the body of her lover in the mountains, she wept so much that her tears formed a torrent and her petrified body was transformed into a tea tree. Even today, that is the explanation given for the year-long humidity and cloudiness of the area.

Tasting notes: The beautiful tender green leaves of Mao Feng tea are a delight to the eye. Whole and tipped by fine buds, they are slightly twisted, as if performing an elegant dance. Their infusion releases delicate aromas of sorrel and raw vegetables. The silky liquid delights with its extremely delicate notes of green bean and artichoke heart. The light finish leaves a gentle vegetal impression in the mouth.

Recommended infusion accessory: A *gaiwan* or small teapot.

Anji Bai Cha | green tea |
Translation: White tea from the region of Anji
Alternative name: An Ji White Tea
Region: Zhejiang Province
Harvest season: Late March to early April
Cultivar: Bai Ye

Contrary to what the name of this tea implies, it is indeed a green tea. The name refers to the plant's leaves, which are a very pale green and almost white. Still largely unknown in the West, it is highly appreciated in China. It has only existed, however, for about 15 years. The cultivar was originally created in the Anji region. However, in recent years it has grown in popularity so quickly that a lot of growers, anxious to take advantage of the trend, have started to use it. We are now seeing teas of the Anji Bai Cha type appear in various regions of China.

Tasting notes: The threadlike leaves of this delicate gem are pale green and uniform. Unfurled they look so tender and perfect that they seem barely plucked from the branch of the tea plant. They release a lush scent of greenery mixed with fresh grass and asparagus with light notes of white flowers. The pale liquid slides suavely and smoothly through the mouth. The sweet and tart attack swells to aromas of ground cherries and fresh beans. The overall sensation is both gentle and dazzling and has a remarkable balance. Fresh and exquisite, the long vegetal finish is undercut with flowers and transports the taster.

Recommended infusion accessory: A *gaiwan* or small teapot.

Huiming | green tea |
Translation: This tea is named after a monk
Region: Zhejiang Province
Harvest season: April to May and September to October
Cultivar: Huiming

The village of Jingning is located on the slopes of Mount Chimu. According to legend, tea production in this area dates back more than 1,100 years, when the monk Huiming built a temple on Mount Nanqan and planted tea trees around it. An ancient plantation of tea trees can still be seen close to this temple.

Tasting notes: The twisted, dark-green leaves are covered in small, downy hairs. The infusion gives off aromas of fresh greenery, sea breezes and osmanthus flowers. The clear, pale-green liquid releases delicate notes of freshly picked flowers and leaves. The gentle attack reveals sweet aromas of fresh soybean and melon skin. This round and smooth tea tickles the senses far into the throat. The long, smooth finish develops into a light note of crocus flowers.

Recommended infusion accessory: A *gaiwan* or small teapot.

Dong Shan | green tea |
Translation/alternative name: Mountain of the East
Region: Jiangsu Province
Harvest season: April to May
Cultivar: Qun Ti Xiao Ye Zhong

This tea is named after the mountain and the village where the famous Bi Luo Chun tea originated. Its recent history dates back only about 10 years. It is produced from the same tea trees as the Bi Luo Chun variety. The leaves are handpicked, but the processing is entirely mechanical. Once the short season of the Bi Luo Chun tea is over, the production of Dong Shan begins. The rich, aromatic potential of the exceptional gardens thus becomes available in a more modest form, so that it can be enjoyed on a daily basis.

Tasting notes: The dark-green Dong Shan leaves produce an infusion with pronounced accents of ripe peaches, sunflower seeds and fresh scallops. Its sturdy liquid is rich and silky. The mouthfeel is intense, conjuring up seaweed and walnut. The persistent finish narrows to a touch of astringency.

Recommended infusion accessory: A teapot.

83

Anxi Tie Guan Yin | wulong |
Translation: Iron goddess of mercy of Anxi
Alternative name: Iron Goddess of Mercy
Region: Fujian Province
Harvest season: Late April to early May
Cultivar: Tie Guan Yin

According to legend, on the way home from his plantation, a grower named Mr. Wei used to pass by a temple dedicated to Guan Yin, the goddess of mercy. Every time he was saddened to see the dilapidated state of the temple and the iron statue of Guan Yin. Although he didn't have the means to restore them, he decided to burn incense there and to sweep the rooms and clean the statue. One night, the goddess Guan Yin came to him in a dream and said, "In the cave behind the temple lies a treasure that will last many generations… Be sure to share it generously with your neighbors." The next day, Mr. Wei searched the cave and found only a small tea shoot. He took it, planted it in his garden and cared for it so well that it became a sturdy bush that bore beautiful tea leaves within two years. When he infused them in a *gaiwan* he noticed a remarkable aroma and a flavor that was pure and lasting even after several infusions. Encouraged by these results he took even greater care of the plant, and after a few years the original tree had produced more than 200 bushes. Now that he had become rich, Mr. Wei was able to have the temple and the statue of the goddess of mercy restored. He willingly shared seeds with his neighbors, and they all

lived comfortably and were able to appreciate the delicate Tie Guan Yin tea.

Another version of the legend claims that Mr. Wei named the tea after both the goddess and the iron pot in which he planted the young shoot. Although this tea is now very famous and produced in many regions throughout China, the best Tie Guan Yin is still found in Anxi.

Tasting notes: In the palm of the hand, the rolled leaves of Tie Guan Yin tea present a delicate composition of shades of green. The infusion envelops the taster in a heady spring bouquet of lily of the valley, hyacinth and clover flowers. The mouthfeel presents gentle vegetable notes of artichoke heart and fresh mushroom before developing into a suave floral fullness. The velvety, very generous liquid is enriched with savory aromas of zucchini and vanilla. The long finish brings together vegetal and floral notes in a refreshing combination.

Recommended infusion method accessory: The *gong fu cha* technique (see page 144) and a *gaiwan* or teapot.

Mi Lan Xiang | wulong |
Translation: Perfume of honeyed orchid
Alternative name: Feng Huang Dan Cong
Region: Guangdong Province
Harvest season: Late April to early May and September to October
Cultivar: Mi Lan Xiang

The history of tea began more than 1,000 years ago in the Feng Huang Mountains (Phoenix Mountains). Indeed, the teas of this region are documented in the *Cha Jing*, a tea classic written by Lu Yu in 780. Since that time, this region has a notion that is found nowhere else: the *dan cong*, the "unique tea tree."

The term *dan cong* describes tea products made from the leaves of one chosen tea tree. The harvest from one plant represents approximately 3½ pounds (1.5 kg) of tea. The older the tree, the more precious the harvest. The oldest of these chosen trees is reputed to be 800 years old.

Another important custom from this region is the use of wild tea trees. Traditionally, this was the only method used. Even today, many growers use a traditional planting method, in groves. Some gardens are also still planted with wild trees that are not pruned. These two customs are, of course, reserved for only the highest-quality teas. Once processed, the teas will be named for their smell. For example, Mi Lan Xiang means "perfume of honeyed orchid," and Huang Zhi Xiang means "perfume of orange blossom," to name two. In order to fully develop and stabilize these rich aromas, the teas generally undergo two firings, which will be as gentle as the quality demands. These teas, which were given in tribute to the emperor over many dynasties, are still rare today.

Tasting notes: The long, dark leaves give off discrete aromas of brown sugar and candied melon. An astonishing procession of lychee, grapefruit, citrus and brioche emanates from the infusion. Heavier notes of toast and morels are carried on this aromatic wave. The peach-colored liquid has the same aromatic exuberance as the leaves. The attack of the mouthfeel is surprisingly strong and full bodied. The aromas of exotic fruit, muscat grape and melon are incredibly persistent. The sweet finish is drawn out into a minty note that is very refreshing.

Recommended infusion method accessory: The *gong fu cha* technique (see page 144) and a *gaiwan* or teapot.

85

Yunnan Hong Gong Fu | black tea |
Translation: Great red tea of Yunnan
Alternative name: Yunnan Black Tea
Region: Yunnan Province
Harvest season: April
Cultivar: Yunnan Da Ye

Contrary to popular belief, black tea has not been cultivated in Yunnan for very long. The cultivation dates back only to the beginning of the 20th century. In spite of that, some of the best black teas in the world are found there. The appellation Gong Fu is reserved for the highest-quality teas from Yunnan. The exceptional teas that have a right to this appellation are characterized by the abundance of buds produced by the trees. The Yunnan Hong Gong Fu variety comes from high-altitude plantations in the Simao region. The leaves are carefully picked in early spring and are only slightly oxidized before being manually dried by pressing in a large heated steel vat.

Tasting notes: The leaves bear an abundance of beautiful golden buds. The gentle twisted shapes release suave aromas of blond tobacco, caramel and scorched earth. The red-orange liquid has a marmalade nose. The mouthfeel is round and slightly sweet. Aromas of tobacco, exotic wood and ripe apricot spread their fullness through the mouth. The long, rich finish is remarkably comforting.

Recommended infusion accessory: A stoneware teapot or a *gaiwan*.

Shou Pu er 1999 | old tea trees |
Translation: Pu er is a town in Yunnan Province. The word *shou* means "cooked," and 1999 is the year of production
Region: Yunnan Province (Xishuangbanna)
Harvest season: April
Cultivar: Yunnan Da Ye

This Pu er tea, produced through accelerated fermentation, has been aged since its production in 1999. Contrary to Sheng Pu er teas, this aging does not significantly improve the tea, but it replaces the hardness of the young Shou with a softness and roundness. It is sold in cake form (bing), produced by the Yunnan Tea Company and stored in Hong Kong. It was produced from leaves picked from ancient trees, which is rare for a Shou Pu er tea. The broad leaves have been compressed in the traditional way and separate easily from the cake.

Tasting notes: Softening as they are rinsed, the leaves give off an intense bouquet of peat, roots and sweet potato. A strong animal undertone suggests wet wool. The liquid is a very dark red-brown. The smooth and unctuous mouthfeel has aromas of ripe fig, spruce and tar. Hazy notes of maple wood, brioche and dark chocolate caress the palate. The gentle persistence of burnt sugar and flint soothes the finish.

Recommended infusion method/accessory: The *gong fu cha* technique (see page 144) and a *gaiwan* or teapot.

SHENG PU ER 1974 HJH 74342 | aged tea |

Translation: Pu er is a town in Yunnan Province. The word *sheng* means "raw," and 1974 is the year of production. Menghai is the main factory where Pu er teas are made. The number 74 indicates the year in which the recipe was first used. The number 34 indicates that the mixture is made up of leaves of grades three and four. The number 2 indicates the Menghai factory.

Region: Yunnan Province (Xishuangbanna)
Harvest season: April
Cultivar: Yunnan Da Ye

This ancient Pu er tea deserves to be called vintage, since it has now been aging for more than 30 years. It should be noted that it has not been compressed into cakes, as the Sheng (raw) Pu er tradition would demand. However, it is still a "tea to keep" that has been carefully aged in a cellar in Hong Kong. Aging leaves loose triggers a faster post-fermentation process than when leaves are aged while compressed into cakes. The tea is brought to maturity faster, but it may also deteriorate faster. Sheng Pu er teas aged as loose leaves first appeared in 1970. This is one of the first of its kind, processed by the famous Menghai factory.

Tasting notes: The medium-sized leaves, ranging in color from dark to light brown, give off the fragrance of beaten earth in the sun. The deep, very dense liquid has an astonishingly fine texture. The mouthfeel is complex, offering earthy aromas of raw beet and potato. These are mixed with more succulent notes of dark chocolate, salty caramel and ground cherries. The long finish leaves a refined mineral sweetness. This is a generous tea whose primitive beauty has been polished by time.

Recommended infusion method/accessory: The *gong fu cha* technique (see page 144) and a *gaiwan* or teapot.

87

Japan

A WORK OF ART AND THE WORK OF A LIFETIME, TEA DRINKING IN JAPAN HAS EVOLVED INTO A SPIRITUAL IDEAL KNOWN AS *CHADO* ("THE WAY OF TEA"). FROM ITS INTRODUCTION TO THE ARCHIPELAGO, TEA WAS ENDOWED WITH GREAT VALUE AND QUICKLY BECAME THE CENTER OF AN ELABORATE RITUAL. TODAY, IN BOTH THEIR METHODS OF CULTIVATION AND THEIR DEVELOPMENT OF THE CEREMONY THAT ACCOMPANIES TEA DRINKING, THE JAPANESE HAVE CREATED A UNIQUE PRODUCT, WORTHY OF THEIR REFINED AND DEMANDING CULTURE. A JAPANESE LEGEND EXPLAINING THE DISCOVERY OF TEA INVOLVES BODHIDHARMA, A SIXTH-CENTURY INDIAN PRINCE AND THE FOUNDER OF CHAN BUDDHISM, WHICH WOULD BECOME ZEN BUDDHISM IN THE 12TH CENTURY. ACCORDING TO THE LEGEND, BODHIDHARMA MADE THE IMPOSSIBLE VOW OF NEVER SUCCUMBING TO SLEEP SO THAT HE COULD DEVOTE HIMSELF TO ENDLESS MEDITATION. HOWEVER, ONE DAY, EXHAUSTED FROM HIS CONSTANT WAKEFULNESS, HE FELL ASLEEP. WHEN HE AWOKE, ENRAGED AT HAVING INTERRUPTED HIS MEDITATION, HE TORE OFF HIS EYELIDS AND BURIED THEM. A FEW YEARS LATER, PASSING BY THE EXACT SAME SPOT, HE SAW THAT TWO MAGNIFICENT BUSHES WITH OBLONG LEAVES HAD GROWN THERE: HIS EYELIDS HAD GIVEN BIRTH TO TWO TEA TREES.

History

Tea was introduced to Japan in the eighth century by monks who had spent time in China studying Buddhism. At the time, tea was already a popular beverage in China, and the monks used it as a stimulant to stay awake during their long hours of meditation. History records the monk Saisho as being the first to have brought the custom back to Japan, so we have reason to believe that Japan's interest in tea was roused at this time. However, because of the strained relations between China and Japan, it was not until the end of the 12th century that Japan could truly be considered as having a tea culture.

In 1191, the monk Eisai (1141–1215), founder of the Rinzai sect of Zen Buddhism, brought a few tea-tree seeds back from a pilgrimage to China. He planted these seeds in the district of Hizen, in the northern part of the island of Kyushu, as well as around the monasteries of Hakata (Fukuoka). Eisai spread the idea that tea should be consumed for its medicinal properties. We are also indebted to him for the first Japanese book on tea, published in 1211. In addition to seeds, he also introduced the Japanese to the tea preparation method that was used in China at the time, under the Song dynasty (960–1279). The tea leaves were ground to a fine powder (matcha) before being brewed. The importance of ritual and discipline as well as the austere nature of Rinzai Zen philosophy no doubt had a great influence on the rigidly codified evolution of the Japanese tea ceremony.

Later, some tea trees were planted on the main island of Honshu, near Kyoto, the former capital of Japan. Originally cultivated by monks to stimulate them during their meditation sessions, tea was soon adopted by intellectuals and statesmen. In the 13th century, while noblemen were meeting to drink tea during ceremonial gatherings, the samurai also made it part of their lifestyle. The fashion for tea-tasting contests began, just like those held in China during the same period. More and more enthusiasts got together to test their ability to recognize different Chinese teas for days and nights on end.

Later, Japanese grand tea masters appeared on the scene. In the 16th century, one of them, Sen No Rikyu, codified the tea ceremony (chanoyu), establishing a close relationship between Buddhist values and the various schools of Japanese tea of that era.

From 1641 to 1853, Japan remained cut off from the rest of the world. It was a policy of isolation, known as sakoku, which forbade anyone from leaving the archipelago and permitted almost no contact with the outside world. For more that 200 years China alone provided the rest of the world with tea. How-ever, the isolation of Japan was not entirely negative because, in addition to contributing to the development of the unique character of Japanese culture, it led to the perfecting of new ways of processing tea. Thus, in 1738, Soen Nagatani created a method of leaf dehydration using steam. Thanks to this method, which brings out the fresh aroma of the leaves, he was able to create a green tea that was very different from Chinese green teas and which rapidly gained in popularity.

In 1859, Japan abandoned its policy of isolation and finally opened up to the international market. It began exporting tea overseas, mainly to the United States, which became a major source of revenue. At the end of the 19th century the archipelago began industrializing its production methods, in particular with the use of heated rotating cylinders invented by Kenzo Takahashi. The production of black tea on Japanese soil also began at this time.

During the years after the First World War, Japanese tea exports set unprecedented records. At that time, Japan exported up to 22,003 tons (19,961 t) of green tea and 11,178 tons (10,141 t) of black tea. But the explosion in demand was short-lived, and Japanese exports of black tea dropped again very quickly.

As the Americans developed a preference for "English-tasting" tea (full-bodied black tea), it became

difficult for the Japanese to compete with the large emerging growers in Sri Lanka, India and Kenya, who could produce tea at very low cost. In the face of this competition, the Japanese market gradually turned more and more toward domestic distribution.

Several studies conducted by Japanese researchers in the 1920s revealed scientific proof that tea contained vitamins and catechins. To promote the sale of tea, the government published these results to encourage the Japanese to drink it on a daily basis, as an integral part of their diet. After the Second World War, various groups and associations of growers continued to promote the benefits of tea, and all

sorts of by-products based on tea began to appear. Later, to facilitate distribution, tea was marketed in tea bags, and a lot of attention was paid to packaging and presentation.

Since then, Japan has increased its productivity considerably by using mechanical harvesting and new techniques for taking cuttings. They have concentrated almost exclusively on the production of green teas.

The Japanese Tea Masters

Various tea masters have made their mark on the history of tea in Japan. Through continual aesthetic and spiritual research, they have steered tea culture in a new direction. The three tea masters presented below are renowned for having developed the Japanese art of preparing powdered tea and for establishing the precepts of the tea ceremony, *chanoyu*.

MURATA SHUKO

The father of the Way of Tea, or *chado* (see page 109), and of the tea ceremony as we know it today, is the Zen monk Murata Shuko (1422–1502). This disciple of the famous and eccentric monk Ikkyu taught his master that the spirit of the Buddha could be present not just in the act of drinking tea but also in the simple gestures involved in its preparation. Shuko was the first to serve tea to his guests himself and to simplify the tasting rules. As official tea master to the shogun Ashikaga Yoshimasa, he introduced the qualities of refinement, rigor, spiritual values and humility into the preparation of tea. He put an end to the use of sophisticated salons and luxurious reception rooms. He himself designed the first building devoted to the tea ceremony, a simple cabin made of rustic materials at the back of a garden.

TAKENO JOO

Having been initiated into the tea ceremony by Shuko's disciples, Takeno Joo (1502–1555) first practiced the tea ceremony according to the principles of the master Shuko, but he then enriched it with the ideal of Zen simplicity. His tearoom, decorated with modest objects like everyday bowls from Japan or Korea, was closer to a personal concept of how to practice the Way of Tea. He eliminated the shelves Shuko used to display precious Chinese objects and replaced them with a piece of calligraphy and a simple floral arrangement. His "simple and natural" ceremony was imbued with honesty, caution and the strict emotional control typical of the *wabi* philosophy.

SEN NO RIKYU

A disciple of Takeno Joo from the age of 19, Sen No Rikyu (1521–1591) radicalized the trend established by his master. The ceremony he offered became a cross between performance art and spiritual practice. While unifying the style of his predecessors, he set down the rules of the *chado* and codified *chanoyu*, the tea ceremony, which he raised to a high degree of perfection. Poverty, humility, modesty and imperfection became the fundamental criteria of the *chado*. Sen No Rikyu reduced the number of utensils used in the ceremony and demanded that the teahouse be built of coarser materials, such as straw, earth or wood still bearing its bark. He also invented the *nijiri guchi*, a small entrance that obliged the guests to bow their head to enter the tearoom.

Though famous for having defined the seven rules of the *chanoyu* ceremony (see page 110), Rikyu went down in history for having been sentenced to commit suicide for treason by the powerful Emperor Hideyoshi. The real reasons for this sentence remain obscure. According to legend, following a final tea ceremony in the company of his faithful friends, he broke his bowl to indicate that "the lips of misfortune had touched it and so no other man should drink from it." Then he committed seppuku (hara-kiri) in silence with honor and dignity.

The Japanese Tea Industry

The Japanese tea industry has gone through several growth phases over time. First established to respond to the tastes of the international market, the industry originally exported a large portion of its production. That is why black tea was still being produced in Japan until the early 1970s. Today, almost all production is reserved for domestic consumption and less than 1 percent is exported. Specializing in the production of green tea, most of which (70 percent) is Sencha, Japan is the seventh-largest tea grower in the world today.

While the younger generations are more interested in coffee — and in spite of the fact that tea drinking is still deeply entrenched in Japanese traditions — Japan is currently witnessing an evolution in consumer tastes. Each year Japan imports several thousand tons of *grands crus* tea from Darjeeling as well as wulong tea from the high mountains of Taiwan. Nevertheless, the Japanese tea industry continues to flourish, thanks to, among other things, many tea-based products, such as toothpaste, pharmaceutical products, pasta, iced tea and polyphenol extract in capsule form.

It is rare to find small-scale growers in Japan who carry out all stages of production, from picking to the final processing of the tea, themselves. The very high cost of machinery forces the growers or processors to specialize in a specific stage of production, fragmenting the traditional chain of production. Thus, the Japanese tea industry comprises several sectors, as shown in the diagram below.

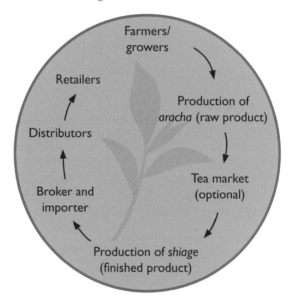

A BRIEF SUMMARY OF THE JAPANESE TEA TRADE

Production area: 119,100 acres (48,200 ha)

Total annual production: 101,500 tons (92,100 t) of green tea

Annual production by province or region: Shizouka, 44,000 tons (39,900 t); Kagoshima, 26,570 tons (24,100 t); Mie, 8,400 tons (7,620 t); Miyazaki, 4,220 tons (3,830 t); Kyoto, 3,275 tons (2,970 t); Nara, 2,790 tons (2,530 t); Fukoka, 2,570 tons (2,330 t); Saga, 2,130 tons (1,930 t); Kumamoto, 1,920 tons (1,740 t); Aichi, 1,060 tons (964 t)

Average production yield: 1,700 pounds per acre (1,910 kg/ha)

Annual exports: 2,105 tons (1,625 t) of green tea; 159 tons (144 t) of other teas

Province that exports the most: Shizuoka

Principal purchasing country: United States, since 1853

Source: Tea Board of Japan, 2007. The data relates to aracha. (Values in imperial units of measure supplied by publisher.)

The tea market in Shizuoka is often bustling with activity as early as five o'clock in the morning.

Japanese farmer-growers maintain their gardens and pick the tea according to the quality and the type of tea desired. Some farmers process the harvest themselves, but usually they sell it or subcontract the processing to specialized companies that turn the leaves into *aracha* (see box below). In turn, these companies take the various batches of *aracha* to the tea market, where it is sold at auction. Many tasters will sample the batches of *aracha*, and they will often separate them into various groupings. (As there are corporate groups that offer exclusivity and certain benefits, some companies sell their *aracha* directly to their partners.) The selected batches of *aracha* will then be sent to various distributors to undergo the different processes required to turn the leaves into a finished product. Finally, brokers and importers will sell the tea to the many distributors and retailers.

ARACHA Processing Japanese green teas involves several stages. *Aracha* is the name given to leaves that have undergone a partial processing that will be completed later. Only 75 percent processed, it is a raw product that includes stems. *Aracha* is used to produce Bancha, Bocha or Sencha teas. The type of tea produced is usually determined in advance, based on the quality of the leaves picked.

A Meeting with Mr. Sato,
Industry Professional

Mr. Sato is the manager of the tea market in Shizuoka, where 110,000 to 220,000 kilos (100,000 to 200,000 t) of tea are traded every day during harvest time.

How long have you been working in the world of tea?
It has been at least 40 years.

What led you to choose this profession?
My father was a tea grower, and when he came to sell our leaves at the market, I was always glad to come with him. Despite coming here so often, I realized that my interest, curiosity and desire to work in this field only grew. I did what I needed to do to apply, and I have been working here now for several decades.

What are your everyday responsibilities?
I supervise trading, make sure that the rules are respected and record sales.

What part of your job do you prefer?
I love to see and to taste all the beautiful teas! I also enjoy the pace of the work, which is often frantic in the high season.

Can you tell us a story related to your job?
During 40 years in the business I have been able to conclude some very large deals, but I remember my first major transaction. I was young, quite new to the market, and I negotiated the sale of 100,000 kilos [220,000 pounds]! That's a lot of tea. There's a lot of pressure in those circumstances, and the seller and the buyer are often pretty tense … Once the deal was concluded I was very proud to have been able to control the situation.

What challenges will the Japanese industry have to face in the coming years?
I must tell you that we are mainly concerned about the excessive popularity of iced teas sold in bottles. Now there are vending machines everywhere. It's a good product, cheap and healthy (in Japan we don't add sugar). However, it is obvious that people, especially young people, are no longer taking the time to drink tea made from leaves in the more traditional way. We must strive to promote interest in high-quality teas that are savored rather than drunk. We would like young people to taste good tea while they are young and remember it all their lives.

What is your favorite tea?
Japanese green teas that have particular and unique characteristics, whether it's a Sencha, a Gyokuro or a Bancha.

How would you define a good tea?
For me, a good tea is often a combination of things: the color of the liquid, the shape and the look of the leaves, a pleasant aroma and a rich taste.

Mr. Sato (at left).

97

Japanese Terroirs

As is the case everywhere, the quality of the terroir is a determining factor in the flavor and character of a tea. Because the sea is never more than 75 miles (120 km) away from the Japanese islands, the sea air imparts iodized notes to the leaves and a marine aroma suggesting seaweed and fresh grass. But, as we will see later, processing methods also contribute to the teas' distinctive flavor.

In Japan, tea plantations are found from the Akita Prefecture in the north to the Okinawa Prefecture in the south. However, the southern islands of Kyushu and Shikoku, as well as the southern part of the main island of Honshu, are the major tea-growing areas. The climate is cooler there than in the rest of the archipelago, 50 to 65°F (10 to 18°C), and annual precipitation can be up to 60 inches (1,500 mm). The

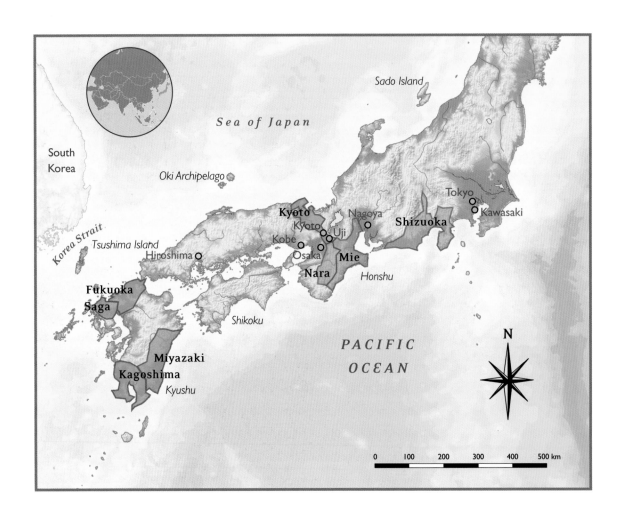

notion of a terroir usually applies less to Japanese teas, except for the *grands crus*. It is quite common to mix harvests from different gardens located in the same region, and sometimes even harvests from different prefectures, before processing them together. The map opposite provides an overview of Japan's main tea-growing areas.

SHIZUOKA PREFECTURE

Located on the Pacific coast, Shizuoka Prefecture is a highly regarded tea-growing region. Covering an area slightly larger than 49,400 acres (20,000 ha), it accounts for almost half the archipelago's production, some 44,100 tons (40,000 t) of tea per year. The region's proximity to the ocean creates harsher weather conditions, a lower mean temperature and variable weather patterns, making Shiuzuoka ideal for growing quality tea. Tea trees raised in tough conditions often have more complex flavor profiles.

This prefecture has a long history in the production of tea, and most of the harvests from other parts of the country are brought here for final processing. Several hundred tea producers are based here, ensuring a very high output and extensive distribution.

KYOTO PREFECTURE

Located in the middle of the island of Honshu, Kyoto Prefecture is characterized by a damp, subtropical climate with mild winters and humid summers. Since the city of Kyoto was the capital of Japan for more than 1,000 years, tea was intensively cultivated in the area. Today the gardens surrounding Kyoto are devoted to the production of high-quality tea and supply roughly 3 percent of Japan's total output.

One of the most prestigious tea-growing areas of the archipelago is Uji, located southeast of Kyoto. The first plants brought back by Eisai at the end of the 12th century were transplanted to this region. As the gardens are concentrated in the inland hills, they are naturally protected from the bad weather of the coastal region. Considered an original growing area and renowned for the rich quality of the teas it produces, the Uji region is famous for its Matcha and Gyokuro teas.

KAGOSHIMA PREFECTURE (ISLAND OF KYUSHU)

The island of Kyushu is in the very far south of the country. The climate is subtropical, so the gardens of this region produce all kinds of teas: Sencha, Bancha, Kabusecha and Gyokuro, as well as an exclusive variety, Kamairicha, which is a green tea that is steamed in vats.

As Kagoshima Prefecture is the main growing region, the teas produced there represent about 20 percent of the country's total output. The other major growing regions on this island are Saga, Miyazaki and Fukuoka.

NARA AND MIE PREFECTURES

The less famous teas of Nara Prefecture are grown on the Yamato plateau, at an altitude between 650 and 1,650 feet (200 to 500 m). They include Sencha, Bancha and Kabusecha varieties. The gardens of Mie Prefecture are at a lower altitude and produce mainly Kabusecha and Sencha varieties.

Japanese Gardens and Plants

The Japanese use a unique method of tea cultivation, which is demonstrated by the beauty of Japanese tea gardens. The tea trees are planted side by side and pruned to form cylindrical hedges of varying heights and with a slightly rounded surface. In order to achieve this hedge formation, the tea trees are planted in twos, back to back and about 1 foot (30 cm) apart, with each group of two separated by a distance of about 2 feet (60 cm).

The gardens are situated on gradually inclined terraces in the foothills of gently sloping mountains. Gardens located on the plains are usually used to produce more industrial teas. To make using machines easier, these gardens are laid out on flat ground without shade trees. Growers spread rice straw between the rows to prevent the soil from eroding or drying out.

In Japan, it takes an average of four to five years before the first buds from new tea trees are ready to be picked, three years if the trees are on the plains. The year before the first picking, the trees are pruned in such a way that the new branches will form the desired rounded profile. This shape provides a maximum picking surface so that a greater number of buds can be harvested. Every five to six years the trees are subjected to more rigorous pruning (*daigari*) after the first spring picking, which strengthens the plant and stimulates growth. After this pruning, the tea trees become dormant and are not harvested from again for one year. The productive life of a Japanese tea tree varies according to its yield, but it is rarely longer than about 30 years.

Fans circulate air above the tea trees.   A garden in the Ashikubo valley.

A widespread technique used in Japan is to install fans to circulate the air above the tea gardens. Strategically placed at a height of about 13 feet (4 m), these fans disperse any layers of fog and retain the heat that accumulates in the soil during the day. They also prevent the formation of dew, which can damage new shoots; in the heat of the sun a drop of dew can act like a magnifying glass and burn the leaves. In addition, when the temperature drops below 32°F (0°C), the dew freezes and can spoil the quality of the leaves. The fans are usually programmed to start up automatically when the temperature reaches 40°F (5°C).

JAPANESE CULTIVARS

Today there are 55 cultivars registered in Japan, of which about 40 are used exclusively for the production of green teas. Despite this variety, most of the Japanese production comes from one hybrid, the Yabukita cultivar. Gokou, Beni Fouki and Samidori cultivars are among the others used.

YABUKITA

Yabukita is a hybrid of the *sinensis* variety that was developed by Hikosaburo Sugiyama in 1954, in Shizuoka Prefecture. Renowned for its resistance to the weather conditions on the islands and its intensity of flavor, which is more suited to Japanese taste, this hybrid quickly spread throughout the archipelago. Almost 70 percent of Japanese tea gardens are composed entirely of Yabukita plants. In Shizuoka prefecture that percentage rises to 90 percent.

In spite of the particular advantages of the Yabukita cultivar, there are certain disadvantages to uniform cultivation. As all the plants carry the same genetic baggage, they have the same qualities but also the same defects, which makes them more vulnerable to diseases and pests. Consequently, growers must take particular care of them.

The widespread use of the Yabukita variety has the advantage of making grouping in batches easier, but it can also give rise to a certain loss of flavor.

GOKOU

Grown on small lots around Uji, in the Kyoto Prefecture, the Gokou cultivar is used primarily for the production of Gyokuro and Matcha tea. It was created by the Center for Tea Experimentation in Kyoto and is renowned for its aromatic qualities.

COVERED GROWING

Tea trees are sometimes covered by special canopies to reduce the plants' exposure to the sun, which triggers a change in the chemical composition of the leaves. Unable to carry out the process of photosynthesis effectively, the trees are forced to compensate by producing more chlorophyll and amino acids. To do this, they must draw more nutrients from the soil. This type of cultivation produces tender, very dark-green leaves that contain more chlorophyll and fewer tannins.

Traditionally, straw was strewn over bamboo structures erected over the tea plants to reduce sunlight. Although straw is still used today, the structures are usually metal and covered with mesh netting made of synthetic fibers. Straw can cut out up to 95 percent of the light, whereas mesh netting blocks about 80 percent of the sun's rays.

Following traditional methods, the shaded plants are not pruned, which maximizes the number of buds along the whole length of the stem. Hence, in spite of the high cost of labor, covered tea plants are picked by hand. The picking takes place later in the spring because the leaves, deprived of light, take longer to reach maturity. The pickers must separate the stems one by one to select the new shoots. Covered gardens are used to produce Gyokuro, Kabusecha, Tencha and Matcha teas, and the duration of covering depends on the type of tea desired.

BENI FOUKI

Originally, the Beni Fouki cultivar was used in Japan for the production of black tea. Today, it is also grown in southern Japan and processed into green tea, which is dehydrated in vats. Some claim it is high in catechins, and this tea is currently enjoying a surge in popularity. Research is under way to prove its medicinal value, particularly in the fight against certain allergies.

SAMIDORI

The Samidori cultivar, fruit of the research of Masajiro Koyama, is mainly used in groupings to create Gyokuro and Matcha teas. Its bright-green leaves produce a richly scented liquid with a hint of bitterness.

HARVESTING

Japanese tea harvests are seasonal and continue from mid-May to September. The first harvests, called *shincha* (literally "new tea"), are eagerly awaited and often the most expensive. High-quality *shincha* picking is done by hand and only the smallest shoots are chosen. Depending on the altitude, four or five harvests will take place each year. It is necessary to wait 45 to 50 days between harvests to allow the new shoots to grow back.

102

Processing Japanese Green Teas

Japanese methods of processing tea were, for a long time, inspired by Chinese practice, but today they are radically different, mainly because of state-of-the-art technologies and specific processing methods that were developed and refined over centuries.

For the production of green teas, the Japanese "fire" the leaf using steam. Also known as the "Uji method," this process preserves extremely fresh aromas with notes of the sea and herbaceous plants.

In order to maintain competitive pricing on the international market in the face of high labor costs, Japanese growers have been quick to adopt technical advances.

To produce Japanese-style green tea, the leaves must first be turned into *aracha*, a raw product that is then sold at auction to companies who complete the processing. After picking, the tea must undergo three essential stages in order to become *aracha*: steaming, rolling and drying.

TRANSFORMING THE LEAVES INTO *ARACHA*

PICKING

Picking is carried out with a machine equipped with scissors and an air compressor, which blows the leaves into a bag. Two workers operate this small cutter, which adapts to the shape of the hedge to ensure precision picking. Faster but less precise, the harvester used for gardens located on the plains can be handled by just one person. Once the leaves are picked, they are quickly sent to the factory for processing.

WITHERING

Usually, the freshly picked leaves are sent straight to the steaming stage. However, some growers let them stand for a few hours.

STEAMING

The leaves are then heated with steam, a process that lasts 20 to 80 seconds. Steaming is extremely important, relative to the aromatic quality of the tea. A short steaming period (20 to 40 seconds) produces a tea in the Asamushi style: leaves are larger, fewer are broken, and they have a full, light taste reminiscent of green vegetables. A long period of steaming (40 to 80 seconds) produces a tea in the Fukamushi style: the leaves have been softened by the long steaming, are more easily broken, are smaller and produce an intense flavor and a darker liquid. This is the style of tea that the Japanese prefer today.

COOLING

After steaming, the leaves are cooled either by being blown through synthetic mesh tubes using air jets or by being placed in large rotating cylinders. This step eliminates excess humidity that could damage the leaves.

FIRST DRYING

The leaves then undergo a preliminary drying process at 210°F (100°C) for about 45 minutes in a rotating cylinder. After this, they spend 30 minutes in a similar machine, where the temperature is lowered from 175°F down to 105°F (80°C to 40°C).

The edges of the cylinder are made of rough bamboo, and during drying, mechanical arms mix the leaves constantly so they brush against the walls. The mixing action is a determining factor in the color of the tea and the release of tannins, which by the same token affects the taste (texture, astringency, etc.) of the tea.

ROLLING

Rolling, which lasts 20 to 30 minutes, softens the stems and releases the natural oils contained in the leaves.

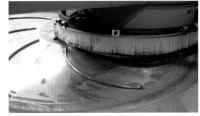

SECOND DRYING

The leaves are dried a second time for 20 to 40 minutes at 80°F (30°C), again in one of the cylinders, in order to reduce the humidity created by the rolling process and to stabilize the oils on the leaves. After this stage, roughly 13 percent of the water remains in the leaves.

Some processors use up to five or six different rotating cylinders throughout the processing, each of which has a different temperature and a different rotation time. The goal is to maintain the leaves at a constant temperature between 85 and 95°F (30 to 35 °C) and to reduce their moisture content gradually.

SHAPING

A machine equipped with mechanical arms gives the leaves a needle shape during a process that lasts between 40 and 60 minutes at temperatures varying from 158 to 248°F (70 to 120°C).

THIRD DRYING

The loose leaves then circulate on a conveyor belt for about 30 minutes as they are heated to 185°F (85°C). It is this third drying that finally produces *aracha*.

FINAL PROCESSING

GROUPING

At the final stage of processing, different batches of leaves are sometimes grouped together and blended.

SIFTING AND SORTING

Next, dust and stems are separated from the leaves, and the leaves are then sorted into different sizes using sieves. The sifting is done mechanically by means of static rollers and mesh. The leaves can also be sifted electronically using several cameras equipped with optical scanners. Each leaf is scanned and, depending on its size and color, is separated from the others by a high-precision air jet.

FINAL DRYING

The final drying stage varies depending on the type of tea and the taste required. The leaves are usually heated to a temperature of about 105°F (40°C) to bring out the aromas. When the firing time is increased, the aroma of fresh grass diminishes and notes closer to those of grilled nuts are released. After the final drying stage, 1 percent to 3 percent humidity remains in the leaves.

PACKAGING

Japanese teas are usually packaged mechanically. Batches of 1 ounce to 44 pounds (25 g to 20 kg) are vacuum-packed, and sometimes nitrogen is added to the bag before sealing to protect the leaves during transportation and to ensure a longer shelf life.

The Local Way of Preparing Tea

Although making tea using the classic method of brewing from loose leaves is still the Japanese national drink, it does not fit well with the lifestyle of young Japanese. New products, such as iced coffee and iced tea, which are widely available from vending machines, are gaining in popularity and drawing the younger generation toward a more instant form of consumption. However, several customs remain fashioable. Restaurants serve Bancha, Hojicha and Genmaicha teas in teapots. For a more upscale tasting experience, Sencha and Gyokuro teas are brewed according to the traditional *senchado* method.

SENCHADO

The broad meaning of *senchado* is "Way of Sencha." *Senchado* is an elaborate ritual method of steeping Japanese teas from leaves. It was created by learned Japanese who wanted to break free from the constraints imposed by the rules of *chanoyu*. They adapted the Chinese method of infusing tea and created a more relaxed and practical context, which was conducive to philosophical and spiritual discussion. Seeking to align themselves with the spiritual lifestyle of ancient Chinese sages from the Ming dynasty, these intellectuals encouraged the practice of certain Chinese arts, such as calligraphy, painting, poetry and music, during their ritual, which often served as a backdrop for these activities. Over time, the growing popularity of loose-leaf tea led *senchado* enthusiasts to make the steeping method of Sencha tea less accessible by introducing, among other things, rules inspired by the *chanoyu*.

Although it is less well known today than the *chanoyu*, the *senchado* ritual continues to be practiced.

BOTTLED ICED TEA   Bottled iced teas can be found everywhere in Japan and are a commercial success. Most are based on green tea, but there are some that use wulong or black tea. Although the tea is brewed and packaged in Japan, it is usually produced from leaves grown in China, Taiwan or Vietnam. The plastic bottles in which it is sold are made from PET plastic (polyethylene terephthalate), so bottled iced teas are popularly known as "pet."

The *Senchado* Brewing Method

Senchado is a tea-brewing method that concentrates the aromas of higher-quality teas, such as Gyokuro or high-grade Sencha. Just like the *gong fu cha* technique (see page 144), this method consists of several successive infusions using the same leaves so that new flavors develop in each brew.

Here are the main steps:

- Prepare and heat the teapot and other utensils required.
- Place the tea leaves in the heated teapot. Use 1 to 2 heaping teaspoons (5 to 10 ml) of tea leaves **1**.
- Pour the water onto the leaves. For best results, ensure the water is between 150 and 167°F (65 to 75°C). To accomplish this, instead of pouring the water directly onto the leaves, it can be poured into a small bowl **2** (one bowl per person) to cool a little. Water cools by about 50°F (10°C) when it is poured into a cold bowl. Using a bowl also ensures that the quantity of water poured onto the leaves will be exactly right **3**.
- Wait approximately 30 seconds. The first infusion is the longest as the leaves are not yet moist. Strain the liquor from the teapot into the bowl. **4**. If you are serving several guests, ensure that the same amount of liquid is poured into each bowl by pouring a little at a time. Empty the teapot completely, or the tea will continue to steep.
- Taste.
- Proceed to the next infusion in the same way. The subsequent infusions should be shorter.

THE KYUSU TEAPOT   A kyusu teapot has a straight handle and a fine interior strainer that filters the leaves when the liquid is poured.

CHADO OR "THE WAY OF TEA"

A genuine way of life directed by a code of ethics and morals in accordance with the very essence of tea, *chado* emerged in Japan during the 15th century. In his marvelous book outlining the close relationship between the spirit of tea and Japanese culture, *The Book of Tea*, Okakuro Kakuzô defines *chado* as follows:

> The Way of Tea is a cult founded on the love of beauty in even the most basic pursuits of our daily life. It teaches us purity and harmony, the mystery of mutual consideration and the romantic element inherent in the social order. … Far from being a simple aesthetic, in the ordinary meaning of the term, the philosophy of tea expresses, at the same time as an ethic and a religion, our global concept of man and of nature. It is a hygiene, in that it demands cleanliness; an asceticism, in that it demonstrates that well-being is to be found in simplicity and not in some expensive complexity; and finally, a system of ethics, in that it defines our sense of proportion in relation to the universe.

Sen No Rikyu defined the four basic principles that sum up the essence of the Way of Tea as follows: harmony, respect, purity and tranquility. He also incorporated *wabi* philosophy, a spiritual and aesthetic concept based on austerity and solitude that leads to a contemplative experience of the relationship between man and objects, into the Way of Tea. In concrete terms, *wabi* involves transcending materialism through human interaction and sees beauty in imperfection and in the suggestion of completeness that can be found in a void. And so the Way of Tea is not restrictive. It is accessible to whoever believes tea to be a way of life that enables us to discover the hidden beauty of people and objects.

THE JAPANESE *CHANOYU* CEREMONY

The *chanoyu* ceremony, an extremely codified ritual consisting of hundreds of different steps, is the most elaborate form of expression of the Way of Tea. Practiced according to the four principles defined by Sen No Rikyu, its purpose is to lead its practitioners to a spiritual dimension by offering and receiving tea in an atmosphere imbued with harmony and humility.

"*Cha no yu*" literally means "water for tea." There are two principal methods of presenting *chanoyu*: *chaji* and *chakai*. *Chaji*, the more formal of the two, lasts three to four hours and includes a maximum of four participants. The guests are first received with great ceremony in the garden before being invited to a meal (*kaiseki*) in the teahouse. After a short pause, the host prepares the most formal moment of the event, the serving of a thick Matcha tea (*koicha*), which is followed, after another pause in the garden, by a lighter Matcha tea (*usucha*). These proceedings are accompanied by expressions of courtesy and respect and long moments of meditation.

A shorter version of *chaji*, known as *chakai*, lasts only 30 to 45 minutes. During this ceremony a light tea is served together with sweets. This is the most appropriate method for a large number of participants.

THE SEVEN RULES OF CHANOYU SET BY SEN NO RIKYU

The seven rules set by Sen No Rikyu present, in the form of statements accompanied by simple illustrations, the procedures that must be respected during the *chanoyu* ceremony. At first glance they seem easy to follow, but, once the underlying essence of each one is understood, it becomes apparent that they require total personal involvement as well as paying close attention to the needs of one's guests.

- "Arrange the flowers as they grow in the fields." Flowers should be arranged in such a way as to suggest nature in all its simplicity.

- "Arrange the charcoal to heat the water." This statement refers to the effort, the ability and the sincerity that the host must devote to this preparation.

- "In summer, evoke coolness." Everything must be done to make guests feel comfortable, including adapting the environment to the mood of the season.

- "In winter, evoke warmth."

- "Take care of everything ahead of time." Every detail must be carefully planned.

- "Be prepared for rain." The host must be prepared for all eventualities.

- "Give every one of your guests your full attention."

A Simple Method to Prepare Matcha

To prepare Matcha, you will need three essential utensils: a *chawan* (tea bowl), a *chasen* (tea whisk) and a *chashaku* (teaspoon).

- Heat the *chawan* and the *chasen* with very hot water. Wait about 30 seconds, discard the water then carefully wipe the *chawan*.
- Sift the required quantity of Matcha in a bowl **1**. The amount of tea for one bowl of Matcha is 2 *chashaku*, or 1 level teaspoon (5 ml). Using a fairly fine strainer, sift the tea with the aid of the *chashaku*. This process is important because, in addition to making the foam of the Matcha smoother, it prevents lumps.
- Pour roughly ¼ cup (60 ml) of water at 167°F (75°C) over the tea **2**, then whisk the tea briskly from the bottom of the bowl to the top

using the *chasen* **3**, taking care not to crush the grounds with the whisk. When a foam begins to form, raise the whisk carefully, making sure to burst any large bubbles that have formed on the surface **4**.
- Enjoy.

Matcha

Matcha is a finely powdered green tea that is traditionally used for the Japanese tea ceremony.

In the 12th century, when the monk Eisai introduced tea to Japan (see "History," page 90), it was the custom in China to grind the leaves to a powder before beating them in a bowl. It was the era of beaten tea. This method of preparation, later abandoned by the Chinese, was adopted by the Japanese, who integrated it into the ritual of *chanoyu*.

The best-quality Matcha tea comes from the covered plantations of the Uji region. After being processed according to the stages described earlier (see pages 104–106), the leaves undergo a specific sorting. In order to produce plant matter that can be easily reduced to a fine powder, the veins of the leaves are removed. This produces Tencha, which is then ground between millstones. There are few "pure" Matcha teas, that is, teas from a single plot of land. Different Matcha teas are often combined, which helps balance their strengths and weaknesses. In the paragraph below we present a tasting-grade Matcha tea.

MATCHA SENDO

Bright green in color, Matcha Sendo gives off an aroma of berries and dark chocolate. In the mouth, its dense texture is rich and appealing. This tea has surprising notes reminiscent of Jerusalem artichoke. It is a very stimulating tea and has a briskness that goes very well with sweet treats.

A Meeting with Mr. Wataru Sugiyama,
Tea Grower

Mr. Sugiyama is the owner of a tea factory in Shizuoka Prefecture.

When did you start working in the world of tea? What has been your career path?

I studied for two years at the national Tea Test Center, after which I started working in my father's factory, where I learned about tea growing and processing under his guidance. My father, Tadahira Sugiyama, is a very influential person in the world of tea and has won several prizes awarded by the Ministry of Agriculture and Forestry. We are indebted to him for all the tea trees that make the famous teas from our gardens.

In 2000, after the death of my father, I took over the family business. Since then, I have participated in several exhibitions, endeavoring to produce the highest-quality tea while using the least amount of pesticides and chemical fertilizers.

How big are your gardens and how much tea do you produce every year?
Do you have many employees?

Our tea plantation covers about 250 hectares [618 acres] and we produce close to 15,000 kilos [33,070 pounds] of tea per year. We have four full-time employees and about 20 pickers that we hire during harvesting.

What are your everyday responsibilities?

To take care of the tea garden! Every day we consider the phases of the moon and decide what needs to be done on the plantation: caring for the tea trees, fertilizing, etc.

Where are your teas sold?
On the local or international market?

We sell our teas directly to the consumer and to specialized tea stores in Japan.

What changes have you seen in the tea industry since you began?

Our town [Shimizu] has been exporting tea for a very long time. When I started out in the industry, the Japanese economy was booming, and our teas were often offered as gifts. There were also companies that bought large quantities of tea. Now, in a less favorable economic environment, our sales have dropped considerably. Because of the popularity of teas sold in plastic bottles, consumers buy less and less loose-leaf tea. A good many people still appreciate high-quality teas, and these are the customers who buy our products.

What is your favorite tea?

Japanese green tea!

The Nomenclature of Japanese Teas

In Japan, the notion of terroir is less important than in China. As we have seen, the practice of mixing different batches of *aracha* in order to create a balanced flavor makes it impossible to determine a precise place of origin for a particular tea. Rather, the names given to teas refer to the methods of production and processing of the leaves. However, in the case of very high-grade teas, there is sometimes a reference to the terroir. There are eight main types of Japanese teas: Sencha, Bancha, Hojicha, Genmaicha, Tamaryokucha, Gyokuro, Kabusecha and Matcha.

SENCHA

Sencha, which means "infused tea," is the most common grade of Japanese tea, representing roughly 80 percent of the country's total production. There are Sencha teas of medium quality, destined for popular consumption, but there are also some high-quality Sencha teas that are rare, complex and subtle in taste.

Bocha (also called Kukicha) is made from batches of Sencha. This type of tea has stems deliberately mixed in with the leaves. Mecha is a variant of Sencha. This type of tea is made from the first harvest of the year which is carefully sorted so that only pieces of leaves and small shoots are retained.

BANCHA

Bancha is usually produced from leaves and stems picked during the late summer or fall harvests. The best quality Bancha teas, however, are made from leaves picked in June.

HOJICHA

Hojicha tea is a Bancha tea whose leaves have been roasted for a few minutes at a temperature of about 390°F (200°C). Although this method strips the leaves of many of their properties, it gives them a honeyed taste reminiscent of hazelnuts.

GENMAICHA

Ganmaicha teas have a green tea base (Bancha or Sencha) with roasted grains of brown rice and popped rice mixed in. Genmaicha teas are usually entry-grade teas ideal for daily consumption. There are also high-quality Genmaicha teas, and the quality of the final product depends on the tea used as the base. Matcha is also added to some varieties.

Hojicha tea leaves.

Matcha.

TAMARYOKUCHA

There are two types of Tamaryokucha. The first, Mushi Sei Tamaryokucha, or Guricha, is subjected to steam dehydration. Produced throughout Japan, this tea tries to imitate the appearance and taste of some Chinese curly-leaf green teas.

The other type of Tamaryokucha is called Kamairi Sei Tamaryokucha, or simply Kamairicha. It is dehydrated in vats and grown mainly on the island of Kyushu. Although most batches are now processed mechanically, there are still some factories that offer batches processed by hand.

GYOKURO

Gyokuro (which means "precious dew") is the highest grade of tea produced in Japan. It is produced from just one harvest per year, in late May or early June. Traditionally, when the new shoots are about ¾ inch (2 cm) long, growers erect a straw canopy over the tea trees for about 10 days. After that period, they add more straw to the canopies, and the trees are left covered in this way for another 11 days, for a total period of about 21 days. The buds are then carefully picked to ensure all the buds growing along the stems are removed. Growers pay such close attention to their crops of Gyokuro tea to encourage the development of a delicate, rich flavor. Gyokuro teas are considered among the most flavorful teas in the world.

KABUSECHA

Shaded growing is also used to obtain Kabusecha teas, but it is done over a shorter period of time. Some growers hang a synthetic cover over their trees, while others place it directly on the plants. The plants are covered for an average of 12 days.

Karigane, a tea similar to Bocha, is produced from batches of Kabusecha. However, unlike Bocha teas, the mixture of leaves and stems comes from shade-grown plants.

MATCHA

Introduced by Buddhist monks at the beginning of the first millennium, Matcha tea was the first type of tea consumed in Japan. Originally, the dried leaves were cut up and then ground between millstones. Today, the best Matchas are often produced from shade-grown leaves.

THE AGING OF GYOKURO AND MATCHA TEAS   Although it is less well known in the West, aging teas is a common practice in Asia, especially in Japan. Whereas Sencha teas are often appreciated for their freshness, liveliness and subtlety, many Japanese tea enthusiasts believe that Matcha and Gyokuro teas are smoother and richer if they are left to mature for a few months after processing.

"Tea is a part of daily life. It is as simple as eating when one is hungry and drinking when one is thirsty."

HAMAMOTO SOSHU

Japanese Teas

Bancha Shizuoka | green tea |
Translation: Third harvest tea and name of the prefecture where it is grown
Production area: Shizuoka Prefecture
Harvest season: June for the best-quality teas and September for the rest
Cultivar: Yabukita

Bancha was the everyday tea for most Japanese until the middle of the Edo era (1603–1868), when Sencha became the most popular tea in Japan. In rural and mountainous regions, every household once grew a small amount of Bancha for its personal consumption.

Tasting notes: The large pieces of leaf that make up the summer Bancha tea (harvested in June) are irregular in shape and produce a humble, robust impression. The dark-green leaves are flattened, and pale-yellow stems are scattered among them. The infusion gives off delicate marine and herbaceous notes with the fruity accent of fresh almonds. The yellow-green liquid is shiny and clear: the mouthfeel is full, smooth and sweet, with hardly any bitterness. Aromas of fresh grass and white fish mingle harmoniously. The finish is a feeling of thirst-quenching freshness.

Recommended infusion accessory: A mid-sized teapot.

Sencha Fukamushi Aji | green tea |
Translation: Infused tea, long dehydration and the name of a hill
Production area: Shizuoka Prefecture
Harvest season: Early May
Cultivar: Yabukita

In Japan, there are two major styles of Sencha tea: Asamushi and Fukamushi. Asamushi is characterized by a short dehydration period and rigorously sorted leaves, which produces a light tea with a delicate, vegetal freshness. Fukamushi teas have a longer period of dehydration and more fine particles are preserved during the sorting, which brings out the strength of the tannins and gives the tea a more iodized flavor. The frank and direct taste of Fukamushi makes it the most popular type of Sencha among the Japanese.

Tasting notes: The dry leaves are a mixture of short flattened needles and finely broken pieces. Infusion transforms their dark-green satiny texture into a dense paste. The nose carries aromas of green vegetables and sea grasses enhanced with a floral touch. The foamy green liquid is slightly cloudy. The mouthfeel is quite full bodied; the attack conjures up freshly cut grass and develops a certain bitterness. Retro-olfaction releases notes of cooked spinach and fresh geranium flowers against a strong background of vegetal and iodized aromas.

Recommended infusion accessory: A small *kyusu* or small teapot.

Gyokuro Tamahomare | green tea |
Translation: Pearl of dew and prestigious
Production area: Uji, Kyoto Prefecture
Harvest season: Once a year, in May
Cultivar: Gokou

Although some sources claim that shaded growing was practiced as early as the beginning of the 17th century, the first Gyokuro tea was officially produced in 1835, in Uji, by Kahei Yamamoto. Gyokuro is the most precious tea produced in Japan. It is processed entirely by hand, and meticulous care is taken at every stage of its production. The distinctive characteristic of its production is that the fields in which it is grown are shaded for three weeks before harvesting, so 80 percent to 95 percent of the sun's rays are blocked. Most growers now use an open mesh to create the shade, however some prefer to use the traditional straw shading for their most prestigious teas. The purpose of shading is to filter the light so that the tea tree, unable to fully carry out photosynthesis, releases more chlorophyll and amino acids (particularly theanine), and fewer tannins, into the leaves.

Tasting notes: The beautiful dried leaves are dark green and glisten in the light. Extremely fine and supple, they vary in size and give off delicate scents of butter, chlorophyll and green vegetables. Infusion releases appetizing aromas of vegetable broth. The same rich bouquet emanates from the thick emerald-green liquid. The smooth, velvety texture of the rounded mouthfeel is surprisingly dense. The generous, heady aromas of chlorophyll, corn salad, broth and oily nuts are quite intense. The fresh, sweet finish, reminiscent of snow peas, is very persistent. It is a remarkably complex tea, with absolutely no bitterness or astringency.

Recommended infusion accessory: A small *kyusu* or small teapot.

120

Sencha Keikoku | green tea |
Translation: Infused tea and valley
Production area: Shizuoka Prefecture
Cultivar: Yabukita
Harvest season: Early May

Sencha, a tea that appeared in the early 17th century, is the most widespread type of green tea in Japan and represents more than 80 percent of the country's total production. Growing extends across many regions, from Kagoshima Prefecture in the south to Ibaraki Prefecture in the north, with the highest concentration in Shizuoka. There are many varieties of Sencha, from the very ordinary to the very refined, and the highest-quality teas are usually harvested between late April and mid-May. The liquid from this tea, whose long, flat leaves resemble pine needles, is vegetal and iodized. The Sencha Keikoku variety is a Sencha of the Asamushi type, which means that it has undergone a short period of dehydration of only about 30 seconds. It comes from an area around the little town of Tenryu, which is dotted with many charming small tea gardens.

Tasting notes: The needlelike leaves are very beautiful. Infusion releases a gentle smell of freshly cut grass, watercress and water chestnut. The cloudy, pistachio-green liquid smells of cooked celery and seaweed. The mouthfeel is of rich, full tannins that coat the tongue with a lively attack that quickly softens. This well-structured tea fills the mouth with vegetal aromas of arugula, leading into a long but light note of pine. The enduring finish of green mango and lime zest is delicate and refreshing.

Recommended infusion accessory: A small *kyusu* or small teapot.

Hojicha Shizuoka | roasted green tea |
Translation: Roasted tea and the name of the prefecture
Alternative names: Bancha Hojicha, Houjicha
Production area: Shizuoka Prefecture
Harvest season: Late in the season, usually September
Cultivar: Yabukita

This tea is a Bancha whose leaves have been roasted until they turn completely brown, which standardizes the flavor of the tea leaves. In Japan, it is customary to serve this tea hot in winter, for comfort, and cold in summer, for refreshment. It is also often used in the commercial production of bottled iced teas. However, it is still common to find a small earthenware pan, used to roast a small quantity of leaves over a gas flame for personal consumption, in Japanese family kitchens.

Tasting notes: The large roasted leaves, mixed in with pieces of stem, are uniformly bronze in color. Infusion releases calming roasted and woody aromas. The clear, amber-colored liquid has the same bouquet. The mouthfeel is delicately sweet. Subtle notes of nut and vanilla, as well as a fine vegetal presence, are overlaid on the woody, roasted base. The texture is aqueous without a trace of tannin. The airy finish is gently honeyed.

Recommended infusion accessory: A medium-sized teapot.

121

Genmaicha Sencha-Matcha | green tea |
Translation: Roasted rice tea, and
Sencha-and-Matcha base
Production area: Shizuoka Prefecture
Harvest season: From spring to fall, depending on
the type of tea desired
Cultivar: Yabukita

Genmaicha tea is a mixture of tea leaves and roasted
and popped grains of rice. It was originally a beverage
drunk by the poor, who supplemented their tea with
rice. Today it is enjoyed by people from all walks of
life. Genmaicha is usually produced from Bancha, but
the variety mentioned here is composed of a delicate
combination of Sencha and Matcha teas.

Tasting notes: The leaves and the grains of rice are
covered in a fine powdered Matcha that gives the
mixture a uniform bright-green color. Some burst
grains of rice, reminiscent of popped corn, are sprinkled
throughout the mixture. Infusion releases a strong
bouquet of roasted rice and a delicate note of sea air.
The Matcha powder makes the liquid cloudy, almost
to the point of opacity. The mouthfeel offers a delicate
attack and a velvety texture. The gentle sweetness of
the rice combines with herbaceous aromas to produce
a full finish that is smooth and calming.

Recommended infusion accessory: A medium-sized
teapot.

Kabusecha Kawase | green tea |
Translation: Shaded tea and the name of the grower
Production area: Shizuoka Prefecture
Harvest season: Early May
Cultivar: Yabukita

Like Gyokuro tea, Kabusecha is a shade-grown tea
cultivated in gardens that are covered by canopies
for about two weeks before the leaves are picked. As
with Gyokuro teas, the goal is to increase the levels of
chlorophyll and amino acids (particularly theanine) in
the leaves, which produces a gentle and complex tea.
However, in the case of Kabusecha teas, the canopies,
made of synthetic material, are less dense and only
block roughly 80 percent of the light. Processing is
more mechanical, closer to that of Sencha teas, to reduce costs and produce a quality tea at an affordable
price. Therefore, Kabusecha teas are a compromise
between Sencha and Gyokuro teas, offering a balance
between strength and delicacy.

Tasting notes: The dry leaves are mixed with needles
and broken particles that are uniformly green. When
they are infused they form a thick paste that gives off
vegetal aromas of fresh grass and cilantro. The dark-
green liquid is clouded by a thick haze of suspended
particles. The vegetal nose is colored by a delicate note
of apricot. In the mouth, the liquid presents brief acidity
and a creamy texture. The strong, herbaceous aromas
combine with a subtle note of raspberry. The dominant
vegetal note, full and intense, leads to a light astringency.
The delicately sweet finish tends gently toward aromas
of green vegetables and berries.

Recommended infusion accessory: A small *kyusu* or
small teapot.

Bocha | green tea |
Translation: Stem tea
Alternative name: Kukicha
Production areas: Shizuoka and other prefectures
Harvest season: May to June
Cultivar: Yabukita

Bocha is produced from a mixture of tea stems and leaves. There are several different grades, as it can be made from different-quality teas, from the simplest Sencha to the most precious Gyokuro. Because the stems contain less caffeine than the leaves, this tea is less stimulating.

Tasting notes: This tea contains no fine particles and is composed mainly of yellow stems mixed with long green needlelike leaves. The scented mixture releases pleasant buttery and fruity aromas. Infusion releases a warm bouquet leading to appetizing notes of corn, crabmeat and nori seaweed. A discreet fruity presence is reminiscent of peach. The pale-green, slightly cloudy liquid is rounded and deliciously sweet in the mouth. The vegetal sweetness of zucchini and corn meld harmoniously with fine seafood notes. It is an appealing tea with a delicate finish of greenery and almonds.

Recommended infusion accessory: A medium-sized teapot.

Kamairicha | green tea |
Translation: Tea heated in vats
Production area: Miyazaki and Kagoshima Prefectures
Harvest season: May to June and September
Cultivar: Yabukita

There are growers on the island of Kyushu who have continued to use the Chinese method of dehydration that gives tea leaves a curly shape. This is the case, in particular, for Kamairicha (*kama* means "vat") teas. Remember that tea was originally introduced to Japan on the island of Kyushu, and so preserving this method of dehydration is probably a way of preserving the Chinese expertise initially handed down to this region.

The origin of Kamairicha tea dates back to the 15th century, when, it is said, Chinese ceramic artists were forcibly sent to Ureshino, on the island of Kyushu, to teach their technique to locals. History recounts that the homesick Chinese artists, prevented from leaving, began to process tea the way they had it in their homeland.

Tasting notes: The small, dark-green leaves have the twisted shape and matte appearance of certain Chinese teas. Infusion reveals roasted aromas of hazelnut, nori seaweed and corn against a green vegetable background. The buttery, vegetal liquid is a luminous yellowish green. The mouthfeel presents a lively, herbaceous attack leading to a slight bitternesswith roasted accents. The full, well-structured liquid reveals a dominant vegetal and sweet taste. The finish offers strong tannins and a lovely after taste.

Recommended infusion accessory: A medium-sized teapot.

Taiwan

ALTHOUGH TAIWAN IS A FAIRLY RECENT TEA-GROWING COUNTRY COMPARED TO CHINA, WHICH HAS A 5,000-YEAR-OLD HISTORY OF TEA CULTIVATION, THE WEATHER AND GEOGRAPHY OF THE ARCHIPELAGO, AS WELL AS THE EXPERTISE INHERITED FROM THE CHINESE, HAVE ENCOURAGED THE DEVELOPMENT OF HIGH-QUALITY PRODUCTION IN THE COUNTRY. TODAY, THE RICH FLORAL FRAGRANCES OF THE HIGH-ALTITUDE TEAS AND THE LUXURIOUS TEXTURE OF THEIR SMALL HARVESTS DELIGHT THE PALATES OF THE MOST DISCERNING ENTHUSIASTS.

History

Taiwan is a small island situated some 90 miles (150 km) off the coast of China, and its history is inevitably linked to the latter, especially as far as the culture of tea is concerned. However, China is not the only country that influenced the development of the Taiwanese tea industry, as various peoples have sought to control the territory, due to its ideal strategic position for exporting goods to Europe. The Portuguese, Spanish, Dutch and English all occupied the island at various points during the 16th and 17th centuries. The Dutch, who occupied Taiwan from 1624 to 1662, were the first to develop the tea trade in this territory.

In 1662, under the Qing dynasty, Admiral Zheng Cheng Gong reconquered the territory, and it was annexed to China in 1683. Following unification, a wave of Chinese immigration into Taiwan completely changed the territory's culture. The new immigrants, most of whom came from Fujian Province, especially the area around Anxi and the Wuyi Mountains, brought with them tea seeds and plants, as well as their expertise in tea growing, which was still unknown in Taiwan.

Many plants were later transplanted to the north of the island, close to the capital, Taipei, as well as in the center of Taiwan. Families began to cultivate small tea gardens close to their homes to satisfy their personal needs and slowly, toward the end of the 18th century, the tea trade started to develop.

Noticing an increase in the importation of tea from the neighboring island, the Europeans — who at that time dealt with the Chinese at Xiamen and Fuzhou (two major Chinese tea-trading ports of that period) — decided to pay closer attention to Taiwan. Then, in 1866, a trader named John Dodd decided to become more involved in trade with Taiwan. He offered financing to Taiwanese peasants who wanted to start tea plantations, and he also set up factories in Taipei so the new local growers would have access to every stage of tea processing. At the time, it was not unusual for tea leaves to be shipped to Anxi or Fuzhou to undergo the final stages of processing. And so Taiwanese tea began to be exported to Europe and the United States, where it was greatly appreciated.

During the first half of the 20th century, under the Japanese occupation that lasted from 1895 to 1945, the black-tea industry was supported in order to take advantage of the high demand in Europe and to avoid competing with Japanese green-tea production.

The Japanese invested heavily in the tea industry in Taiwan, giving fertilizers and numerous tea plants to Taiwanese peasants. They offered training courses and encouraged the mechanization of processing, creating an environment in which the industry could thrive.

With the arrival of the Chinese, who drove the Japanese out of the territory at the end of the Second World War, the industry was oriented toward the production of green teas, which were exported to North African countries. Around 1965, Taiwan also began to export tea to Japan. During the 1970s, because of the strong competition from China and

WILD TEA TREES IN TAIWAN   Although the tea trees cultivated in Taiwan today come from China, various types of wild tea trees have been found in the south of the island, close to Kaoshan.

FORMOSA "Discovered" in 1590 by the Portuguese, who named it Formosa ("the beautiful"), Taiwan is a small, mountainous island. This ancient name was also once applied to Taiwanese teas, which were called "formosas," but this usage is no longer common. The island's highest summit is Mount Yu Shan, which peaks at 12,966 feet (3,952 m).

the self-sufficiency of the Japanese, Taiwan could no longer find an international outlet for its green tea, so the government decided to stimulate the domestic market. These new trading conditions forced the tea industry to turn to the production of wulong teas, which were the local favorite. In addition, the average income of the Taiwanese had increased considerably over this period, so growers decided to concentrate on quality rather than quantity.

The Taiwanese Tea Industry

Today, Taiwan produces some of the best wulong teas in the world, and almost all the production is consumed locally. To satisfy demand, and despite an 18 percent tax on tea brought in from outside the territory, Taiwan imports more than three times as much tea as it exports each year. This commercial activity extends beyond the island's borders, as some Taiwanese businessmen are now investing in tea production in Vietnam, Thailand and China. The Taiwanese inherited a genuine art of tea tasting from the Chinese through the *gong fu cha* ceremony, a simple and refined ritual that uses a special "sniffing" cup to enhance the heady aromas released by wulong teas.

Moreover, since the late 1990s, Taiwan has been one of the hubs of the Pu er tea trade. Some of the major Pu er collectors are Taiwanese, and they have contributed to the recent explosion of this market.

Unlike in other countries, such as India, China or Sri Lanka, where many tea gardens extend over several thousand acres, the Taiwanese tea industry is fragmented among a number of small growers. Today there are more than 30,000 growers, who are, for the most part, small family businesses of no more than two to eight employees.

The Tawainese industry produces some 18,700 tons (17,000 t) of tea per year, mostly wulong. This production is not much compared to the output of other tea-growing nations, especially since Taiwan must import several thousand tons of tea to satisfy local demand. However, local weather and geographical conditions are not appropriate for high-volume production. Some gardens located high in the mountains, like those of Da Yu Lin, for example, can only be harvested twice a year.

Until the beginning of the 1980s, roughly 80 percent of Taiwanese production was shipped abroad. To keep the industry alive in spite of competition from neighboring countries and to free the country from its dependency on exports, the Taiwanese government decided to try to redirect production toward the domestic market. It managed this very skillfully by channeling growers into high-quality teas and introducing many popular educational programs (museums, tea contests, festivals and the like).

This transformation of the industry gave growers the impetus to form groups and to sell their tea directly to consumers, which eliminated the need for middlemen. This stimulated the emergence of a local

A BRIEF SUMMARY OF THE TAIWANESE TEA TRADE

Production area: 37,861 acres (15,322 ha) in 2009

Total annual production: 18,497 tons (16,780 t) in 2009

Principal growing region: Nantou, with a production area of 18,649 acres (7,547 ha) and a total anual production of 12,321 tons (11,177 t) in 2009

Percentage of production per family of tea: wulong, 93%; green tea, 4%; black tea, 3%

Average production yield: 1,006 pounds per acre (1,128 kg/ha)

Annual exports: 2,901 tons (2,632 t) in 2010; 2,646 tons (2,400 t) in 2009; 2,581 tons (2,341 t) in 2008

Source: Taiwan Agricultur and Food Agency, COA, Taiwan Tea Production Association. (Values in imperial units of measure supplied by publisher.)

tea culture and a gradual reduction of exports. The Taiwanese are now free of the yoke of competition. They export only a very small proportion of their harvest (about 12 percent) and consume the bulk of it themselves.

Today, almost all growers take great care of their gardens, from the choice of the tea trees to meticulous processing in order to produce the best possible quality. They then enter their high-quality leaves in contests that usually take place twice a year, in May and November, in various growing regions, where they are judged and compared by eminent specialists. These contests can be very lucrative for a grower because, in addition to conferring fame and prestige, winning a prize increases the market value of a tea.

Although there are still pockets where black tea is produced (particularly the east coast, close to Sun Moon Lake), as well as several low-grade imitations of quality Chinese green teas, Taiwan now specializes in one single tea, wulong.

A grower from the Chushan region exhibiting his teas.

BUBBLE TEA Bubble tea, which is very popular in Taiwan, is an exotic mixture of tapioca pearls and fruit syrup diluted with a cold infusion of tea (Pu er, black tea, wulong, green tea or jasmine tea).

A Meeting with **Ms. Lin Mei Yen**,
Tea Industry Professional

Ms. Lin Mei Yen is a judge at the Lugu tea competition.

*How long have you been working
in the world of tea?*
Actually, I have always worked in areas associated with the tea industry, but I decided to dive into it completely in 1984.

What attracted you to this profession?
I am a tea grower. I hoped to develop my competencies further by becoming a judge. I particularly wanted to acquire the knowledge and skills that would help me better understand my everyday work.

*What are your daily responsibilities
during a contest?*
First of all, I weigh the teas and check the uniformity of the leaves. Next I examine the dry leaves (color, shape, nose) and the infused leaves, and then I taste the infusion. Finally I grade the teas.

What do you like best about your job?
The possibility of tasting high-quality teas in the company of well-qualified colleagues!

*Can you tell us an anecdote or a story
about your work?*
Sometimes we taste several hundred teas in one day. Previously, the tasting room wasn't air-conditioned. In the afternoon the room got quite hot, and the judges could get irritable by the end of the day, which could have an adverse effect on the results … Also, meals (rather bland with no spices) are now provided by the organization. Before, judges brought their own lunch and sometimes the food was much too spicy!

*What challenges will the Taiwanese industry
have to face going forward?*
It is essential that growers work to preserve the unique style of their teas, of their region. Here, in Lugu, thanks to this kind of contest, we are partcularly keen to promote firing wulong teas, which represents the distinctive mark with which the grower signs his tea.

What is your favorite tea?
I love to brew Bao Zhong style wulong teas according to the *gong fu cha* tradition. I also like Bi Luo Chun green tea.

How would you define a good tea?
The most important thing is a balance between the aromas and the flavors. The liquid must fill the mouth as well as being tasty and smooth in the throat.

Taiwanese Terroirs

With several mountain ranges with peaks soaring to over 6,550 feet (2,000 m), a temperature that rarely drops below 55°F (13°C) and a mean rainfall of more than 79 inches (2,000 mm) a year, the climatic and geological conditions of Taiwan are perfectly suited to the cultivation of tea.

The Zhong Yang Shan Mai mountain range, in the middle of the island, creates a natural protective barrier against the typhoons and other storms that come in from the ocean, so most of the tea gardens are concentrated in the west of the island. However, the best *crus* are grown in the northern regions and on the western slopes of the highest mountains in the center of the island: Ali Shan, Shan Lin Xi and Li Shan, an 8,070-foot (2,460 m) summit where one of the highest tea gardens in the world can be found.

THE DISTRICT OF NANTOU

The district of Nantou, in the center of the island, is Taiwan's principal tea-growing region. This district produces roughly 12,100 tons (11,000 t) of tea per year, representing more than half the output of the entire country. Apart from the teas grown on certain famous mountains, such as the celebrated Mount Dong Ding and Mount Shan Lin Xi, where there are some exceptional gardens, the tea from the Nantou district is mostly of medium quality, in part because of the high volume produced. A lot of harvests from other parts of the island are also shipped here, and industrial processing methods are highly advanced. Small harvests of black tea, such as Sun Moon Lake tea, from the area around the eponymous lake, are also produced here.

MOUNT DONG DING

The celebrated Mount Dong Ding rises up close to Lugu in the region that pioneered tea growing in Taiwan. The first plantations on this mountain date from the middle of the 19th century. Now famous around the world, the mountain is entirely covered in tea plantations; 4,000 to 5,000 growers produce tea

in this region at altitudes that range from 1,650 to 2,600 feet (500 to 800 m). In addition to being an important tourist destination, the region attracts many Taiwanese consumers who buy tea. The government has also contributed a great deal to the promotion of the tea trade in this region. A festival is still held to present the new harvests for tasting and to teach the basics of the *gong fu cha* tea ceremony (see pages 144–145).

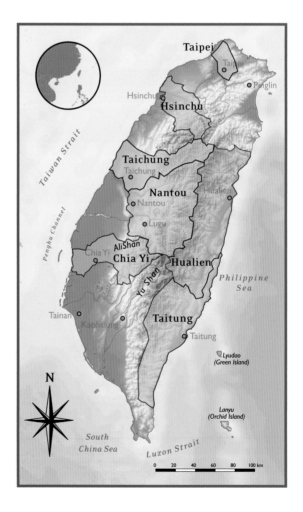

Mount Dong Ding.

A garden at Shan Lin Xi.

MOUNT SHAN LI XII
Mount Shan Lin Xi, where the highest plantations rise to 5,400 feet (1,650 m), is also in the district of Nantou. Celebrated for its beauty, especially its many bamboo forests, it has developed rapidly over the last 20 years. A lot of land has been cleared, and new plantations have appeared. The best gardens are on the steep mountain slopes that have all the ideal conditions for tea cultivation. An interesting characteristic of the region is that all the gardens are named after the animals of the Chinese astrological signs (dragon, goat, etc).

THE DISTRICT OF TAIPEI
The district of Taipei, located in the north of the island, is the second-most-important growing region in the territory. Whereas most of the gardens were previously centered around the capital (Taipei) — which was the longtime point of departure for tea headed to overseas markets — they migrated south to the district of Nantou as heavy industrial and residential development took over Taipei. Today, the best harvests are produced close to the town of Pinglin and in the Mucha Mountains.

PINGLIN
Located in the massif of the Wen Shan Mountains, some 30 minutes from Taipei, Pinglin is a very popular village, and many residents of the capital go there regularly to buy their favorite tea. Because of this high demand, the prices of the tea from this region have increased considerably, and there is reason to believe they may now be somewhat inflated. Pinglin does, however, produce a style of wulong tea with twisted leaves that is rarely still found in Taiwan: Bao Zhong (see "The Origin of the term *Bao Zhong*" on the following page and "Pinglin Bao Zhong" on page 152). Today, the preferred method of processing wulong leaves is the bead method, which makes it easier to ship and store the tea.

THE MUCHA MOUNTAINS
Around 1875, two brothers from Anxi, China, planted a few shoots of the famous cultivar Tie Guan Yin in the Mucha Mountains, south of Taipei. Thanks to the persistence of these two brothers, Tie Guan Yin tea is found in Taiwan today. The originality of the tea produced in Mucha is due to the cultivar grown there, but also to the intense firing it undergoes over several days, which gives it unique roasted notes.

THE DISTRICT OF HSINCHU

Located in northwestern Taiwan, the district of Hsinchu is an area of plains at an altitude of approximately 650 feet (200 m). The region is famous for its wulong black teas, which are oxidized at a rate that varies between 40 percent and 60 percent. This oxidization darkens the appearance of the leaves and creates a beautiful coppery color when they are infused. Great classics come from this area, including Bai Hao (Oriental Beauty) and the Wulong Fancy teas, which are of a lower quality.

THE DISTRICT OF CHIA YI

Although tea growing only started in the district of Chia Yi 20 years ago, it is renowned for its production of Gao Shan Cha (see "Gao Shan Cha: A High-Altitude Tea" on page 135). A little less than 10 percent of the country's total production is harvested here. It is in this district that the great massif of the Ali Shan Mountain begins before merging with lofty Mount Yu Shan.

ALI SHAN MOUNTAIN

Without a doubt one of the most famous mountains on the island, where high-quality, high-altitude teas are grown, Ali Shan has several gardens located between 2,300 and 5,600 feet (700 to 1,700 m). This region was known for its giant evergreens. During the Japanese occupation many were felled for the Japanese market. The Ali Shan region is now a protected area. There is a natural park with luxurious vegetation. At the foot of the mountain, palm trees, banana trees and a number of fruit trees gently sway.

YU SHAN MOUNTAIN

Although Yu Shan Mountain soars to 12,966 feet (3,952 m), the plantations are at approximately 4,250 feet (1,300 m). Tea growing began there about 20 years ago and — contrary to other regions, such as Shan Lin Xi, where growing areas have expanded from year to year — the growth in the number of plantations on Yu Shan appears to be stable and limited.

THE DISTRICT OF HUALIEN

Located on the east coast in an area hit by typhoons and other ocean storms, the district of Hualien produces a meager output of tea. The region produces a number of different kinds of tea, including wulong, black, green and floral teas. While the gardens of Hualien are generally located at low altitudes, some operate at 3,300 feet (1,000 m). Over the last few years, there has been a strong trend toward organic cultivation in this region. Moreover, in a rather rare phenomenon in Taiwan, growers in this district often produce more than one tea family.

THE DISTRICT OF TAITUNG

On the east coast, south of Hualien, lies Taitung, a small growing area of relatively little importance.

THE DISTRICT OF TAICHUNG

The district of Taichung contains the central massif of the island, including the mountains of Li Shan and Da Yu Lin. High-quality, high-altitude teas are produced here. This new, rapidly expanding, growing region has only been producing tea for around 15 years.

THE ORIGIN OF THE TERM *BAO ZHONG* The term bao zhong means "wrapped in paper" and appears to come from China (Anxi) where, more than 150 years ago, a merchant by the name of Wang Yi Cheng used to present a certain type of twisted leaf tea wrapped in paper. This custom, taken up again by the Wen Shan in Taiwan, was later associated with the name of the tea.

A garden on Li Shan Mountain

A garden on Ali Shan Mountain

LI SHAN MOUNTAIN

Li Shan Mountain, or "Pear Mountain," includes several growing areas located between 5,250 and 8,700 feet (1,600 to 2,650 m). Fruit trees have been grown here for a long time, but the growing of tea is fairly recent. Farmers are increasingly switching to tea growing because of the high demand and the high prices for tea produced in the area. However, to avoid excessive expansion, the government controls and limits the number of new plantations.

On Li Shan, the two annual harvests are rather late compared to other harvests carried out on the island. The spring picking takes place at the end of May, and the winter picking at the end of October.

The gardens of Da Yu Lin Mountain, located nearby, are among the highest in the world, at an approximate altitude of 8,500 feet (2,600 m).

GAO SHAN CHA: A HIGH-ALTITUDE TEA   The tea trees that grow at more than 3,300 feet (1,000 m) are referred to as Gao Shan Cha, which means "high altitude tea." Taiwan and Sri Lanka are the only countries to distinguish between high-altitude and low-altitude teas, although the region of Darjeeling in India also produces them. Teas grown at higher altitudes are highly sought after, since the higher the altitude at which the plant is grown, the more complex its aromatic properties and flavors will be. The weather conditions at high altitudes are obviously different. It is colder, which slows the growth of the tea trees but increases the concentration of aromatic oils in the leaves. In addition, thick fog filters the sun's rays in the morning and at night, as well as during part of the day, thus reducing the amount of sunshine to a few hours each day, resulting in the plants producing young, extremely dark-green shoots that contain more amino acids and nitrogen compounds. Moistened by this fog, the leaves are also more tender and, unlike leaves that grow at lower altitudes, they remain supple, which is a good quality for further processing.

135

Taiwanese Gardens and Plants

By devoting themselves almost entirely to the production of wulong teas, Taiwanese growers have managed to develop a tea culture that is specific to their taste and their terroir.

In new plantations, tea trees are spaced about 12 to 20 inches (30 to 50 cm) apart and rows are about 6 feet (1.8 m) apart. The ideal planting time is after Chinese New Year. This is usually a rainy season, which helps the roots of the young plants to take hold. To protect the tea trees from winter snows, especially in high-altitude gardens, growers plant high grasses along the paths between the rows of trees.

The age of the trees is also a factor that growers take into consideration. A new plant will take 5 years to become productive. It will then be in its "Golden Age" a term used by the Taiwanese for trees that are 10 to 15 years old. At 30 years old the trees will be uprooted and replaced. The use of organic substances to care for the garden can help prolong a tea tree's useful life.

Growers must wait 45 to 60 days between pickings in order to obtain perfect leaves. Taiwanese growers usually harvest four times a year.

Taiwanese Cultivars

Although the first cultivars to be grown on the island of Taiwan were of Chinese origin, over the years the Taiwanese have developed their own cultivars. Some, like the Si Ji Chun variety, are the result of natural hybridization, while others, such as the Jin Shuan cultivar, were developed by the Taiwanese Tea Experiment Station (TTES). Although roughly a hundred cultivars have been recorded, only a few are commonly used today, and they include the Qing Xin, Si Ji Chun, Cui Yu, Jin Shuan and Tie Guan Yin varieties.

QING XIN (ALSO CALLED "CINGSHIN" AND "LUANZE")

The Qing Xin cultivar is recognized by and appreciated for the fragrances the leaves reveal during processing. It is the undisputed favorite of Taiwanese growers. It is most often planted at high altitude, at about 2,600 feet (800 m), and preferably in newly cleared soil. In order to encourage the growth of this temperamental cultivar, it is best to use rich soil that has never been used to cultivate other plants, preferably on sloping ground, where regular drainage will help the roots take hold.

SI JI CHUN

Discovered by chance in northern Taiwan and officially recognized in 1981, the Si Ji Chun variety is said to be a natural hybrid produced from two Qing Xin varieties (Qing Shin Dapan and Qing Xin). The name given to this local variety means "tea of the four springs" and refers to its exceptional productivity: five or six harvests per year, depending on the geographic region and the altitude of the plantation. With a great ability to adapt to all soil types, on the plains as well as in the mountains, and a strong resistance to parasites and disease, this variety is grown more and more widely in Taiwan. The leaves of Si Ji Chun teas are rich in aromatic substances that release an explosive floral attack when infused.

CUI YU (ALSO CALLED "TZUIYU" AND "TAI CHA NO. 13")

This cultivar is the result of a forced hybridization, recorded in 1981, between the Yingchi Hungshin and Tai Cha No. 80 varieties. Cui Yu is another local variety grown mainly on the plains and in the Nantou region. This cultivar offers high yields and gentle floral aromas, but it does not seem to enjoy the same popularity as Si Ji Chun tea among either Taiwanese growers or consumers.

JIN SHUAN (ALSO CALLED "CHINSUAN," "MILKY WULONG" AND "TAI CHA NO. 12")

This cultivar is sturdy, has plentiful buds and is adaptable. It is reputed to have an aroma reminiscent of milk, hence its nickname "Milky Wulong." Very popular in the 1980s and 1990s, this variety seems to be less popular among growers today, as a glut on the maket caused prices to tumble.

TIE GUAN YIN

The Tie Guan Yin cultivar originated in China is now also found in Taiwan. It was planted there by the Tsang brothers around 1875. It is grown only in the north of the island, in the Mucha region.

Unfortunately, Taiwanese consumers seem to be moving away from the roasted version of Tie Guan Yin, preferring wulong teas with their delicate floral aromas. The Tie Guan Yin tea trees are now very old, and, given their declining popularity, growers will probably turn to other varieties of tea when the time comes to replace their crops of Tie Guan Yin. We may be witnessing the final years of the Mucha Tie Guan Yin variety.

Processing Green Wulong Teas

As previously noted, it is the process of oxidation that determines which of the six families a tea belongs to. The wulong family of teas consists of semi-oxidized teas that can be categorized somewhere between green teas and black teas. This family of teas, which is less well-known in the West, is widely grown in China (Fujian, Guangdong) and in Taiwan, where it is something of a specialty. A wulong tea can be closer to a green tea or a black tea depending on its degree of oxidation. This is why we distinguish between green wulong teas, which generally undergo 30 percent to 50 percent oxidation, and black wulong teas, which can be up to 70 percent oxidized. Of course, these different degrees of oxidation develop very different aromas. It is easy to tell the vegetal and floral bouquet of a green wulong from the sweet, woody notes of a black wulong.

The processing of black wulong teas is described in the section on China (see pages 62–63), and below is a description of how green wulong teas are processed.

THE FIRST DAY

On the first day, as soon as the freshly picked leaves arrive at the factory, skilled workers concentrate on the oxidation process, which will take up the better part of the day.

PICKING

Although most of the first picking takes place in April, some growing areas on the plains at an altitude of 330 feet (100 m) can be harvested as early as mid-February. If the factory is producing a wulong tea, the buds need to have reached a certain stage of maturity. The final bud must have opened before it can be picked, along with the three following leaves. Picking is done manually by women, especially at plantations on steep slopes. On the plains, machines are often used.

WITHERING

Once the leaves have been picked, they are spread out on large sheets, usually outside, to undergo the first stage of processing: withering. This stage consists of drying the leaves slightly so the moisture they contain does not damage them. Depending on the weather conditions, they may be left to stand for 30 minutes to two hours. If the sun is too strong, light canopies are placed over the leaves to protect them.

WULONG   The literal translation of wulong is "black dragon," and it refers to the black snakes that were sometimes found wrapped around the branches of tea trees. It is said that adults would try to comfort children who were afraid of the snakes by telling them that the snakes were little black dragons.

OXIDATION

The next stage of processing, oxidation, is an extremely delicate step, as it largely determines the final flavor of the tea. It is during oxidation that aromas are released and begin to stabilize on the leaves. The leaves are spread out on woven bamboo trays about 3 feet (1 m) in diameter in an environment where the temperature is maintained at 68 to 77°F (20 to 25°C) and the humidity at 60 percent to 85 percent. The leaves are lightly stirred at regular one- to four-hour intervals. This stirring action is very important, as the friction of the leaves against the bamboo trays breaks down the cellular structure of the leaves and releases oils that contain aromatic substances, thus triggering the process of oxidation. This stage can last from 10 to 18 hours.

This process is instinctive, as only the experience of the grower, who touches and sniffs the leaves, tells him when it is exactly the right time to stop the oxidation process.

FIRING

Next, the leaves are fired. This process, as with green teas, is intended to stop oxidation by destroying the enzymes that cause it. Once the leaves have reached the required degree of oxidation, they are placed in a heated rotating cylinder that looks like a large clothes dryer, where they undergo a preliminary heating/stirring. The leaves will be heated to about 572°F (300°C) for five to seven minutes.

ROLLING

As soon as they are taken out of the rotating cylinder, the still-warm leaves are rolled for the first time. A mechanical arm attached to a rounded dome rotates swiftly, causing the leaves to brush against the walls of the machine and release their fragrance. This first rolling lasts three to five minutes.

DRYING

Drying stabilizes the aromas of the leaves. It also prevents excessive residual moisture from damaging the leaves. Drying starts at about 158°F (70°C), for five or six minutes, and then continues for 20 to 30 minutes at 212°F (100°C).

Finally, the leaves are spread out on large bamboo trays and left to stand for six to eight hours.

THE SECOND DAY

On the second day the leaves undergo three basic stages, which will be repeated several dozen times: heating/stirring, rolling and compression.

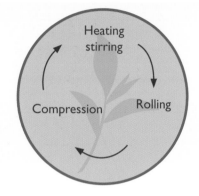

HEATING/STIRRING

The leaves are first placed in a rotating cylinder for a few minutes to soften them.

ROLLING

Next, the leaves are formed into a 44-pound (20 kg) package and wrapped in a special fabric. This mass of leaves is placed in a machine equipped with four rotating rollers that compress it into a round shape.

COMPRESSION

Still wrapped in the fabric, the leaves are then placed in another machine, where they will be turned and rolled for about 10 minutes while being compressed.

These three steps are repeated 10 to 20 times with a rotating cylinder that is full of air heated to 140 to 392°F (60 to 200°C) and 30 to 40 times with a non-heated cylinder. This is how, after a great deal of work, the distinctive wulong bead shape is obtained.

FINAL DRYING

Later, the final drying will stabilize the aromas on the leaves and allow the grower to ensure that no more than 2 percent to 3 percent moisture remains in the leaves. This drying phase lasts five to ten minutes at a temperature ranging from 212 to 248°F (100 to 120°C).

SORTING

At the sorting stage, the leaves are separated from the small stems that are still attached. Although there are machines that can do this work, sorting is usually done by hand. It is an extremely tedious process that does nothing to enhance the flavor of the tea according to some growers; however, it remains important to those who want their tea to look perfect. After the sorting, the processing is complete.

ROASTING

In Taiwan, current practice is to leave the tea intact, without roasting it. However, at the request of customers, many producers heat the leaves one last time. It is often tea merchants who carry out this last step. With the help of an electric oven or bamboo baskets placed over a heated base, the leaves are heated at temperatures ranging from 167 to 320°F (75 to 160°C) for two to 60 hours, depending on the intensity required. There is no need to rotate the leaves in a convection oven, but if a bamboo basket on an electric heater is used, the leaves must be stirred at 20- to 30-minute intervals in order to ensure an even firing. Firing plays an important role in the taste and color of a tea. It can add woody, sweet, even caramelized aromas. In addition, it gives the liquid more balance, reducing the astringency as well as the level of caffeine. At the request of some older customers, who claim that roasted wulong teas "eliminate moisture" from the body, several growers fire

their teas in the fall. This type of wulong gives that impression because, by reducing the "greenness" of the tea, firing makes it easier to drink and to digest.

Although it may look like a simple operation at first glance, roasting is an art in itself, as it involves adding heat-induced notes without overpowering the other aromatic accents present in wulong tea.

STEMS IN WULONG TEAS It takes one person no fewer than 10 hours to remove the stems from 26½ pounds (12 kg) of tea. Once the stems have been removed, only 20¾ pounds (9.4 kg) of tea remain.

Tea leaves with stems.

Tea leaves without stems.

AGED WULONG TEAS

Just as there are aged Pu er teas, there are also wulong teas that are called "aged" after several years of maturing. The creation of this type of wulong tea is probably a direct result of the humid climate of the island. Because of the climate, unsold harvests had a tendency to become saturated with moisture and to deteriorate. It is likely that certain growers, seeking to remedy this situation, came up with the idea of firing in order to conserve their teas. Combined with the effect of the aging of the leaves, the annual roasting gives rise to new flavors quite different from those that were present at the outset.

THE AGING PROCESS

The process of aging wulong teas consists of subjecting them to firing annually or every two to three years. As a skilled worker decides instinctively for how long and at what temperature the firing should take place, it is difficult to make any connection between the age of the tea and the intensity of the roast. However, after 20 to 25 years of aging, mineral notes begin to appear, creating similarities with aged Pu er teas. Further aging progressively confirms the mineral notes.

Today, the production of aged wulong teas is quite rare and unfortunately, due to economic factors, this tradition could disappear entirely in a few years. The high demand for wulong teas leaves producers with very little surplus. Harvests are now vacuum-stored, further reducing the risk of deterioration. In addition, as the price of aged teas is relatively low, growers no longer see any advantage in conserving and processing a small quantity over a long period of time to finally obtain a price only slightly higher than that of fresh tea. However, as tea enthusiasts, let us hope that this unique tradition, rich in gustatory pleasure, will be continued.

BEFORE ELECTRICITY In the past, small pieces of coal were used for roasting. Today, few growers still resort to this method; however, it is sometimes possible to discover teas fired in this way in specialty stores.

The Local Taste and Method of Preparing Tea

The Taiwanese are proud of their wulong teas, and many of them travel long distances to buy tea from their favorite mountain garden. However, there has been a discernible change in consumer habits. Although tea was previously an integral part of daily life — at home, at work and in public places — the younger generation, who view tea as an outdated and outmoded drink, are gravitating toward coffee and energy drinks. In the face of this change of attitude and the rise in popularity of coffee in large cities, the values associated with tea seem old-fashioned.

However, tea remains at the heart of a very important social ritual. In almost all Taiwanese households, it is customary to welcome visitors by offering them the best tea in the house. In addition, growers continue to make every effort to promote the popularity of tea, as they have done since the 1970s, by organizing many festivals and contests. These events also offer educational activities that promote socializing and teach participants the fundamentals of the *gong fu cha* ceremony (see pages 144–145). Tea parties, which are like large outdoor receptions, are just one of the activities organized in Taiwan to popularize tea culture. These events, which take place in parks or other large public spaces that are conducive to meditation, aim to bring together a large number of people around various themes connected to tea.

Moreover, tea-growing villages organize a lot of tasting events, and small teahouses serving local teas can be found everywhere, sometimes tucked away in unexpected places.

Taiwan is full of tea enthusiasts and well-informed connoisseurs who use the specific method of infusion known as *gong fu cha* to bring out the extraordinarily rich flavor of wulong teas.

CHA XI Still relatively unknown in the West, *cha xi* is a practice that consists of surrounding the preparation of tea with beauty by creating an aesthetic environment conducive to tasting. The choice of tea, accessories and ornaments, as well as the arrangement of these objects, is of prime importance. The idea is not to show off expensive possessions, so there is no need for luxurious accessories. The focus is more on the materials used and on the harmony of their placement.

The *Gong Fu Cha* Ceremony

The Chinese symbols for *gong fu* are the same as those representing the martial arts: they represent mastery of time and movement. The literal meaning of *gong fu* is "the time for tea," and it refers to the time that is needed to achieve mastery of the art.

The first mention of this ceremony can be traced back to the early 17th century in China. At that time, four utensils were used: a teapot, a charcoal burner, an earthenware kettle and a few small porcelain bowls. Over time, the method has undergone several developments that have led to better control of the infusion. Today, for example, a sniffing cup is used, allowing the taster to

follow the development of the aromas that stabilize on the rim. This method of infusion, ideal for the preparation of wulong and Pu er teas, enables repeated infusions of the same leaves so that each stage reveals a different characteristic. Tasting a tea prepared in this method is both a journey and a discovery.

THE UTENSILS USED FOR *GONG FU CHA*

As many as 11 utensils may be needed for the preparation of tea following the *gong fu cha* method. Here are the most important ones:

- A small, ½- to 1-cup (100 to 200 ml), teapot
- A *cha chuan* bowl into which the teapot can be placed
- A *cha hai* (a container equipped with a spout) or a spare pot
- A sniffing cup or a tasting cup (*wen xiang bei* or *cha bei*)
- A kettle ——

To these objects one can add a spoon, a small napkin and a box in which to place the tea

1

2

Here are the steps of the *gong fu cha* method:

- Heat the utensils. Place your teapot in the *cha chuan* and pour a little simmering water into it. Put the lid back on and pour the contents into the spare pot. Once your teapot is well rinsed, add the required quantity of tea (2 or 3 teaspoons/10 to 15 ml).

- Rinse the leaves. Pour simmering water over the tea leaves and then discard this water. At this point you can smell the first aromas released by the moistened leaves.

- Infuse the leaves. Refill the teapot with simmering water until it overflows **1**, place the lid back on the pot and pour water over the outside of the teapot to get rid of the foam. Meanwhile, empty the spare pot to prepare it to receive the liquid.

- Wait as long as you wish. The first two infusions should last only 20 to 60 seconds, but the following infusions can last one to three minutes. Note that a bubble will usually form at the end of the teapot's spout, and after a short while it will slide back into the teapot as if it is being sucked in. This phenomenon is due to the fact that the leaves soak up the water and are "drinking" the liquid, so to speak. This indicates it is time to transfer the infusion.

- Pour the liquid into the spare pot. Be sure to drain the teapot so that no liquid remains inside **2**.

- Fill the sniffing cup, which has an elongated shape **3**, then transfer the liquid into the tasting cup **4**. Inhale the different fragrances that emanate from your now empty sniffing cup. Linger over the aromas that cling to the sides of the cup.

- Taste.

This tasting technique will allow you to infuse the same leaves several times and to discover different fragrances every time. The fundamental principles require patience, attentiveness and meticulousness. However, there is no set rule for a successful *gong fu cha* tasting. Tasters can adapt the technique to suit their own specific approach, bearing in mind that it is by taking time and paying close attention to the task at hand that the most sublime moments can be lived.

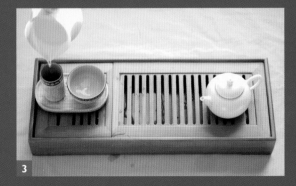

3

4

145

A Meeting with **Mr. Chen Nen Yu**,

Tea Grower

Mr. Chen Nen Yu is a tea grower in the district of Nantou.

What lead you to work in the world of tea?
How and when did you begin? Do you come
from a tea-growing family tradition?
I was born into a family of tea growers. Both my grandfather and my father were growers. I learned from them how to cultivate tea, to manage a garden and to process the leaves. I also received state-sponsored training in the tea industry. It has now been 17 years since I took over the family business.

Do you have a large tea garden? How big is it?
My tea garden covers 2 hectares [5 acres].

How much tea do you produce annually?
Do you have employees?
I produce about 5,000 kilos [11,000 pounds] of tea per year. In addition to the 30 pickers that I need during harvest time, I have three full-time employees who take care of the garden and five other seasonal employees who work in the processing plant.

Do you have your own store to sell your tea?
No, I don't.

To whom do you sell your tea? To the local
or international market?
I sell most of my tea on the local market.

What kind of tea do you produce?
I produce Qing Shin wulong tea in Lugu as well as a little Jin Shuan. I also have two gardens in Shan Lin Xi.

Have you noticed changes in the industry and in
your clientele since you started out?
Yes, in my father's and grandfather's time, the garden was small, the business was small, salaries were lower and almost all production was done by hand. Now we have high-tech equipment that allows us to manage a bigger garden and produce a lot more tea. The tendency in the industry now is toward specialization in a specific area, either cultivation, processing or trading tea.

T-18 Black Tea from Taiwan

Created by the Black Tea Experimentation Center in Taiwan, T-18 is a hybrid produced from a tea tree from Burma (Myanmar) called Ashamu and a wild tea tree from southern Taiwan. After 40 years of research and observation, T-18 stood out from other similar hybrids because of its superior sensorial characteristics, and so it was finally launched on the market in 1999.

Today it can be found mainly in the region around Sun Moon Lake (the largest natural lake in Taiwan), as well as on the east coast of the districts of Hualien and Taitung. This tea plant produces a whole-leaf black tea of unrivaled flavor. The liquid is rounded, full bodied, smooth and slightly minty, with generously fruity notes of prune and raisin. Intended primarily for the local market, only minimal quantities are produced, which partly explains the high price of this tea. However, its originality and growing popularity bode well for increased production that should lead to more reasonable pricing.

The Processing of T-18

After withering for 16 to 22 hours, T-18 needs four periods of mechanical rolling lasting 30 minutes each. The tea will then be oxidized for two hours in a room where a temperature of 77°F (25°C) and a level of humidity of approximately 95 percent will be maintained as consistently as possible. Two stages of drying will follow, lasting 30 minutes each at a temperature of around 210°F (100°C). Lastly, the tea will be sorted, most often mechanically. The finest batches will sometimes be sorted with tweezers to prevent hands from transferring undesirable aromas to the leaves.

Taiwanese Teas

Shan Lin Xi | wulong |
Translation: Coniferous forest close to the stream
Production area: Nantou, at an altitude of 3,300 to 5,400 feet (1,000 to 1,650 m)
Harvest season: April, June, September and November
Cultivar: Qing Xin

Tea plantations did not appear on the steep slopes of Shan Lin Xi Mountain until the early 1980s. Although recently introduced, tea growing in the region has expanded more than anywhere else on the whole island of Taiwan. The mountainsides are covered with green and thriving gardens that radiate health. Their energy is reflected in the rich and spirited temperament of the teas they produce. The most interesting teas are made from spring and winter pickings.

Tasting notes: The small beads of shiny leaves, barely softened by the heat of the water, fill the air with fragrances of ground cherry and luxurious flowers. The vegetal base of the infusion bursts with the rich aroma of hyacinth. The nose, while still heady with flowers, offers appetizing notes of candied fruit and melted butter. In the mouth, the liquid is supple and rounded with a sweet, vegetal attack. The finish leads us delicately to a vegetal and fruity silk embellished with candied melon and coconut.

Recommended infusion method and accessory: The *gong fu cha* technique and a *gaiwan* or teapot.

Dong Ding | wulong |
Translation: Frozen peaks
Alternative name: Tung Ting
Production area: Nantou, at an altitude of 1,650 to 2,600 feet (500 to 800 m)
Harvest season: April, June, September and November
Cultivar: Qing Xin

Since the 1970s, the Taiwanese government has actively encouraged the production of tea in this region. A festival is still organized so that people can taste the new harvests and learn the basics of the *gong fu cha* preparation method. This festival follows the annual spring tea contest. There are more than 4,000 growers in this region who use the Dong Ding name for their teas, even if it is not actually grown on the mountain. About 20 years ago the government designated three "official" Dong Ding growing regions. They are Zhang Yu, Yong Long and Feng Huang.

Tasting notes: The satiny leaves rolled into tight beads are a very dark green. The infusion gives off a powerful bouquet of lilac, vanilla and clover honey. The golden liquid gleams with lovely hints of pale green. Aromas of narcissus and peony fill the mouth against a background of ripe peach and butter. The unctuous texture leads to a long finish in which the floral aftertaste combines with a fresh vegetal note.

Recommended infusion method and accessory: The *gong fu cha* technique and a *gaiwan* or teapot.

149

Si Ji Chun | wulong |
Translation: Tea of the four springs
Production area: Mainly Nantou, at an altitude of 650 to 2,600 feet (200 to 800 m)
Harvest season: March to November
Cultivar: Si Ji Chun

It is said that Si Ji Chun is a natural hybrid resulting from a crossing of Qing Shin Dapan and Qing Shin wulong cultivars. Approved in 1981, it was discovered by chance in northern Taiwan by a farmer from the Mucha region. The Si Ji Chun variety offers certain advantages: it adapts well to various soil types; it provides up to five harvests per year; and its leaves release heady floral fragrances. These positive characteristics explain its growing popularity and the spread of its use on the island, on the plains as well as in the mountains.

Tasting notes: The explosive floral bouquet releases aromas of lilac, narcissus and hyacinth. The swelling floral attack is enriched with notes of spice and fresh grasses mixed with delicate aromas of browned butter and candied fruits. The texture is rich and unctuous, and the finish offers a long, sweet aftertaste.

Recommended infusion method and accessory: The *gong fu cha* technique and a *gaiwan* or teapot.

Ali Shan | wulong |
Production area: Chia Yi, at an altitude of 2,600 to 5,600 feet (800 to 1,700 m)
Harvest season: April, June, September and November
Cultivar: Qing Xin

Ali Shan is an important tourist destination in Taiwan. The huge mountain, rising to a peak of more than 8,500 feet (2,600 m), is equipped with an elaborate infrastructure to handle the thousands of visitors that flock there every year to watch the sunrise from the summit, to hike in the forest or to take the local steam train. The highly renowned tea gardens are located on various lower slopes.

Tasting notes: Rich and heady floral aromas are released from the emerald-green leaves. The delicately vegetal infusion gives off notes of fruit and pastry. In the mouth, aromas of coconut, exotic fruit and vanilla combine in a luxurious bouquet. The whole fades into a long, sweet finish of flower nectar. The texture is smooth and supple.

Recommended infusion method and accessory: The *gong fu cha* technique and a *gaiwan* or teapot.

Bai Hao | wulong |
Translation: White down
Alternative name: Oriental Beauty, Fancy Wulong
Production area: Hsinchu, at an altitude of 500 to 2,000 feet (150 to 600 m)
Harvest season: June to July
Cultivar: Qing Xin Dapan

The hint of muscat grape that characterizes the taste of this tea is the effect of a tiny insect, *Jacobiasca formosana*. When the plant is bitten by this insect, it defends itself by secreting a specific hormone. The aromatic potential of the hormone is then released by the intensive oxidation of the leaves, which can reach 50 percent to 60 percent. To take advantage of this insect, gardens must be located at low altitudes with sufficiently warm temperatures. The insect only attacks during the summer season, and only the bitten leaves are picked.

Tasting notes: The fine, dark-red twisted leaves dotted with numerous silver buds delight the eye even before they release any aroma. The aromatic complexity of the bouquet mingling honeyed, floral and fruity notes announces more smooth delights to come. The coppery, remarkably clear liquid is full and velvety. The mouthfeel opens on a note of orchid and muscat grape followed by a harmonious succession of aromas of apple, nutmeg, autumn honey and exotic wood. It is a treasure trove of seemingly endless delights.

Recommended infusion method and accessory: The *gong fu cha* technique and a *gaiwan* or teapot.

Li Shan | wulong |
Translation: Pear Mountain
Production area: Tachung, at an altitude of 6,550 to 7,900 feet (2,000 to 2,400 m)
Harvest season: May and October
Cultivar: Qing Xin

The little village of Li Shan is nestled in a magnificent landscape. It is surrounded by mountain slopes covered in pear, peach and apple orchards. In fact, tea has been cultivated for less than 20 years in this region and is not the principal crop, although it is certainly increasingly popular. The tea gardens are planted at very high altitude, up to 6,550 feet (2,000 m). At this altitude, growers plant long grasses between the rows to protect the tea trees from winter frosts.

Tasting notes: Once they are rinsed, the leaves release appetizing odors of melted butter and caramel flan. A flood of floral aromas combining peony, white lily and hyacinth arises from the infusion. This heady bouquet is finished with notes of brioche and barley sugar. The full liquor, swelling with persistent floral aromas, has a pleasantly oily texture. The finish carries a long aftertaste of flowers and candied zest. This is an elegant, sophisticated tea reminiscent of the most beautiful spring days.

Recommended infusion method and accessory: The *gong fu cha* technique and a *gaiwan* or teapot.

151

Pinglin Bao Zhong | wulong |
Translation: Wrapped in Pinglin paper
Alternative name: Wen Shan Bao Zhong
Production area: Taipei (Wen Shan), at an altitude of 1,300 to 2,000 feet (400 to 600 m)
Harvest season: April, June, September and November
Cultivar: Qing Xin and sometimes Cui Yi

Situated in the Wen Shan mountain massif, about 30 minutes from Taipei, Pinglin is a very popular village. Many residents of the capital go there regularly to buy their favorite tea. This high demand has pushed up the prices of the tea from this region considerably. It is interesting to note that Bao Zhong is one of the only wulong teas that is becoming hard to find in Taiwan. Today, the twisted-leaf style is being replaced by leaves rolled into small beads.

Tasting notes: When the long, twisted leaves are rinsed they release generous fragrances of lilac, lily of the valley and vanilla. The infusion produces a nose with a dominant floral aspect enhanced with a gentle vegetal note of chlorophyll. The straw-colored liquid has a sweet and delicate attack and offers a mild acidity reminiscent of cooked peach. Aromas of flowers and melon develop in the mouth, culminating in a full roundness. The still-flowery finish stretches into a sweet note of birchwood. The aromas released by this tea are remarkably persistent.

Recommended infusion method and accessory: The *gong fu cha* technique and a *gaiwan* or teapot.

Gabacha | wulong |
Translation: Tea containing GABA
Alternative name: Jia Yeh
Production area: Taipei (Wen Shan) and Nantou, at an altitude of 1,300 to 2,000 feet (400 to 600 m)
Harvest season: Two weeks before and after the Duan Wu holiday, which falls on May 5 in the lunar calendar
Cultivar: Qing Xin

This tea was introduced and developed in Taiwan following Japanese research on the GABA molecule during the 1980s. According to some studies, this molecule, which is found in the human brain, helps to reduce stress and anxiety. Thanks to a special method of production that includes vacuum-processing, this tea has a very high GABA content. In addition, this unusual processing method helps to bring out a very interesting, distinctive taste.

Tasting notes: The large, irregular, twisted leaves are brown and dark red in color. Their generous spicy and fruity character is delightful, even before infusion. As the leaves unfold, they release smooth fragrances of stewed fruit, nutmeg and licorice against a woody background. The balance of acidity and sweetness in the mouth combines notes of dried apricot and marmalade to which aromas of fresh tobacco and brown sugar join, producing a rounded, silky texture.

Recommended infusion method and accessory: The *gong fu cha* technique and a *gaiwan* or teapot.

Gui Fei | wulong |
Translation: Imperial concubine
Alternative name: Zhuo Yan Cha
Production area: Nantou, at an altitude of 1,500 to 2,300 feet (450 to 700 m)
Harvest season: June and September
Cultivar: Qing Xin

This tea appeared quite recently and in the most unlikely circumstances. Following the devastating earthquake of 1999, many plantations in the Nantou region were temporarily abandoned. Untended, the gardens fell prey to the invasion of numerous parasites. One of these, *Jacobiasca formosana*, is a tiny insect that is one reason for the renown of the Bai Hao tea grown in the northwest of the island. When the growers realized the insects affected how the leaves taste, they decided to process the leaves that had been bitten by the insects. The leaves are rolled tightly, in accordance with the style of the region, and 30 percent to 40 percent oxidized, which brings out the distinctive character of the bitten leaves. Gui Fei tea thereby combines in a highly original way two great classic Taiwanese teas: Bai Hao and Dong Ding. As well as creating a new style of tea, the growers were looking for a way to take advantage of the summer harvests, when the level of oxidation is lower, and the teas are often less interesting.

Tasting notes: The leaves are rolled into beads that have a prettily marbled green and copper appearance. The infusion releases aromas of cinnamon, flowers and oxidized apple to form an attractive bouquet topped off by a powerful fragrance of roses. The luminous golden liquid offers the nose delicious notes of honey and muscat grape. The texture is smooth and round in the mouth, opening onto a delicate fruity note. The light finish extends into a base of marzipan and honey.

Recommended infusion method and accessory: The *gong fu cha* technique and a *gaiwan* or teapot.

153

India

THE BRITISH ESTABLISHED AN INDUSTRY IN INDIA THAT, TO THIS DAY, RESPONDS TO A STRONG INTERNATIONAL DEMAND FOR TEA WHILE MAINTAINING EXCEPTIONAL QUALITY STANDARDS IN SOME OF ITS GROWING REGIONS. HOWEVER, THE DISCOVERY OF WILD TEA TREES IN THE JUNGLES OF ASSAM INDICATES THAT INDIA IS ONE OF THE BIRTHPLACES OF THE TEA TREE.

History

The true beginning of the history of tea cultivation in India can be attributed in part to Major Robert Bruce. In 1823, as an employee of the East India Company, he discovered wild tea trees growing in the state of Assam, close to the border with Burma (Myanmar). Major Bruce had noticed certain tribes chewing the leaves of tall trees that were identified as wild tea trees, but to his knowledge there were not enough of these to produce a significant harvest, nor were there any plantations. However, at that time the British were looking for ways to get around supply problems related to their tea imports, including the Japanese market being closed to the outside world, the long shipping route between China and England (which often resulted in tea spoiling while still aboard the ships) and the exorbitant prices demanded by the Chinese, who enjoyed a monopoly on the trade (see "The End of the Chinese Monopoly: The Opium Wars" on the facing page). And so, in response to their need to find new tea-growing regions, the British took a serious interest in Robert Bruce's discovery.

Even before Bruce's discovery, several attempts had been made to grow tea trees in India. As early as the beginning of the 19th century, C.J. Gordon had brought back approximately 80,000 *Camellia sinensis* var. *sinensis* seeds from China, which he introduced in Darjeeling, Kumaon, Assam and southern India, long before the tea tree discovered in Assam was recognized as a variety of *Camellia sinensis*. However, this first attempt to grow tea failed due to a lack of experience.

Establishing and developing a new tea supply chain was, of course, a challenge fraught with many difficulties, but — motivated by the problems arising from trade with China and the high global demand for tea — the British plunged into the venture. In 1834, Charles Alexander Bruce succeeded in creating India's first plantation, carrying on the project started by his brother, who had died in the intervening years. Some four years later he made his first delivery to England — 12 cases of tea. Received with much curiosity, this first shipment was sold at auction for a good price, although it did not quite live up to British expectations. It was not easy, after just a few years, to compete with the Chinese, given their level of expertise.

The British decided to send spies to China to try to discover the secrets of growing tea. Botanist Robert Fortune, disguised as a tea merchant, managed to gain access to the gardens and pick up enough clues to understand the mysterious process that produced China's famous black tea and the important phenomenon involved, oxidation. In 1848, he returned with 20,000 plants, essential information regarding the processing of the leaves and a Chinese labor force of about 80 workers, who were to prove invaluable to the creation of new plantations. It was at this point that the cultivation of tea in India really got under way.

Next, a huge deforestation program in the region of Assam cleared the way for vast gardens. Moreover, the British applied the experience they had acquired during the agricultural revolution in Europe in the 17th century to the management of the plantations, which led to industrial methods of production being adopted more quickly in India. Consequently, by the early 1860s, Indian production was sufficient to meet

THE END OF THE CHINESE MONOPOLY: THE OPIUM WARS   Queen Elizabeth I founded the East India Company (EIC) in 1600, hoping to dominate trade with Asia. The company was supposed to give the British control over the tea trade with China. When the EIC managed to establish its first trading post in Canton in 1684, tea became the main export, mostly in response to the huge demands of the English market, as tea had become extremely popular in England. However, the Chinese were self-sufficient and wary of foreign trade, so they demanded payment in cash, rather than in exchange for goods. This did not suit the British, as they were rich in goods, produced mainly in their Indian colonies, but not in money.

To encourage the Chinese to export their tea, the British began to exchange it for opium. This trade not only destabilized the Chinese market, it made the population dependent on foreign trade (since they could only obtain opium through foreign trade). This trade proved to be an absolute disaster for China. As early as 1729, the Chinese instigated various prohibitionist measures to fight against the opium trade. In 1796, Emperor Jia Qing established the death penalty for opium trafficking. In spite of these efforts, the drug trade continued to spread like wildfire. It is said that by 1830, the British had exported more than 1,650 tons (1,500 t) of opium to China.

In 1839, the Chinese government managed to fight back by confiscating and burning stocks of opium. Next, all ports involved in the opium trade were closed, including the port of Canton. In reaction to these measures, the British initiated a series of military interventions historically referred to as the first Opium War (1840–1842). This war destroyed Chinese defenses and, in effect, terminated their trade monopoly. The conflict was resolved by the Treaty of Nanjing, which forced the Chinese to restart the opium trade with Britain. The Chinese also had to turn over the island of Hong Kong to the British and give them access to five major ports, including Fuzhou, Canton and Shanghai. When the Chinese failed to respect the terms of the treaty the British launched the second Opium War (1856–1860), hoping to obtain further concessions from them. This second war was even more disastrous for the Chinese. They were then obliged to sign the Treaty of Tianjin, which greatly favored the British.

British needs. Regions that were suitable for better-quality harvests were also established in the mountains of Darjeeling and Nilgiri.

Specializing in the production of black teas, the British were able to launch an industry that would explode over the following decades, increasing from a few hundred tons in the early 1860s to more than 198,400 tons (180,000 t) in 1914. The invention of crush, tear, curl (CTC) processing, which facilitates mechanical handling of the leaves, paved the way for high-volume production.

On August 15, 1947, the former British colony of India was partitioned into two independent nations. As a result, the tea-growing gardens and processing plants that had belonged to the English gradually came under Indian control. In 1951, the Indian government signed the Plantation Act in law, ensuring better working conditions for plantation workers. Today, the active involvement of the Indian tea industry in the field of research makes it a world leader both in terms of the quality of its teas and the quantity of its output.

The Indian Tea Industry

With annual production of 1,081,170 tons (980,820 t), India is the second-largest tea producer in the world after China. The tea industry is a vitally important sector of the Indian national economy, directly employing more than a million workers. Before its independence in 1947, India kept only about 30 percent of its output for the domestic market. Today, the reverse is true: a large majority of Indian production is sold on the local market. Only 21 percent is exported. Although tea gardens can be found throughout the country, most of them are concentrated in the states of Assam, Western Bengal, Tamil-Nadu and Kerala.

Home to 900 gardens, some of which spread over several thousand acres, Assam is the largest tea-growing region in the world: more than 550,000 tons (500,000 t) of tea are produced there annually, sometimes even glutting the market. Luxury teas, like Darjeelings, are reserved for the export market. Japan, Great Britain, Europe and, more recently, North America, are the major importers.

The industry's rapid growth was made possible by the development of highly efficient black-tea processing methods. The CTC method, which consists of grinding the leaves into very small pieces, allows growers to produce a uniform standard of tea — ideal for the industrialized market. This led to the creation of tea bags (see "Tea in Bags," on facing page), a product that is extremely important in the industry today. Very high domestic demand, growing at a rate of 3 percent to 4 percent per year, has encouraged the use of the CTC method, which allows for very high productivity, if not high quality.

In addition to the product destined for local consumption, India produces more and more high-quality teas that are based on seasonal harvests and the specific tastes of importing countries looking for more upscale teas. The Darjeeling region is a good example of this trend.

THE TEA INDUSTRY IN DARJEELING

Although the market it serves represents only 3 percent of the total tea production of India, the Darjeeling tea industry occupies a unique position. Realizing that they could not compete with the high volumes produced in other, milder, regions of the world, growers decided to perfect their product in order to produce an exceptional black tea that would give them access to a global market.

A garden in Darjeeling produces about 445 pounds of tea per acre (500 kg/ha) per year, three times less than a garden in Assam, for example. In order to

A BRIEF SUMMARY OF THE INDIAN TEA TRADE

Total growing area: 1,429,400 acres (578,458 ha)
Total annual production: 1,081,170 tons (980,820 t)
Principal growing region: Assam, with 537,373 tons (487,497 t)
Percentage of production by type of tea: CTC, 90%; orthodox, 8.9%; green tea and wulong1.2%
Average production yield: 1,521 pounds per acre (1,705 kg/ha)
Annual exports: 223,900 tons (203,120 t)

Source: 2008 data from the Tea Board of India. (Values in imperial units of measure supplied by publisher.)

A CTC factory in Assam.

The organic section of the Coonoor Garden in the Nilgiri Hills, Tamil Nadu.

ensure the viability of the industry, growers pay special attention to each harvest throughout the year.

By producing ever more complex and unusual teas, which have allowed growers to demand higher prices, the Darjeeling region has built up an excellent reputation. However, in spite of its reputation, a flourishing international market and the rapid growth of the local market (thanks to an increasingly affluent middle class), Darjeeling tea survives in a fragile context. Political instability and very high production costs have created serious problems for growers. Every year, several gardens are forced to close or are bought out by other owners.

TEA IN BAGS The invention of tea bags is attributed to Thomas Sullivan, a New York tea trader and distributor. In June 1908, as he was preparing several samples for prospective clients, Sullivan came up with the idea of putting a little of the tea leaves into small silk bags. To taste it, he thought, they would just need to remove the tea from the bags. But when the clients received the samples, they plunged the bags directly into the boiling water. Pleased with the result, they asked Sullivan for more tea "in bags." From there, the idea took hold.

Today, some 130 million cups of tea are brewed from tea bags every day, but the packaging was modified many times before it achieved popular acceptance. This was the case particularly in England, where deeply ingrained consumer habits had to be changed. Thomas Sullivan himself made one of the first changes, when he replaced the silk with gauze, which was just as effective but less expensive. Another important change originated in Boston, where, in 1930, William Hermanson invented a bag made of heat-sealed paper fibers. But the greatest change came after the Second World War, when Joseph Tetley and Co. (1953) began mass-producing tea in bags. Ever since, the tea-bag market has continued to flourish. Tea bags have taken on new shapes, round, pyramid shaped, etc., and now contain many different varieties of tea.

TEA TASTERS   The world of tea could not manage without tea tasters. They make significant contributions throughout the production process of tea, right up until marketing, especially in relation to the evaluation of a harvest and the processing methods. Tea tasters can fulfill many roles, depending on the different needs of the companies. Some of them, who are also called "tea blenders," specialize in the creation of blends, such as when a uniform tea is required or to test the quality.

THE DISTRIBUTION SYSTEM

Most of the Indian tea that is destined for export is sold at auction in Kolkata (formerly Calcutta). All the tea-producing companies deal with a broker who hires professional tea tasters to evaluate the quality of a harvest and the price that it could fetch. A buyer who wishes to source an Indian tea must go through a broker, who will provide a list of the available teas.

The buyer can then enter the tasting room. Over the following days, the buyer will decide which batches he or she would like to purchase. The buyer will then attend the auction and bid on the chosen batches.

Taster-importers, who enjoy a privileged relationship with growers, can visit the gardens directly. They can thereby sample and buy the grower's latest batches before they are even sent to Kolkata.

THE APPELLATION SYSTEM   India is currently trying to apply the first tea appellation system in the world. Developed by the Tea Board of India in collaboration with the Darjeeling Tea Association, the system has been put in place in response to copies of famous teas, such as those of Darjeeling. Note that the market currently offers approximately four times as much tea under the Darjeeling label than is actually produced in the region every year. In order to increase volume, teas from other more productive regions, such as Assam, are added to Darjeeling teas. The appellation system obliges growers to indicate the geographic origin (garden), the name of the cultivars used and the processing method used for any given harvest. In spite of the good intentions of the tea producers, a lot remains to be done to ensure that this standard is respected.

The Temi Garden in Sikkim State.

A Meeting with Mr. Kavi Seth,

Industry Professional

Mr. Kavi Seth is the head taster for J. Thomas, India's most important tea broker in Kolkata.

How long have you been working in the tea industry?

I began working in the tea industry in August 1985.

What brought you to this line of work?

In the beginning, when I was finishing my studies at the college of New Delhi, I knew nothing about the workings of the tea market. However, one of my uncles was a general manager with J. Thomas & Company Private Limited, and he invited me to join the company.

What are your everyday responsibilities?

The work of a taster may appear monotonous, but it is up to each of us to make it interesting. We must taste and evaluate the teas, attend the auctions, collect information about the market and interact with the buyers and sellers.

What do you like best about your profession?

The auctions! Even if it is sometimes mentally and physically exhausting. Also, the fact that every tea is different, especially the Darjeeling teas. There can be an enormous price difference between the batches.

What challenges will the Indian tea industry need to meet in the years to come?

Over the past few years, the tea industry has experienced a steep drop in prices because of inflation in the Indian economy. Fortunately, 2008 was a good year and prices reached record highs. The major challenge for our industry is to re-establish a strong presence on the export market, which has been declining for several years now.

What is your favorite tea?

A second harvest from Darjeeling, for its unique muscat grape characteristic.

How would you define a good tea?

For me, not only does a good tea look good, it tastes good and can be kept for a long time.

Indian Terroirs

Tea growing in India began in the northeast of the country, with the discovery of wild tea trees (see page 156), and spread along the banks of the Brahmaputra River to the foothills of the Himalayas. Darjeeling and Assam are the most famous production regions. Some high-quality harvests come from the south, where the Nilgiri Hills are located. Other lesser-known growing regions, such as Dooars, Teraï, Kangra, Cachar, Travancore and Sikkim, produce high-volume harvests that are mainly destined to supply the domestic market.

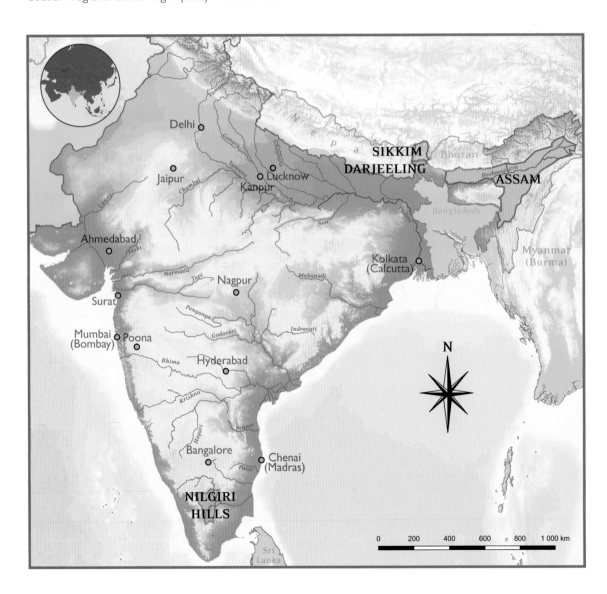

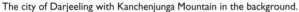

The city of Darjeeling with Kanchenjunga Mountain in the background.

Workers picking tea leaves in tropical rain, in Assam.

THE DARJEELING REGION

Suspended high in the foothills of the magnificent Indian Himalayas, Darjeeling (the land of storms) is a district of Western Bengal. The town of Darjeeling itself is perched at an altitude of 6,890 feet (2,100 m). From this amazing vantage point, three of the four highest peaks in the world can be seen: Everest, Kanchenjunga and Lho-Tse. To the west, the Singalila River separates Darjeeling from the Kingdom of Nepal. The region of Sikkim lies to the north, with Tibet beyond.

The first recorded plantations in Darjeeling date from 1856. Twenty years later there were more than a hundred. Today, the district of Darjeeling alone contains 86 tea gardens. These are the only gardens that are recognized by the Darjeeling Planters Association, having the right to sell their tea under the international appellation of Darjeeling.

Running down the mountainsides of the Himalayan foothills, this region is blessed with undeniable natural advantages. The gardens are planted on the steep slopes of the valleys, which provide excellent soil drainage, and they grow at altitudes from 1000 to 7,500 feet (300 to 2,300 m), with the majority located at over 3,300 feet (1,000 m).

The soil is rich and slightly acidi,c with a pH of about 5.5. With temperatures averaging 77°F (25°C) in summer and 46°F (8°C) in winter (the high-altitude regions are frequently affected by frost), and rainfall that varies from 63 to 158 inches (1,600 to 4,000 mm) (in the south), the tea trees grow in ideal conditions. The intense high-altitude sunlight is filtered by frequent cloudy periods, which prevents the leaves from drying out or burning. The almost constant fog during the monsoon season and the presence of a light breeze that cools the atmosphere help the new shoots to develop.

Today, this magnificent region enjoys unprecedented fame. The delicacy of the teas it produces have earned it the nickname of the "Champagne of Black Teas."

THE ASSAM REGION

The Assam State lies in northeastern India, 125 miles (200 km) east of Darjeeling, close to the borders of Burma (Myanmar) and Bangladesh. It is here that the *Camellia sinsensis* var. *assamica* was dis-covered, a tea with large leaves that brews into a full-bodied, dark liquid with a lot of character. This highly fertile tropical region is covered at low altitude by a vast jungle through which flows the Brahmaputra River.

165

It contains some 900 gardens, stretching from the Himalayas in the north to the mountains of Naga and Patkoi in the south.

Approximately 118 inches (3,000 mm) of precipitation falls on the 370-mile (600 km) valley every year. Between October and March, the temperature remains stable, at a mild 68 to 77°F (20 to 25°C). During the monsoon — from April to September, when the temperature can soar to 95°F (35°C) — the valley becomes a kind of natural hothouse in which the pickers work in extremely difficult conditions. In spite of that, more than half of Indian tea is grown here, most of it processed using the CTC method. Most of the plantations are in the vast plains along the Brahmaputra River.

These are the leaves most often used to create the "British-taste" teas, that is, teas destined for sale in tea bags and to be enjoyed with the addition of a little milk. Assam teas can be drunk just as they are, but their natural spicy, astringent and malty flavor makes them an excellent base for the preparation of chai (see Indian Chai recipe on page 244). Some "orthodox" teas are still produced in Assam, and they have surprisingly rich aromas and body.

THE NILGIRI HILLS

High on the plateaus of southeastern India, the Nilgiri Hills are part of the western Ghat range known as the "Blue Mountains." This is the third-largest tea-growing area in India. Beginning in the middle of the 19th century, it has produced teas that are well structured, slightly fruity and spicy. Because of the tropical climate, growing is continuous and harvesting takes place all year long. About 80 percent of the cultivars used are *C. s. var. assamica*, and the best harvests are picked in January and February. Almost all the tea is grown for the domestic market and processed by the CTC method.

There more than 30,000 gardens in this growing region. Although some gardens, like the Tiashola Estate, cover several hundred acres, most are no larger than 25 acres (10 ha). In spite of the high number of growers, the industry is currently going through a difficult phase. Many gardens are being abandoned and investment is rare.

Some parts of the Nilgiri Hills are located at high altitude, where excellent growing conditions and a particularly rich soil favor the cultivation of very high-quality teas. For now, only a few growers seem interested in this rich potential. Let us hope they will be able to revitalize the industry.

THE SIKKIM REGION

Just north of Darjeeling, between Nepal and Bhutan, is Sikkim State. One single garden, Temi, is responsible for the increasing renown of this area. Following a government project about 30 years ago that called upon the expertise of the Darjeeling growers, this garden was planted with cultivars from the Darjeeling region.

Temi is at the top of a mountain that borders the Teesta River, which marks the boundary between Sikkim and Darjeeling. The harvests from this region, which are processed according to the orthodox method, (see page 172) have the well-structured taste and explosive aromas typical of Darjeeling teas.

Lunch awaits the pickers at Hunwal, in Assam.

Indian Gardens and Plants

The first governor of Darjeeling, Dr. Campbell, was the first to experiment with tea planting in the region, in 1835. Campbell planted his own garden with some seeds and cuttings (*Camellia sinensis* var. *sinensis*) that had come mostly from China. These samples were distributed by the governor general, who was trying to encourage tea growing on Indian soil. There were other samples, belonging to the *C. s.* var. *assamica* variety, that were discovered in the northeastern jungles of India by Scottish Major Robert Bruce.

Since these two varieties thrived in their new environment, they were planted on newly cleared land in the same district. It soon became obvious that the Darjeeling region was an exceptionally favorable tea terroir. Despite the lack of sunlight, damp atmosphere and cold mountain climate, which shortened the growing season, the tea trees produced leaves of extraordinary flavor. The teas of this region are blessed with rare aromatic complexity and richness.

Several tea gardens in Darjeeling have preserved sections of the original plantations that date back to 1860 or even earlier. Growers are proud to show visitors areas of their gardens that contain "pure" *C. s.* var. *sinensis*. The teas harvested in these sections are sometimes referred to as "*grands crus*," as in the case of the Singell garden, for example, which contains a "heritage" section that grows only original trees.

However, as many of these trees are reaching the limit of their productive life, their yield has diminished considerably. (A slowing of the sap's flow seems to be partially responsible for this phenomenon.) Currently, replanting represents a major challenge in Darjeeling.

In order to establish new plantations, a large number of cultivars have been selected to correspond to the needs and climatic conditions of certain areas. The India Tea Research Association at Jorhat (Assam) nurtures and distributes young tea trees grown from cuttings (about 30 for Darjeeling, 30 for Assam and another 30 for the Nilgiri Hills). The cultivars are chosen according to various criteria, including production capacity, adaptability to different soils and climates, and the aromatic complexity of the leaves.

The *Camellia sinensis* var. *sinensis* cultivars are used most frequently in high-altitude plantations, like those of the mountains of Darjeeling, where weather conditions are harsher. The *C. s.* var. *assamica* cultivars are more often used on the plains, at an altitude of around 1000 feet (300 m).

Unfortunately, tea trees obtained from cuttings have a much shorter life span. Tea trees grown from seed have a much more highly developed root system, which allows them to extract more nourishment from the soil, giving them a productive life of 120 to 150 years. Cultivars produced from cuttings have

INDIAN TEA TREES AND STRESS   For a plant that originated in the tropical forests of south China, the rigorous conditions found in the mountainous regions of Darjeeling can be difficult. However, this stress contributes to the development of exceptional aromas. Here is the opinion of S.E. Kabir, founder of the Department of Tea Studies at North Bengal University: "The high level of volatile components that produce aroma (VCPA) found in the tea trees of Darjeeling can be attributed to the 'meeting' between the Chinese variety and the agro-environmental conditions of the region. The misty atmosphere — high humidity, short periods of sunlight, etc. — favors the synthesis of the precursors responsible for the biosynthesis of the enzymes necessary for the production of the volatile components and, therefore, of the taste." The unfavorable weather conditions of the Himalayan foothills would appear to be essential for the development of the aromatic characteristics of Darjeeling teas.

Camellia sinensis var. *assamica* in the Nilgiri Hills.

Camellia sinensis var. *sinensis* in Darjeeling.

a useful life of only about 40 years. Moreover, their shallow roots can quickly drain the soil of mineral resources, endangering later generations of trees. For these reasons, although two-thirds of the plantations in Darjeeling have been created from cloned cultivars, many growers are now choosing to seed certain sections of their gardens.

More than 30 cultivars are grown in India today. Among them, T78, originated in the famous garden of Tukdha in 1978, is one of the most widespread. Although its popularity is in sharp decline because its productivity and quality decrease with age, it has been a star cultivar for the past few years. Most popular today, the AV2 (Ambari Vegetative 2 from the Terai garden) and P312 (Phoobsering 312) are also used regularly, although both are a little more delicate and require good fertilization and adequate water.

VARIOUS DARJEELING HARVESTS

Since tea is a seasonal product, the quality of a harvest depends largely on the growing conditions of the trees. Rainfall, sunlight and temperature all have an effect on the lengthening of the shoots and the unfurling of the leaves. Gardens are picked at intervals of four to seven days, depending on weather conditions. The timing of the intervals between pickings is crucial. Growers must strike a balance between productivity and the health of the plant because excessive picking can endanger the tea tree. In Darjeeling there are three main harvests, each of which produces a distinctive taste representative of the season.

FIRST FLUSH

The first picking period of the year begins between mid-March and the end of March, when the spring rains have stimulated plant growth, and it ends around the second week of May. This first harvest yields light-bodied teas with explosive aromas. The moment when the first new leaves appear depends on the weather and varies from one garden to another. Some growers irrigate to artificially stimulate the growth of the trees, as early as February, in order to obtain advanced harvests.

FINE PICKING   In Darjeeling, the usual method of harvesting is fine picking, which means that only the final bud and two leaves are picked.

While global enthusiasm was previously center-ed on Second Flush teas, a new market for excep-tional teas was created when the world turned its attention to the First Flush. Consequently, growers strive to create ever more complex fragrances. In Darjeeling, the fresh quality of the young spring shoots is enhanced by a shorter period of oxida-tion (which preserves the herbaceous aroma), an explosive attack and a sweet aftertaste. Over the last 15 years, the First Flush teas of Darjeeling have become a growing phenomenon.

The first harvest lasts from six to eight weeks, after which the tea trees are trimmed and lightly pruned then left to rest for a few weeks, according to the natural cycle of each garden. After the picking, the plants naturally fall dormant, and growers cannot undertake another harvest until the trees awaken.

SECOND FLUSH

The second harvest takes place from the end of June until mid-July, and it yields a higher volume. Some growers delay the second harvest in order to slip an in-between picking between the first and second harvests. Although they are new, the leaves picked during this second harvest are firmer. They are processed using a longer oxidation period, which gives them a full-bodied liquid with a malty fragrance reminiscent of ripe fruit.

After the second harvest, another pause (*banjhi*) is necessary so that the tea trees can regenerate before the third harvest.

AUTUMN FLUSH

After the monsoon, which lasts until September, and just before the tea tree goes into winter hibernation, the final harvest of the year, the fall harvest, takes place, in October and November. A heightened interest in methods of cultivation and processing has lead to a discernable improvement in quality. As growers seek to increase the number of quality teas they produce, they are paying more and more attention to second and third harvests.

THE CHEMISTRY OF BLACK TEAS   Polyphenols are essential components of tea leaves. In the fresh leaf they are colorless and acrid, but during oxidation these enzymes are transformed into theaflavins and thearubigins, the two elements that give tea its color and astringency. Oxidation develops brown, red and black pigments and reduces the leaves' astringency.

Processing Indian Black Teas

In order to compete with the low production costs of the Chinese, who had access to a very cheap labor force, the British had to reinvent every stage of processing. They needed to reduce costs by turning their tea plantations into industrial enterprises.

As we have seen, the first methods of processing black tea appeared in China during the 17th century. To produce satisfactory results, this method required the repetition of numerous steps. The British were able to develop techniques that were far simpler and more efficient by mechanizing the whole process. Taking inspiration from Chinese traditional methods, at the end of the 19th century they created the first industrial technique, the orthodox process. This mechanized process requires expertise and intuition and allows for greater control over the different variables that affect the chemistry of tea leaves. This process is still used today to produce extremely high-quality teas, such as those from Darjeeling.

THE ORTHODOX METHOD

Developed by the British in northeastern India around 1860 and constantly improved upon since, the orthodox method is one of the oldest mechanized methods of black-tea processing. It consists of five steps: withering, rolling, oxidation, dehydration and sorting. More complex than the CTC method, the orthodox method is used to process the best black-tea harvests.

WITHERING

Withering reduces the water content of the leaves, softening them and changing the waxy texture so they can then be rolled without breaking. While dehydration changes the physical structure of the leaves, the natural activity of the enzymes begins to subtly change the chemistry of their flavors. This triggers, among other reactions, an increase in amino acids. The freshly picked leaves are evenly spread out in withering vats on metal, jute or plastic grids that allow air to circulate freely. The ambient humidity, ventilation and temperature are constantly monitored to ensure successful withering. After 14 to 17 hours, the moisture content of the leaves will have been reduced by 60 percent to 70 percent.

ROLLING

The following stage, rolling, consists of breaking the outside membranes of the leaves in order to release the oils and enzymes they contain. For 10 to 20 minutes, the piles of leaves are held in copper vats inside enormous machines. These machines roll the leaves under pressure until they form a compact mass. Next, with the aid of a rolling machine, various levels of pressure are applied to the leaves following a precise cycle until their cellular membranes are broken, releasing the oils they contain. As soon as these oils are exposed to the air the phenomenon of oxidation begins. If rolling is too intense, the leaves will be discolored and dull, and if rolling is too light the leaves will be dry, gray and dusty and brew into a pale and tasteless liquid.

OXIDATION

On contact with oxygen, the enzymes contained in the oils of the leaves trigger a chemical reaction called "enzymatic oxidation" or fermentation. This process of chemical change will determine the flavor, strength, body and color of the tea.

The rolled leaves are spread out on trays made of stainless steel, ceramic or glass in a humid environment and at a temperature between 68 and 86°F (20 to 30°C). Depending on the moisture content of the leaves, they will be spread in a thin layer (for quick oxidation at low temperature) or in a thick layer (for slower oxidation). The temperature and humidity are sometimes controlled by humidifiers in order to maintain a minimum of 90 percent humidity in the room. Oxidation time can vary considerably, according to the ambient temperature and the type of tea being produced. While 15 to 30 minutes can be enough for First Flush Darjeeling teas, certain teas from the Assam region need to oxidize for up to four hours. This is a critical stage and requires workers with expertise and good intuition because they must strike a perfect balance for the different tea flavors. Excessive oxidation will result in a liquid that is thick, strong and has a wine-like (fermented) taste, while too little oxidation will produce a green and raw infusion with a thin liquid. Often, in order to make the process easier to manage, the oxidation is slowed down to prolong the period during which the aromas are at their peak. According to many factory managers, this moment is recognizable by a surprising and very specific smell of apple. When the precise moment to stop the oxidation arrives, the leaves are ready to be dried.

DRYING

Dehydration puts an end to the process of oxidation by altering the enzymes that causes it. The leaves are placed either on conveyors or on a series of revolving trays in a large machine that is heated to a temperature of 248°F (120°C). If drying is incomplete the oxidation process can continue uncontrolled, while if it is too intense the leaves will burn and acquire a smoky taste. The process lasts 20 to 30 minutes, until the moisture content of the leaves is reduced to 2 percent to 6 percent.

SORTING

After the drying stage, the leaves are sorted. Vibrating grids of varying sizes placed one on top of another separate the leaves into different grades. The largest leaves remain on the top grid while the crushed leaves (fannings) and dust fall to the ground. The intermediate leaves are caught by the other grids.

In Darjeeling, all teas, regardless of the quality, are sorted in this way. The grade a tea is given is therefore an indication of size, not quality. Sorting is, however, an essential step, as each size of leaf requires a different infusion time and will have different characteristics.

THE CTC METHOD

The method of processing called CTC, which stands for crushing, tearing and curling, is an industrial method that was developed in India by Sir William McKercher. In the 1930s, borrowing ideas from existing machinery, Sir William perfected a system of industrial processing that would speed up the oxidation process and produce higher yields more quickly.

The CTC method consists of three simple steps. After a brief withering process, the leaves are cut and then crushed in metallic cylinders equipped with blades. During the next step they are torn apart by a machine called a Rotorvane. Finally, the leaves are sent to a *ghoogi*, a large barrel in which they are rolled into small beads.

At first used only for coarser leaves, this method gained in popularity in the middle of the 20th century, with the invention of tea bags. Although this method thoroughly revolutionized the tea industry, it was inevitably at the expense of quality. Furthermore, the majority of the leaves used in the CTC method are of an inferior picking quality.

Most tea-growing regions have adopted modern and highly mechanized production methods that aim for high volume and uniform quality. Hence, this method of production of black teas is now found in practically every country that produces high volumes of tea.

THE LOT CONCEPT   After picking, the harvest must immediately be sent to the processing plant to be treated in order to bring out its specific flavor. If the leaves are left to stand for too long they will become oxidized and unusable. Therefore, nearly every garden has its own processing plant. In Darjeeling, growers identify each daily harvest taken from their garden by a lot number. For example, the appellation "Darjeeling Singell First Flush DJ2" means that the tea comes from the second lot or "invoice" number processed during the first spring picking in the Singell garden of Darjeeling. It should be noted that a lot might come from just one section of a garden or be composed of a grouping from two or three sections.

MELLOWING When tea leaves the factory, the aromas of the first harvests are not yet completely stabilized. Growers will even maintain sufficient moisture in the leaves for a slight oxidation to continue, creating a process called mellowing. Thus, the tea will continue to develop over a period of up to three months after processing, after which the reaction will gradually stop. Some enthusiasts are passionate about the green aspect of the immature leaves and the floral character of the aromas reminiscent of muscat grapes, while others prefer the moment when the aromas are stabilized and the liquid acquires its full roundness.

GRADES OF BLACK TEA

There are three major systems of grading black teas. The grades refer more to the state of the leaves (whole, broken or crushed) than to their taste qualities. Usually, whole leaves will result in a more complex and aromatic infusion, whereas broken leaves create a darker liquid with a simpler flavor profile.

Here is the grading system used in Darjeeling to indicate the grade of a whole-leaf tea. In this case, the most important aspect is the number of buds (pekoes). The more buds a tea contains, the more letters there are in its appellation.

SFTGFOP: Special Finest Tippy Golden Flowery Orange Pekoe
FTGFOP: Finest Tippy Golden Flowery Orange Pekoe
TGFOP: Tippy Golden Flowery Orange Pekoe
GFOP: Golden Flowery Orange Pekoe
FOP: Flowery Orange Pekoe
OP: Orange Pekoe

Tippy refers to the abundance of flowering buds.
Golden refers to the tips that turn golden after oxidation.
Flowery refers to the slightly floral aroma released by the buds.
Orange is a purely historic reference to the Dutch royal family of Holland-Nassau, who were among the first to import tea into Europe.
Pekoe comes from *pak-ho*, meaning "white down." Also used to describe the hair of newborn babies, here it refers to the final leaf on a branch (final bud), which is covered in a fine white down.

The numeral 1 sometimes appears at the end of the grade of certain batches. Like the letter S, the garden manager adds the number one if he considers the batch to be exceptional.

DARJEELING WULONG TEAS Some experienced growers will test new processing techniques to obtain teas with different aromatic characteristics. By reducing oxidation time, they have developed teas that are clearer and lighter and contain greener leaves. This has led to the creation of wulong teas from fall harvests and to teas with floral aromas from the first harvests.

175

The Darjeeling Singell "Heritage"

Located in the heart of Darjeeling, the Singell garden was one of the first to be sown in India, in the 19th century. Although more and more cloned trees are being planted there, it was originally planted with Classic China-type trees that are said to have been brought back from China by British botanists. Proud of this heritage, the growers have managed to pre-serve a section of the garden, called "heritage," that remains planted only with these first trees.

Now 150 years old and grown from seeds rather than cuttings, these trees have plunged their roots deep into the soil, which gives them greater resistance to weather conditions. In this way they derive nourishment from the mineral reserves of the terroir.

Illustrating the pure and classic character for which Darjeeling teas are internationally renowned, the teas produced by the heritage section of the garden are also remarkable for the quality of their taste. The leaves release intense fragrances of pastry, and their well-balanced liquid has a silky texture and a pronounced floral character with notes of clover honey and muscat grape.

Local Preparation

When the English established tea in India, the product was destined mainly for the export market. Before the 1850s, the people of India drank almost no tea, whereas now they consume almost 79 percent of what they grow. Now considered the national drink, tea is the most affordable and available beverage in India. Indians usually choose an inexpensive lower-grade black tea, either loose or in tea bags. They are not as concerned about the quality of the tea because they usually add milk, sugar and spices to it and make chai (see recipe on page 244).

Comparative Tasting

Invented by the professional sector and used in tasting salons during contests or to batch teas, comparative tasting is a method of observing, smelling and tasting various teas and comparing them to each other. The teas are subjected to the same conditions and prepared according to identical parameters (quantity of leaves, water temperature and infusion time), so that their essential characteristics can be more easily compared.

For each tea to be tasted you will need the following accessories:

- A cup with a lid for the infusion
- A bowl to receive the infused liquid
- A small dish or a sheet of white paper on which to observe the dried leaves
- A scale for weighing each tea and a timer to time the infusion

Carry out the tasting in a well-lit spot close to a window, as this will make it easier to distinguish the different shades of the leaves and liquids. To make it easier to taste the differences, the teas are

1

2

3

4

usually presented in ascending order, from mildest to strongest.

- Weigh the tea. In the case of black tea, it is customary to use $1/12$ ounce (2.5 to 3g) and a 4-fluid-ounce (120 ml) infusion cup **1**. The aim is to concentrate the flavors, as their distinctive characteristics will be easier to detect. You should also place a small quantity of each tea in a small dish or on a sheet of paper.
- Pour the water on the leaves in the cup **2**. In the case of black tea, use almost-boiling water, about 203°F (95°C). Place the lid on the cup as soon as you finish pouring the water.
- Wait three minutes. This is the standard infusion time and is best for this type of tasting. Remember that the goal is not to get the best results for each type of tea but to submit them to the same conditions.
- Tip the cup with the lid into the tasting bowl **3**. The liquid will flow through the opening in the rim of the cup, and the leaves will be held back.
- Flip the cup over quickly so the leaves are caught on the back of the lid, and inhale the fragrances released by the freshly infused leaves **4**.
- Taste. First smell the liquid using a spoon or directly from the bowl **5**, then take a sip **6**, rolling it around your mouth to cover all the taste buds and the tongue. With the liquid in your mouth, breathe out completely through your nose to allow all the aromatic elements to come in contact with the olfactory gland through retro-olfaction. Follow the development of the liquid in your mouth, the texture, suppleness, etc.

Note: In India, milk is added when tasting teas that are produced to be consumed that way. The addition of milk is essential for the evaluation of the color of the liquid, an important consideration for that market sector.

5

6

A Meeting with Mr. H.K. Panjikar, Tea Grower

Mr. Panjikar is the manager of the Gopaldhara garden in Darjeeling.

*How and when did you start to work
in the world of tea?*
When I had finished my studies I was looking for a stimulating job. As my older brother worked in the world of tea, I could see the challenges I would face and I decided to get involved. My brother helped me. And so, on January 5, 1988, I began working in the Poobong garden in Darjeeling.

What have you done since then?
After being hired as an assistant at Poobong, I worked in several gardens, such as Pussimbing, Singtam and Singbulli, as assistant to the factory director. I was then promoted to principal assistant to the director, and I worked at Selimbong then at Gopaldhara (2000) where I was interim manager until I became manager in 2002. That is the position I hold today.

What are your everyday responsibilities?
Very early in the morning I tour the garden. After lunch I go to the factory to direct operations. In the afternoon I return to the garden to check on things again. In the evening I taste the teas and decide on a strategy for the following days.

*What is your involvement with the tea
industry?*
My goal has always been to improve the garden I manage as much as I can. To do that I don't necessarily follow the theory. For example, a few years ago I ordered very radical pruning of the trees in a section of the garden. Several Darjeeling growers criticized me for it. Everyone thought that I would lose at least half of the section pruned. A year later, seeing how the plants had grown back, several growers followed my example. I have also created many of the new teas that are found on the market today, including Wonder Tea, Clonal Gold and Red Thunder. In Darjeeling I am considered an innovator.

*What changes have you seen in the tea industry
since you began?*
Since the beginning of my career in the tea industry, I have seen three major trends. First, between 1988 and 1991 the industry concentrated on quantity rather than quality. We used a lot of chemical products. The Russians were buying a lot of Indian output, and quantity was more important than quality.

Secondly, between 1992 and 1998, with the dissolution of the Soviet regime, the Russians withdrew from the Indian market. The Europeans became our principal customers. From then on, quality was more important. Important measures have been put forward to prevent the use of chemicals. We have created a standard MRL (minimum residue level) for export.

Thirdly, a new period began in 1999. Garden owners began organic growing. Since then all the gardens have reduced their use of chemicals, and most of them now practice some level of organic cultivation. Tea production today is based on quality.

What is your favorite tea?
Wonder Tea (a wulong) and Red Thunder (an autumn black tea).

Indian Teas

Darjeeling Samabeong First Flush
| certified organic black tea and a fair-trade product |
Production area: Darjeeling, Western Bengal
Harvest season: April
Cultivar: AV2, P312

This small isolated garden, one of the highest in the Himalayan area, is located in the far east of Darjeeling. Founded in the early 19th century, it has a rich and colorful history. In the 1930s, Samabeong produced tea bricks for the Tibetan market. The garden changed hands several times and was inactive for a long time before being acquired by the current owners in the early 1990s. At that time, the garden was certified as an organic fair-trade business. The garden contains 80 percent original Chinese varieties (*C. s. var sinensis*). The rest is mainly planted with recent clones, such as AV2 and P312.

Tasting notes: This harvest yields a remarkably green tea with a lovely fresh quality. The large, lightly rolled leaves are delightfully bright and release smooth notes of fragrant hay and daisies. The mouthfeel is light, and the liquid is lively with an interesting minty attack. The harmony of the spicy, fruity and floral aromatic notes reveals a remarkable complexity underlined by a rich texture with almost perfect balance.

Recommended infusion accessory: A teapot or *gaiwan.*

Darjeeling Sungma First Flush | black tea |
Production area: Darjeeling, Western Bengal
Harvest season: Mid-March
Cultivar: AV2

The ancient garden of Sungma is directly opposite the Gopaldhara garden, on the other side of the valley, where the Balasun River flows. It is administered by a professional agronomist, Mr. Jah, one of the most experienced and respected managers in the region. Planted in 1863, the garden is still composed of 80 percent original Chinese varieties to which clones (15 percent) and *C. s. var. assamica* (5 percent) hybrids have been added. Over the past few years, this garden has become one of the best in the region and regularly produces high-quality tea. Supported by a high proportion of ancient Chinese plants, the classic teas it produces are among the best there are.

Tasting notes: The dry, uniformly shaped leaves, ranging from light brown to pale green, look cared for and include many silvery buds. The liquid is dark for a first picking and gives off a fragrance of wild flowers. The mouthfeel is well structured, revealing pronounced aromas that open onto a fruity note. The unctuous texture shows remarkable balance. The full finish leads to aromas of muscat grape and delicate accents of peach.

Recommended infusion accessory: A teapot or *gaiwan.*

Darjeeling Castleton Second Flush | black tea |
Production area: Darjeeling, Western Bengal
Harvest season: June
Cultivar: Classic China

Castleton is one of the oldest gardens in Darjeeling. It is composed mainly of Chinese trees from the 1860s, which give the teas produced here a unique character and complexity. In recent years, many growers have chosen to replant old sections with hybrids that yield higher volumes. This situation has created a controversy in the tea community, in relation to the importance of preserving at least some of the ancient trees. In spite of their lower productivity and slower growth, these trees are an irreplaceable resource in the production of quality teas. Their genetic qualities are the result of centuries of improvement in China, long before they were introduced to India in the middle of the 19th century.

Tasting notes: The dark-brown uniform leaves are sprinkled with golden buds. On infusion they release rich fragrances of walnut, caramelized figs and gingerbread. The amber liquid reveals an immediate aroma of muscat grape that is typically present in second harvests. This aroma is carried through to the finish. The mouthfeel is full, unfolding a harmonious succession of malt notes reminiscent of brown sugar and cocoa. It is a full tea with a delightful aromatic complexity.

Recommended infusion accessory: A teapot.

Darjeeling Autumn Gopaldhara "Red Thunder" | black tea |
Production area: Darjeeling, Western Bengal
Harvest season: October
Cultivar: AV2, P312, B157

Known as Red Thunder, this tea requires very specific harvest conditions that occur only a few days a year. Only a very small quantity is produced. It is picked in the highest section of the garden, the famous Wonder Tea section, which produces Gopaldhara's renowned wulong. Unlike the wulong, Red Thunder is harvested in the fall and undergoes more intense oxidation.

Tasting notes: The robust-looking leaves, rolled by hand and broad and irregular in shape, display various tones of copper and include numerous buds. The woody nose conjures up stewed red fruit. The supple, dark mahogany liquid has a pleasant floral attack. Comforting aromas of fruit and spices gently combine to create a good balance. The peppery finish, typical of Gopaldhara teas, gives way to a long, delicately aromatic aftertaste.

Recommended infusion accessory: A teapot or *gaiwan*.

Darjeeling Avongrove | certified organic white tea |
Production area: Darjeeling, Western Bengal
Harvest season: July
Cultivar: *C. s. var assamica* hybrid

Black tea is the most famous product of the Darjeeling region and accounts for 99 percent of production. However, over the past few years, some unusual yet noteworthy teas from other families have appeared. That is the case with this delicious white tea from the Avongrove garden. It is produced from fine picking on sections of Assam trees that have been radically pruned. The buds are separated from the leaves, and both are left to wither for about 72 hours. The withering is done naturally, without the use of hot air. Next, the delicate buds are dried at 248°F (120°C). A final manual sorting removes any remaining leaves.

Tasting notes: The long buds covered in fine silvery down look very well cared for. Infusion releases a delicate floral bouquet with spicy accents. The pale, shiny liquid has a nose of fresh mushroom, vanilla and white chocolate. In the mouth, the elegant attack combines aromas of orange blossom and pepper. The complex liquid coats the mouth with a velvety texture and has delicate notes of fresh hay and honey. Beautifully balanced, the finish is distinguished and mild.

Recommended infusion accessory: A teapot or *gaiwan*.

Darjeeling Gopaldhara Wonder Tea First Flush | wulong |
Production area: Darjeeling, Western Bengal
Harvest season: Late March
Cultivar: A blend of clones B157, AV2, P312

This tea comes from one of the highest areas of the Darjeeling plantations, at an altitude of more than 7,200 feet (2,200 m). It is in this particular section of the Gopaldhara garden that Wonder Tea is grown. The Gopaldhara garden has adapted the methods of processing black tea that have made this region famous to the production of wulong tea. The whole leaves undergo prolonged withering and partial oxidation of about 35 percent. Darjeeling expertise being adapted and applied to a very high-quality raw material has led to the development of an exceptional tea that is constantly gaining recognition in the industry.

Tasting notes: The coppery-green leaves are remarkably large and whole, attesting to the care taken in their processing. Infusion releases a heady aromatic bouquet, a floral combination with accents of hay and oxidized apple. The golden liquid distils smooth, fruity notes. The floral dominant, sustained through to the finish, has aromas of fresh peach and melon combined with notes of celery and pepper, typical of Gopaldhara teas. This tea has exceptional balance and a long and full mouthfeel that is relaxing and delightful.

Recommended infusion accessory: A teapot or *gaiwan*.

Assam Duflating Orthodox | black tea |
Production area: Assam
Harvest season: June
Cultivar: *Assamica* hybrid

Assam is one of the largest tea-growing regions in the world, and Duflating is one of the largest gardens in Assam. It has several thousand employees and an annual output of close to 2 million pounds (1 million kg). As with most gardens in the region, it mostly uses CTC production and creates teas intended for mass distribution. However, a small portion of the garden is reserved for the production of higher-quality orthodox teas. This remarkable tea is one of the finest Assam *grands crus*. Unusually for this region, it is made from a fine-picked harvest and undergoes rigorous sorting.

Tasting notes: The small, twisted leaves seem to consist only of delicate golden buds. Infusion releases rich fragrances of grains and blond tobacco. The shiny liquid is a dark reddish orange. The texture in the mouth is thick and silky. A slight bitterness carries a malty dominant harmonized with the fruity aromas of ground cherry and almond as well as a subtle note of raw sugar. The supple tannins offer structure and balance. A light astringency accompanies a long aftertaste of burnt sugar.

Recommended infusion accessory: A teapot.

Nilgiri Coonoor | black tea |
Production area: Nilgiri Massif ("Blue Mountains")
Harvest season: February to June
Cultivar: *Assamica* hybrid

This tea is the result of an increasing trend in India. More and more large plantations are developing specialty teas along with their standard commercial teas. Produced in low volumes, these teas are destined for sale in the specialty tea stores that are opening everywhere. Nilgiri Coonoor tea is an unusual black tea that is part of this trend. Few teas of this region have a similar style or light aromatic character. Indi Khanna, a veteran grower in Assam, took over a small section of the famous Coonoor garden. He immediately began organic cultivation of Assam hybrid plants. The leaves are treated in a small custom-built factory using machines from China that reproduce manual processing.

Tasting notes: The large leaves of this tea have a striking appearance. The nose is a fruity bouquet of stewed papaya and peach with a subtle hint of osmanthus flowers. In the mouth, the lively liquid with well-structured tannins is slightly malty. Aromas of pepper, coriander seed, orange peel and cooked fruits delicately unfold. The finish is long and coats the mouth with pleasantly fruity tannins.

Recommended infusion accessory: A teapot.

185

Sri Lanka, Nepal, Vietnam and the East African Coast

IN ADDITION TO CHINA, JAPAN, TAIWAN AND INDIA, MANY OTHER COUNTRIES AROUND THE WORLD GROW TEA. FOLLOWING IS A DESCRIPTION OF SOME OF THE TERROIRS IN SRI LANKA, NEPAL, VIETNAM AND TWO EAST AFRICAN COUNTRIES, KENYA AND MALAWI.

Sri Lanka

The Democratic Socialist Republic of Sri Lanka, formerly known as Ceylon, occupies an entire tropical island situated 25 miles (40 km) off the southeastern tip of India. Although Sri Lanka is now one of the world's major tea exporters, and the appellation "Ceylon Tea" is still in use, its tea industry is relatively young. Before 1860, not a single tea tree grew on the island. It was entirely covered with coffee plantations, which represented the country's primary economic resource.

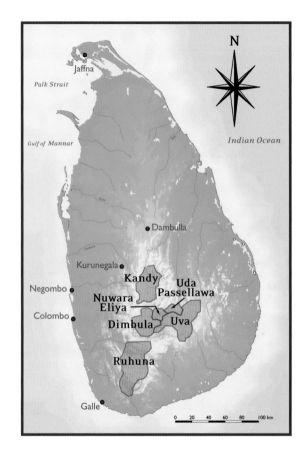

The establishment of the first tea gardens on the island is attributed to a young Scot, James Taylor, who worked for a large coffee grower. Taylor managed to obtain a few tea-tree seeds from the Royal Botanical Gardens of Peradeniya, with which to try to create a first plantation. Throughout the 1860s he experimented with different growing and leaf-processing methods, on a few acres of the Loolecondera Estate, which were referred to as Field No. 7. This garden, in Kandy, is considered the pioneer of tea growing in Sri Lanka. However, Taylor's work would probably have gone unnoticed if a sudden epidemic had not devastated the coffee trees.

Starting in 1869, a parasitic fungus (*Hemileia vastatrix*) that attacked the leaves of coffee plants swept the entire island and completely wiped out the coffee plantations in a couple of decades. Looking for a substitute crop, growers copied Taylor and turned to tea trees. With an already established agricultural system and experienced growers, the transition from coffee to tea growing happened quickly. In fact, tea-producing areas grew from 1000 acres (400 ha) in 1875 to 300,000 acres (120,000 ha) in 1900.

Consisting of just two small crates, the first exportation of Sri Lankan tea took place in 1872. After that, high demand from the British stimulated the industry's expansion. In 1890, the explosion of the tea-growing industry was also encouraged by Thomas Lipton, who, sensing a bargain, arrived on the island to snap up plantations for a song. He invested in industrial machinery for cheaper high-volume production and concentrated on developing packaging that would be attractive to customers.

During the 1990s, after the break up of the USSR, Sri Lanka benefitted greatly from the business coming in from the new republics.

Their tea industry has become well organized and highly regulated by the government. All teas are sold through the auctions in Colombo.

Recent years have seen Sri Lanka become one of the world's top exporters, but tea production for the industrial market is increasing in many other countries. With Sri Lanka's relatively high costs of production the quality control is becoming their essential distinction.

THE SRI LANKAN TEA INDUSTRY

With a favorable climate that allows growers to produce several harvests per year, Sri Lanka is the fourth-largest tea grower in the world. Its annual output of 2 million pounds (223 million kg) of tea (according to 2008 data from the Tea Board of Sri Lanka) represents 6 percent of global production. Dependent on the export market and tailoring its product to the high standards of importing countries, Sri Lanka exports almost all of its production.

THE GARDENS

Stretching from the mountains down to the southern plains of the country, plantations cover more than 544,000 acres (220,000 ha) of the island. Most of the gardens are in the south of the island, on the eastern and western slopes of the high plateaus. They fall into three groups, according to their altitude:

- The low-grown gardens, from sea level to 2000 feet (600 m).
- The medium-grown gardens, from 2,000 to 4,000 feet (600 to 1,200 m).
- The high-grown gardens, situated between 4,000 and 6,500 feet (1,200 to 2,000 m).

GROWING AREAS

Although plantations can be found throughout the island, there are three major quality growing areas in Sri Lanka: Nuwara Eliya, Dimbula and Uva.

The highest peaks are found in the region of Nuwara Eliya, a mountainous valley in the center of the island, and culminate in a plateau at 6,500 feet

A garden in Heputale.

(2,000 m). The climate is hot and humid, yielding several harvests throughout the year. The best harvests, however, are gathered from January to the end of March.

Recognized as one of the foremost plantations in Sri Lanka, the growing area of Dimbula was established in the 1870s, during the epidemic that would completely destroy the coffee trees. The gardens are located at altitudes that vary from 3,300 to 5,600 feet (1,000 to 1,700 m). The harvests destined for the production of high-quality teas also take place from January to March.

High on the eastern slopes of the central mountains, the plantations of the province of Uva are also situated at an altitude of 3,300 to 5,600 feet (1,000 to 1,700 m). Because this area is affected by a different weather system, the best harvests are gathered from August to October.

189

Nepal

"The Nepalese believe that every morning and evening, Siva, who lives at the top of Mount Kachenjunga, blows a gentle breeze onto the gardens, giving the tea its exceptional quality," said a Nepalese grower.

Sandwiched between China to the north and India to the south, Nepal is nestled in the heart of the Himalayas. With several peaks soaring higher than 26,200 feet (8,000 m), Nepal experiences weather conditions similar to those of Darjeeling. In fact, tea growing began there around the same time (late 19th century). However, whereas Darjeeling benefited from investment and production geared to the export market, the tea industry in Nepal suffered from inefficient government management that severely hampered the transition to privatization.

Nevertheless, over the last 10 years, the Nepalese industry has experienced rapid growth. The surface area of plantations has multiplied almost fivefold, increasing from 8,600 acres (3,500 ha) in 1996 to more than 37,000 acres (15,000 ha) in 2004, while production has increased at the same rate, going from 3,202 tons (2,905 t) in 1996 to 12,843 tons (11,651 t) in 2004. In addition, the industry's prospects for the future are very promising, as many recently planted estates will soon be ready for harvesting.

Nepalese tea is produced primarily for the domestic market and consists mostly of black CTC-processed tea (see page 174). Most of these teas are grown on the Terai Plains and at an altitude of no more than 1,000 feet (300 m). However, some plantations produce teas according to the orthodox method (see page 172). These have aromatic qualities similar to those of Darjeeling teas and are also produced for the export market. They are found mostly in the mountainous regions of Ilam, Panchthar, Taplejung and Dhankuta. The districts of Ilam and Dhankuta produce Nepal's premium-quality teas.

Although Nepal is already producing quality teas and its production is still developing on a more commercial level, the industry must overcome several hurdles before it can truly thrive — the precarious political situation, abject poverty and very bad roads do not encourage investment. However, it appears that some investors working in the tea sector in Darjeeling are showing more interest in the growing regions of Nepal, where conditions are similar to their own. If their plans come to fruition and they bring their knowledge and experience to Nepal, it would not be surprising to see the appearance of *grands crus* teas grown in these famous mountains.

Nepalese pickers getting ready to start their workday.

Vietnam

Just as in China, the cultivation of tea in Vietnam springs from a long tradition. Some local legends recount that the first tea trees were brought to Vietnam from what is now known as the Golden Triangle — Chinese border, Laos, Burma (Myanmar), Thailand and Vietnam — more than 1,000 years ago. Today, tea growing is well established on Vietnamese soil, and the industry employs roughly two million people. Over 197,000 acres (80,000 ha) are reserved for tea plantations, producing an output that has exploded over the last two decades to reach 99,200 tons (90,000 t) in 2004. The tea produced here is often produced for the domestic market and priced to be affordable for the local population.

GROWING AREAS

From the central tropical regions to the mountains of the north, tea is grown in more than 30 provinces throughout the country. Vietnamese production consists mainly of black teas (60 percent, of which a small proportion is produced using the orthodox method — see page 172), green teas (35 percent) and a miscellaneous category that includes jasmine tea, lotus tea and wulong teas. The northern provinces grow about 65 percent of the national output. In the southern regions of the country, especially in the mountains, more and more wulong teas are being produced, thanks to Taiwanese investment.

THAI NGUYEN

Thai Nguyen is the principal growing area and one of the only regions reputed for the excellence of its tea production. The tea gardens in this province are located at altitudes between 1000 and 1,650 feet (300 to 500 m) and are more numerous than rice or corn plantations. Sometimes organized into small cooperatives, the tea industry in Thai Nguyen consists of small groups of artisans who nearly all process the tea themselves. Some of them also sell and distribute their own product, but most sell their tea to larger companies who package it for sale in supermarkets.

THE GARDENS

Vietnam is blessed with many natural advantages (climate, soil quality) that have helped it develop tea growing. Tea gardens in Vietnam are small, usually no more than 5,400 square feet (500 m²). Between pickings, the tea trees are pruned to keep them at a height of about 24 inches (60 cm). The trees are planted about 8 to 12 inches (20 to 30 cm) apart, and the space between rows is only 16 to 24 inches (40 to 60 cm), so the small gardens are densely grown. Harvests take place from March through to early November, and the best pickings are gathered in April and September.

CULTIVARS

The tree recognized as the local tea tree is called Trung Du La Nho ("small middle tea leaf"), and it is used in almost 70 percent of the plantations in the north of the country. Other cultivars are also grown, including LDP1 and TLE777, both from China. Created in Vietnam from a hybrid of these two, LT is another cultivar in widespread use.

Final sorting of a Vietnamese green tea.

African Countries

As happened in many countries that turned to tea growing in the 19th century, the establishment of tea cultivation in Africa was a direct result of European colonization. The first tea gardens to be planted on the African continent were created on an experimental basis in the 1850s in South Africa (Natal region), and the first commercial plantations appeared in 1877, in the Stanger. Although these first attempts yielded interesting results, it was not until the 1920s that tea growing really got under way. Today, more than 10 African countries produce tea, most of them using the CTC method. Among the major tea growers are Kenya, Tanzania, Uganda, Burundi, Malawi, Mozambique and Rwanda.

Yielding very high output — nearly 1 ton per acre (2 t/ha), whereas China produces barely 1/3 ton per acre (0.7 t/ha) — African production is concentrated almost entirely on black teas.

Today, with the development of the specialty tea market, several experiments to improve quality are in development, using mainly the orthodox processing method (see page 172). In addition, new families of teas, especially white and green teas, are appearing. These experiments are taking place mainly in Kenya and Malawi, currently the only African countries that offer high-quality teas.

KENYA

A serious part of the industry since the beginning of the 20th century, Kenya is now the foremost tea grower on the African continent and the third-largest in the world. More than 370,000 acres (150,000 ha) of gardens are now devoted to the cultivation of tea, with an annual output of more than 375,000 tons (340,000 t). Most of the gardens are situated in mountainous regions at altitudes from 5,000 to 6,500 feet (1,500 to 2,000 m), as well as west of the Rift Valley. In 2008, Kenya exported more than 353,000 tons (320,000 t) of tea throughout the world. The most famous gardens are Milima, Marinyn and Kangaita, which all use the orthodox and CTC processing methods.

MALAWI

One of the first African countries to market its tea production, Malawi is still one of the major African growers. The industry is composed mainly of small artisans, who produce more than 49,600 tons (45,000 t) of tea per year. After cotton, tea is the country's major commercial crop.

The first plantations were established in 1878 and gradually spread to the regions of Malanje and Thyolo. At the time, tea trees from the Natal

ROOIBOS   Exclusively grown in South Africa, rooibos is a beverage that the local population has been consuming for centuries. It is prepared using a plant of the family of pulses (*Aspalathus linearis*). This plant, which is grown on the plains in the Cedarberg region, is a bush that grows 3 to 6 feet (1 to 2 m) in height and is covered in small branches. The leaves and stems are harvested then cut, crushed, oxidated and dried in the sun. Commonly called "red tea," rooibos is rich in minerals and vitamins. Its bright-red liquid is fruity and acidic.

A tea garden in Malawi.

region of South Africa were transplanted, but, due to Malawi's unpredictable weather, these trees did not live up to expectations. During the 1920s, trees of the *assamica* variety, better suited to the subtropical climate of Malawi, were imported from India, where the development of cultivars was already very advanced.

Today, growing areas are found mainly in the southern regions of the country, around Thyolo and Mulanje (in the Shire Highlands). Mulanje is the most important growing region in the country.

Malawan teas are still relatively unknown. They are used primarily in tea blends. Most plantations belong to foreign companies that export their production primarily to Europe. Harvesting takes place during the southern hemisphere summer, from October to April.

A Sri Lankan Tea

Ceylan Uva Adawatte | black tea |
Region: Uva
Harvest season: July to October
Cultivar: *Assamica* hybrid

Sri Lanka is blessed with a terroir that is ideal for the cultivation of tea and an expertise inherited from the great tea plantations of India. The Uva region is traditionally famous for its high-grown *grands crus*. Although it is grown at a slightly lower altitude, the low-grown garden of Adawatte has shown astonishing energy and dynamism, contributing to the revival of quality teas in Sri Lanka. This tea is produced from the leaves of pure Assam hybrids planted in the 1930s, and it is processed following the orthodox methods that have established the reputation of the teas from this classic terroir.

Tasting notes: The dark, beautifully regular leaves are twisted and hardly broken. Infusion releases an exceptionally aromatic bouquet and creates a bright vermilion liquid. The nose combines woody and fruity fragrances with accents of molasses. In the mouth, the slightly acidic attack is reminiscent of sun-dried tomato. The round liquid against a woody background develops a gentle bitterness. Mild peppery aromas and minty notes of wood tea and eucalyptus form a surprising combination in the full mouthfeel with personality and a pleasant astringent finish.

Recommended infusion accessory: A teapot.

A Nepalese Tea

Nepal Fikkal | certified organic green tea |
Region: Ilam
Harvest season: April to June
Cultivar: Yabukita (Japan) and AV2 (Darjeeling)

The Nepalese tea industry produces mostly black teas. This plantation is entirely devoted to the cultivation of organic green tea, making it an unexpected find. A recent project, it is a collective effort on the part of a group of resolute growers who planted a small garden with hybrids of trees from Japan and the nearby region of Darjeeling. The tiny processing plant was built and equipped with small Japanese machines. This unusual project is still in the experimental phase, but its long-term goal is to produce high-quality green tea on Nepalese soil. Several varieties of green tea are available, but Nepal Fikkal offers a surprising "Japanese-style" tea.

Tasting notes: Infusion of the small needle-shaped leaves releases a rich herbaceous bouquet that is lightly iodized. The clear, very pale-green liquid has a discreet vegetal nose. Round in the mouth, it gives off sharp aromas of fresh grasses with a slight bitterness, revealing shades of ash and cocoa. Notes of green bean and celery form the heart of this vegetal palette. The finish leads into a delicate astringency with notes of minerals and sea air.

Recommended infusion accessory: A teapot.

A Vietnamese Tea

Tan Huong LT | green tea |
Translation: Name of the growing cooperative and the name of the cultivar
Region: Thai Nguyen
Harvest season: March to November
Cultivar: LT

Tan Huong LT tea comes from the Thai Nguyen region north of Hanoi. Tea is the principal crop here, and the garden is well tended. Indeed, almost every family in this rural region owns a small tea garden. In the early 1980s, the growers joined together to form cooperatives, with all the members working together to process each member's tea. Their efforts gave rise to this invigorating tea, grown without chemicals.

Tasting notes: The long, twisted, gray-green leaves look clean and robust. Infusion releases appetizing aromas of smoked meat and corn. The generous nose is reminiscent of bok choy and cooked broccoli. In the mouth, the light and vegetal attack echoes the nose and develops full vegetal aromas that are sweet, slightly herbaceous and smoky. The tannins build a slow finish of sweet and sour contrasts.

Recommended infusion accessory: A teapot.

An African Tea

Kenya Kangaita | fair-trade black tea |
Region: Kinrinyaga district of Kenya
Harvest season: All year
Cultivar: *Assamica* hybrid

The tea-processing plant in Kangaita was built in 1965. Located at high altitude, close to 6,250 feet (1,900 m), it processes the leaves of some 3,700 small growers. The product of *assamica* tea trees, Kenya Kangaita tea is processed according to the orthodox method (see page 172), unusual for this region, where teas are usually produced using CTC processing.

Tasting notes: The dried leaves are broken and regular with a classic appearance. Infusion releases warm fragrances of malt and spices. The nose is dominated by notes of oats and caramel, enlivened by a touch of bay leaf and pepper. The attack is lively and clear in the mouth with a strong flavor of lightly roasted grains. The strong tannins develop a long finish with a touch of the bitterness of citrus zest. A robust tea, it shows strength without being coarse.

Recommended infusion accessory: A teapot.

197

PART THREE

FROM CUP
TO PLATE

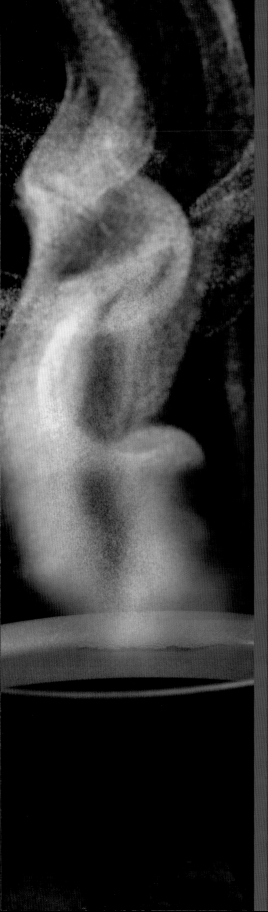

The Art of Preparing Tea

TOWARD THE END OF THE 16TH CENTURY, SEN NO RIKYU, ONE OF THE GREATEST JAPANESE TEA MASTERS, MADE THE FOLLOWING REMARK: "TEA IS NOTHING MORE THAN THIS: HEAT THE WATER, PREPARE THE TEA AND DRINK IT PROPERLY. THAT IS ALL YOU NEED TO KNOW." THE EXTREME SIMPLICITY OF THIS STATEMENT IS RATHER SURPRISING COMING FROM THE MAN WHO ESTABLISHED THE BASIC PRINCIPLES OF WHAT IS KNOWN TODAY AS "THE WAY OF TEA." ALTHOUGH FOR RIKYU THIS SIMPLICITY DEMANDED TOTAL PERSONAL INVOLVEMENT, IT IS TRUE THAT IN ESSENCE, TEA PREPARATION IS A SIMPLE PROCESS. HOWEVER, EXPERIENCE TEACHES US THAT TEA IS "MOODY," SO, IN SPITE OF BEING PREPARED IN AN IDENTICAL WAY, ONE DAY IT CAN TURN OUT PERFECTLY AND THE FOLLOWING DAY IT CAN BE LESS SUCCESSFUL.

Teapots

For centuries, tea masters and tea enthusiasts the world over have sought the perfect method of preparing leaf tea. Either as part of a ritual or simply to obtain the best possible beverage, each culture has developed its own art of tea, adapted to its specific lifestyle. Of course, the practice of drinking tea is essentially personal, but it is possible to enhance and develop the preparation of leaf tea and adapt it to daily consumption. The teapot is best suited to this purpose. Here, then, is an overview of different kinds of teapots, some of which are linked to a specific culture or ritual.

YIXING TEAPOTS

Earthenware Yixing teapots come from the Chinese county of the same name. Thanks to the porous nature of the clay from which they are made, they have the capacity to "remember" the teas that have been infused in them, and so they are called "memory teapots."

Objects fashioned from clay date back to the Han dynasty (206 BCE to 220 CE), but it was in the middle of the Ming dynasty (1368–1644), around 1500, that a significant production began. Toward the end of the 17th century, Yixing teapots arrived in Europe. High demand from European clients led Chinese craftspeople to create some of their pieces with them in mind.

Yixing is a town in Jiangshu Province, to the west of Shanghai. Famous for the quality of its clay as well as for the incredible creativity of its potters, Yixing still produces teapots that enjoy a solid reputation in China and abroad. The center of production is in Dingshan, a community close to Yixing. In addition to the small workshops of craftspeople who work entirely by hand, there are large manufacturers who mass-produce teapots.

Yixing teapots are particularly suited to the preparation of black, wulong and Pu er teas.

YIXING CLAY There are three main types of Yixing clay: *zishani* (purple), *hongni* (red) and *banshanlu* (yellow). The following natural characteristics make Yixing clay a distinctive raw material:

- Its malleability, which makes it easy to work with and has allowed craftspeople to develop a technique to make the teapots entirely by hand. Note that Yixing teapots are rarely formed using a pottery wheel; they are usually shaped by hand.
- Its porous quality, which means that a Yixing teapot should only be used for a single family of teas.
- Its high concentration of ferrous oxide is easily visible on the surface of the teapots.

The clay is made from rocks that are extracted, crushed, cleaned, kneaded and sifted, then mixed together. The colors of the three types of Yixing clay vary according to where and from what depth the rocks were extracted, as well as the firing method used by the potter. The sound made by the teapot when it is tapped gently with its lid is also distinctive and can often be a test of quality. The sound should be clear and metallic.

THE MEMORY TEAPOT   When they are hot, the sides of a Yixing teapot absorb the tannins in the tea, creating a deposit that builds up over successive infusions. This is how the memory teapot acquires its coating. The more the teapot is used, the better it will reveal the wealth of aromas in the teas infused in it.

THE THREE-LEVEL RULE

If a Yixing teapot for the *gong fu cha* ceremony is well made, it will conform to the three-level rule: the tip of the spout and the top of the handle will be level with the rim of the teapot. In addition, the lid should fit the opening in the teapot as closely as possible, so it does not move, and the handle and spout should be perfectly aligned.

The seal (or signature) of the potter is printed on each teapot. It is usually on the bottom of the teapot or under the lid, and sometimes it is under the handle.

KYUSU TEAPOTS

Japanese Kyusu teapots are distinguished by their hollow lateral handle, which is meant to facilitate handling and, according to the Japanese, provide a more ergonomic design. Light and elegant, they are often made of sandstone clay fired at a high temperature, which enhances the flavor of fine Japanese green teas. They are sometimes made of porcelain or even glass. Note that Japanese potters originally made teapots from porcelain and only started to use local sandstone in the 19th century. It was at this time too that the hollow lateral handle appeared.

Kyusu teapots are usually equipped with a very fine mesh that is useful for infusing finely cut Japanese green teas, as it keeps the leaves in the teapot. Handcrafted teapots often have an integrated clay strainer, whereas the strainer in industrially mass-produced teapots is often made of stainless steel.

Kyusu teapots vary in size. The largest are used for classic infusions, while the smallest are used for the *senchado* tastings (see page 108) commonly practiced in Japan.

ENAMELED CERAMIC TEAPOTS

Ceramic has long been recognized for its quality and delicacy. The enamel coating makes these teapots suitable for all families of teas. They are particularly recommended for fragile, delicate teas, such as white teas or Chinese green teas, which are renowned for their delicacy and subtlety.

METAL TEAPOTS

There are many types of metal teapots, and their quality varies significantly. North African teapots are perfectly suited to brewing mint tea. Unfortunately, they may give tea a slightly metallic flavor, so they should not be used for the infusion of delicate teas. Stainless steel is the most suitable metal for teapots.

ENAMELED CAST-IRON TEAPOTS

Originally used in China as kettles, enameled cast-iron teapots are suitable for many types of tea. The enamel coating makes them easy to clean and prevents the tea from coming in contact with the cast iron. However, they are not recommended for delicate teas.

GLASS TEAPOTS

Glass teapots offer the same advantages of neutrality and versatility as ceramic teapots. Their smooth surface is suitable for the infusion of all types of tea and will not affect the taste. In addition, thanks to the transparency of the glass, the leaves can be seen unfurling and dancing in the water and the color of the infusion can be fully appreciated. Most designs are equipped with an infusion strainer that is removed when preparing tea in bags.

CHOOSING A TEAPOT   As pottery is an art in which, as in the art of tea, many manufacturing techniques and various quality standards exist, there is a wide choice of teapots on the market. Here are the main criteria that should be considered in terms of the material, the size, the shape and the quality of a teapot:

* **The material.** Cast iron, clay or ceramic? First you must decide what kind of tea you want to drink. Ceramic and enameled cast-iron teapots are suitable for many types of tea. Clay teapots are ideal for black, Pu er and wulong teas. Because they are porous and "remember" the tea, clay teapots can enhance a tea's flavor.
* **Size.** Do not buy a teapot that is too large. Some delicate teas need to be infused in a small quantity of water to release their precious fragrances. A Chinese saying claims that the smaller the teapot, the better the tea.
* **Shape.** To enhance your tea-drinking experience, choose a teapot that is suited to your hand. Handles come in many different shapes and sizes, so always lift a teapot before purchasing it to ensure it will pour well and that you like the grip.
* **Quality.** A good teapot will age well. Beware of cheap teapots, especially in cast iron or clay, as they may deteriorate quickly.

Preparing Tea in a Teapot

Tea reacts to various factors that one must keep in mind in order to get the best possible flavor from an infusion. The ratio of tea to water, the temperature of the water and the length of the infusion are all important factors to consider, regardless of the infusing method being used. Following the instructions below will help you prepare tea that tastes perfect nearly every time.

- Start by warming your teapot with hot water: fill to about a third, wait 30 seconds, then discard the water. You can also warm the outside of the teapot **1**.

- Add the leaves. The basic recipe requires one heaping teaspoon (5 ml) — the equivalent of $^1/_{14}$ to $^1/_{10}$ ounce (2 to 3 grams) — for every 1 cup (250 ml) of water **2**. You can place the leaves directly into the teapot. If you use a tea strainer, make sure it is as large as possible in relation to the teapot. The more space the leaves have to unfurl in the water, the better the tea will be. Tea eggs are not recommended, as they compress the leaves.

- Pour the water over the leaves **3**. Water quality and temperature are important. You should never

pour boiling water on tea leaves, as it can scald the leaves and destroy their delicate aroma. The higher the quality of a green or white tea, the less resistance it will have to hot water.

- Let the leaves infuse for the required time, which is usually between three and seven minutes. Small, broken leaves will infuse more rapidly.
- Stop the infusion by pouring the liquid into another container or by removing the filter used for infusion **4**. An infusion must be controlled to be successful. If it is too short, the character of the liquid will not be revealed; if it is too long, the bitterness of the tannins will overwhelm the aromas.
- Serve and savor **5**.

The table on the following pages presents general guidelines for the preparation of tea.

Tips for Successful Infusion

FAMILY	APPEARANCE OF THE LEAVES	QUANTITY	TEMPER-ATURE	LENGTH OF INFUSION	COMMENTS
WHITE TEAS Bai Hao Yin Zhen, Yu Xue Ya	Non-rolled, fine, needle-shaped buds covered in white down.	¹/₁₀ oz. (3 g) tea to 1 cup (250 ml) water (2 teaspoons per cup/10 ml per 250 ml)	149 to 167°F (65 to 75°C)	5–7 minutes	White teas should be infused in a small volume of water (e.g. in a *gaiwan*) to bring out all their subtlety.
Bai Mu Dan, Hong Xue Ya			167 to 176°F (75 to 80°C)	5–7 minutes	These can take a larger volume of water.
Avongrove Darjeeling, Malawi Satemwa	Silver and slightly blackish leaves.		176 to 194°F (80 to 90°C)		These can take a larger volume of water.
YELLOW TEA Jun Shan Yin Zhen	Slightly silvery and pale-green buds and leaves.	¹/₁₀ oz. (3 g) tea to 1 cup (250 ml) water (1½ teaspoons per cup/7 ml per 250 ml)	167 to 185°F (75 to 85°C)	4–5 minutes	Infused in a *gaiwan*, a yellow tea will be as strong as a green tea; in a teapot it will be as mild as a white tea.
GREEN TEAS Pan fired in vats (Chinese method) Huiming, Yuzan, Bi Luo Chun, Dong Shan, Fuding Mao Jian, Xin Yang Mao Jian, Tan Huong, Wuyuan Zi Mei, Kamairicha	Small but dense leaves with varied shapes (rolled, flat, twisted), varying from dark green to greenish yellow.	¹/₁₂ oz. (2.5 g) tea to 1 cup (250 ml) water (1 teaspoon per cup/5 ml per 250 ml)	167 to 185°F (75 to 85°C)	3–5 minutes	A higher-quality tea with a greater number of buds, use less water at a lower temperature. The best way to infuse Chinese green teas is in a *gaiwan*.
Huang Shan Mao Feng, Long Jing, Anji Bai Cha, Lu An Gua Pian, Tai Ping Hou Kui, Huo Shan Huang Ya, Tian Mu Qing Ding, Lu Shan Yun Wu, Xue Ya, Wu He	Large, bulkier leaves with varied shapes (twisted, curly, flat), varying from dark green to greenish yellow.	¹/₁₀ oz. (3 g) tea to 1 cup (250 ml) water (1½ teaspoons per cup/7 ml per 250 ml)	167 to 185°F (75 to 85°C)	4–5 minutes	
Steam dehydration (Japanese method) Sencha, Gyokuro, Kabusecha	Fine flat leaves, varying from dark to bright green. Leaves only, whole or broken.	¹/₁₂ oz. (2.5 g) tea to 1 cup (250 ml) water (1 teaspoon per cup/5 ml per 250 ml)	140 to 167°F (60 to 75°C)	3–4 minutes	The *senchado* technique is recommended for the highest grades of this tea.
Bocha, Bancha	Stems and leaves.	¹/₁₂ oz. (2.5 g) tea to 1 cup (250 ml) water (1 teaspoon per cup/5 ml per 250 ml)	167 to 185°F (75 to 85°C)	4–5 minutes	

FAMILY	APPEARANCE OF THE LEAVES	QUANTITY	TEMPER-ATURE	LENGTH OF INFUSION	COMMENTS
WULONG TEAS Dong Ding, Si Ji Chun, Tie Guan Yin, Shan Lin Xi, Ali Shan, Da Yu Lin, Ma Yuan Shan, Yu Shan, Cui Yu, Jin Shuan, Gui Fei	Tightly rolled leaves (balls, pearls, beads), varying from forest green to blue green to deep black.	1/10 oz. (3 g) tea to 1 cup (250 ml) water (2 teaspoons per cup/10 ml per 250 ml)	203°F (95°C)	4–5 minutes	Rinse the leaves so they can unfurl more easily.* Use a container large enough to allow the leaves to unfurl freely. The *cha* technique is ideal for the infusion of wulong teas.
TWISTED-LEAF WULONG TEAS Rou Gui, Shui Xian, Da Hong Pao, Bai Hao, Qi Lan Xiang, Mi Lan Xiang, Qian Li Xiang, Zhi Lan Xiang, Shui Jin Gui, Pinglin Bao Zhong	Twisted leaves, varying from blue green to dark brown.	1/10 oz. (3 g) tea to 1 cup (250 ml) water (2 teaspoons per cup/10 ml per 250 ml)			
BLACK TEAS Darjeeling (all gardens, regardless of picking season), Assam, Nilgiri, Kenya, Jin Zhen, Qimen, Zhenghe Hong Gong Fu, Ceylan	Crushed, broken or whole small or medium-length leaves, varying from brown to black, sometimes with golden or silver tips (buds). Some first-harvest Darjeeling teas have green or brownish-green leaves.	1/12 oz. (2.5 g) tea to 1 cup (250 ml) water (1 teaspoon per cup/ 5 ml per 250 ml)	203°F (95°C)	3–4 minutes	For Darjeeling First Flush teas, the temperature can be lowered to 194°F (90°C). The color of the liquid will vary (from amber to red) according to the type of tea. If the leaves are very broken or crushed, shorten infusion time.
Yunnan Hong Gong Fu, Jin Die, Bai Lin Gong Fu	Whole leaves with many golden buds.	1/12 oz. (2.5 g) tea to 1 cup (250 ml) water (1 teaspoon per cup/ 5 ml per 250 ml)	185 to 194°F (85 to 90°C)	4–5 minutes	Chinese black teas with many golden buds should be infused in cooler water.
PU ER Sheng Pu er teas less than 10 years old	Longish leaves or compressed shapes (nest, cube, cake, brick).	1/12 oz. (2.5 g) tea to 1 cup (250 ml) water (1 teaspoon per cup/ 5 ml per 250 ml)	194 to 203°F (90 to 95°C)	3–5 minutes	Rinse for 5 seconds.* If the leaves are very broken, shorten the infusion.
Shou Pu er (any age) and Sheng Pu er over 10 years old	Longish leaves or compressed shapes (nest, cube, cake, brick).	1/10 oz. (3 g) tea to 1 cup (250 ml) water (2 teaspoons per cup/10 ml per 250 ml)	203°F (95°C)	4–6 minutes	Rinse twice for 5 seconds.* If the leaves are very broken, shorten the infusion.

* Rinsing: Certain teas, especially Pu er and wulong teas, need to be rinsed for a few seconds before they are infused. Rinsing gives a more balanced infusion. To do this, pour almost-boiling water, 194 to 203°F (90 to 95°C), over the leaves (enough to cover them), then discard the water a few seconds later and make your infusion.

A Short Tasting Guide

INTIMATELY LINKED TO OUR EXPERIENCES AND OUR EATING HABITS, TASTE IS ONE OF THE MOST FUNDAMENTAL CULTURAL TRAITS. IT ENABLES US TO PERCEIVE, CONSCIOUSLY OR NOT, THE ENTIRE RANGE OF FLAVORS WHILE CREATING DIRECT LINKS BETWEEN OUR PAST AND OUR PRESENT. IN OTHER WORDS, IT ALLOWS US TO TRAVEL IN TIME AND SPACE BY ASSOCIATING OUR PERCEPTIONS TO OTHER SENSORIAL AND CULTURAL DOMAINS. ON THE OTHER HAND, TASTE IS NOT AN INFALLIBLE SENSE, AS OUR PERCEPTIONS CAN CHANGE ACCORDING TO THE CONTEXT AND ENVIRONMENT. BUT SINCE WE ARE EQUIPPED WITH THOUSANDS OF TASTE BUDS THAT ACT AS RECEIVERS AND REGENERATE EVERY 10 DAYS, WE HAVE THE CAPACITY TO EDUCATE AND REFINE OUR TASTE.

Visual Analysis

Our first contact with tea is usually made through sight. Although it is not always a reliable indicator of the richness of a tea, the appearance of the leaves (their shape, texture, color, the presence of buds) still gives us a first impression.

A close observation of a tea's leaves can give us some idea of its taste. The presence of white tips formed by buds can be an indication of quality, as can a brilliant, shiny color, which is often a sign of freshness. On the other hand, dull, grayish leaves without luster can indicate processing or storage defects.

Tasting is first and foremost a quest for sensorial pleasure, but it is also a way of appreciating taste. It allows us, through our sensory organs, to identify the components that make up a fragrance and to then analyze and communicate our taste impressions.

It is not easy to learn how to identify and dissociate impressions, especially as certain fragrances may be imbued with happy or unhappy memories, leading our brain to make associations that may have nothing to do with the inherent qualities of the food or drink that we are trying to taste. The point of tasting is, therefore, to go beyond first impressions (it's good, it's bad, I like it, I don't like it) so we can more precisely evaluate the quality of whatever we are tasting. No special talent is needed to do this. With a little effort, we can all develop our tasting ability. That being said, it is helpful to understand the basics of the complex mechanism of taste in order to properly appreciate the tasting experience. Here, as elsewhere, theory enhances practice, increasing the pleasure to be derived.

Taste

Taste is a combination of several complex sensations. It mainly involves two of our sensory systems: olfactory receptors (the nose) and gustatory receptors (the tongue).

After visual analysis, the second critical step of tasting is to sniff the fragrances released by the tea leaves. In addition to preparing the brain to receive tasting information, this step provides important information that the tongue alone cannot detect. Our olfactory system is far more complex than our gustatory system. Most of the information relating to taste is impossible to perceive without a sense of smell (such as when your nose is blocked).

Let us briefly review how the olfactory system works.

Olfactory sensations can be perceived in two ways: by direct olfaction or by retro-nasal olfaction. In both cases, they must reach the olfactory gland, where the information is processed.

In the case of direct olfaction, volatile molecules pass through the nasal cavities and go directly to the receptors of the olfactory gland, giving us a first impression or an indication of the taste. As for retro-nasal olfaction, this occurs once the liquid is in the mouth. Aromas rise through the pharynx toward the nasal cavities to reach the olfactory gland. This gives a more intense perception of the aromatic aspect of a tea.

SMELL AND AROMA "Smell" is used to describe sensations perceived by direct olfaction, while "aroma" defines perception through retro-nasal olfaction.

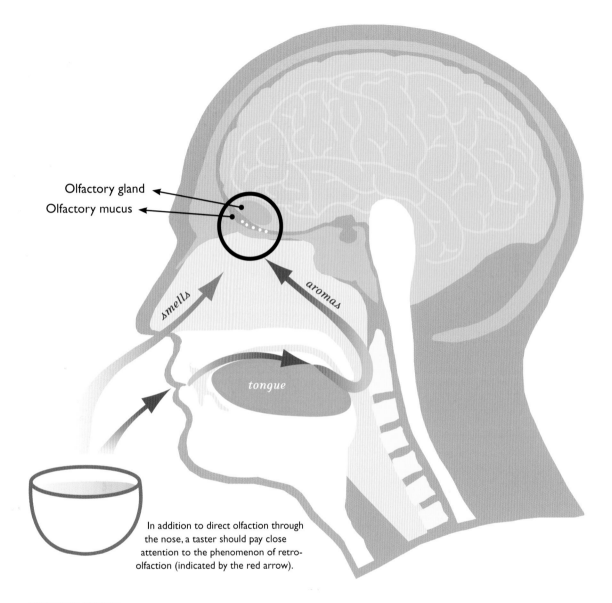

Olfactory gland
Olfactory mucus

smells

aromas

tongue

In addition to direct olfaction through the nose, a taster should pay close attention to the phenomenon of retro-olfaction (indicated by the red arrow).

THE TONGUE

While aromas are perceived primarily by the sense of smell, flavors are detected mainly by the tongue, which is covered with gustatory receptors (these are also found in other parts of the mouth, such as the soft palate). These receptors lie under the taste buds. The tongue is equipped with some 10,000 of these, and each represents a bouquet of 50 to 100 cells that react to all flavors.

Human beings detect only five essential tastes: sweet, salty, acidic, bitter and umami (which means "tasty" in Japanese). Each of these tastes is detected to different degrees, and the perception of one can be affected by another. That is why we generally refer to a gustatory "continuum."

THE PERCEPTION OF FLAVORS
ON THE TONGUE

As taste buds are not specialized, any taste bud, whatever its position on the tongue, can detect all tastes.

As taste is also defined by sensation, other sensory receptors in the oral cavity are involved. Among other things, they allow us to determine texture, temperature, freshness and astringency.

It should be noted that the temperature of a tea can affect our perception of its flavors. At very high temperatures bitterness is less noticeable and sweetness is accentuated. However, heat has no effect on the perception of acidity.

The Way of Tasting

If you wish to enhance the experience of drinking tea, the first thing to do, before even wetting your lips with the fresh infusion, is to sniff the leaves before and after infusion, inhaling the subtle fragrances they contain. Next, study the color and texture of the liquid, then bring the bowl very close to your nose to smell the fragrances released by the liquor. You can use the "little dog" technique, involving repeated rapid sniffing. Concentration is important at this moment, as the first impressions derived from the smells are often very revealing.

Now that you have inhaled the aromas of both the leaves and the liquor, you are ready to take your first sip. Once you are ready to drink, take a small sip and then expel air through your nostrils to facilitate retro-olfactory perception. Pay special attention to the sensations the liquid creates throughout your mouth. Of the five essential tastes, salty is rarely found in tea. Bitterness, however, is present in varying degrees in almost all teas because of the tannins and the caffeine, which give structure to the liquid. But that is not a bad thing! For a Western palate, bitterness is perhaps an acquired taste, but it is not a defect as such. Study how the bitterness is balanced with other aromas in the tea. Link the flavor to others it reminds you of. Try to go beyond your first impression. Allow your sensations to guide you while maintaining your concentration so as not to lose these precious first impressions. Finally, try to define the sensations so as to better understand and remember them.

All the senses are involved in tasting. It is not just about the nose and the tongue. Hearing allows us to hear the "song of the water" and know that it is ready for infusion. Vision tells us how the tea looks. So the environment, the music, the lighting, the other people present, our own mood are all elements to take into account if you are to succeed in truly tasting. In the wrong conditions, even tasting a *grand cru* can be an unpleasant experience.

FLAVOR   Flavor is the combination of olfacto-gustatory sensations derived from consuming a food.

Words for Tasting

Apart from the wealth of knowledge and cultural and personal experience he or she possesses, a taster must be able to summon up several skills. One of them is knowing how to structure sensations in order to express them clearly.

When one inhales a fragrance, an image or an emotion comes to mind more readily than a word. Unfortunately, without the help of the right vocabulary, an emotion can be difficult to interpret. Learning to describe our sensations as precisely as possible helps us to refine our senses and enrich the perception we have of a tea (or any other food). Associating a smell with a word allows us to classify it, to categorize it so that it will be easier to recognize later. It is necessary therefore to build up a gustatory memory. The greater the precision of the terms used, the easier it will be to detect shades of taste and for the brain to remember taste experiences.

Learning the right vocabulary is, therefore, fundamental. At first, it may seem a tedious exercise, but with patience and training it soon becomes clear that it is not that difficult. By developing our olfactory memory every day and becoming aware of the smells around us, our senses will naturally learn to be more precise. Group tasting also creates the opportunity to exchange tasting terms and to detect certain elements that a solitary taster cannot at first appreciate. Sharing and expressing sensations is part of the pleasure of tasting; in some ways, this is the goal.

Naming the aromas of a tea is much more difficult than detecting the various flavors, for a very simple reason: an infusion of tea releases several hundred volatile molecules. Bombarded with all this information, the brain has to sort and summarize.

THE NOTES OF TEA

The smells released by tea are not perceptible at the same time or in the same way. Their degree of volatility changes their persistence and tells us how the taste of a tea evolves.

- Head notes are volatile notes that are often fleeting and give us a first impression of the taste of a tea. We perceive them immediately.
- Body notes are those we perceive when the liquid is in the mouth. They structure the liquid and give it its character. Powerful and stable, they are responsible for the overall impression we have of a tea.
- Tail notes are those that remain in the mouth and linger in aromas after the liquid is swallowed. When a tea is rich in flavors, the tail notes can show either its persistence or the evolution of the flavor, which will sometimes culminate in complex sensations.

After having sniffed the tea and having tried to detect as many aromas emanating from the leaves or the liquid as possible, the second challenge is to describe the texture as well as the general impression that it leaves.

FAMILIES OF AROMAS

To learn how to use the vocabulary of tasting correctly, it is a good idea to start by getting to know the various families of tea aromas. The aim is not to learn by heart all these terms and definitions, but to better understand the groups of smells according to their olfactory characteristics. Of course, the fragrances of tea are not set, and they can belong to several families and often mingle different shades of various aromas, mystifying us and enhancing our pleasure.

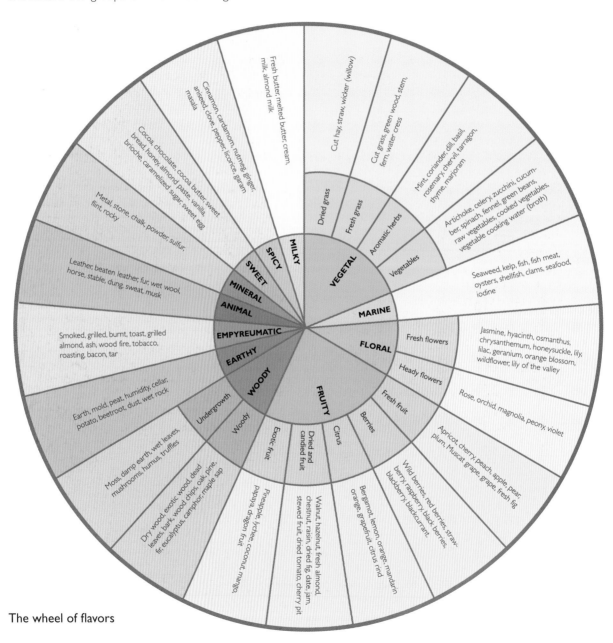

A Brief Lexicon of Tasting

Ample: Round texture, generous liquid, quite long in the mouth.

Aromatic: Rich in aroma, very fragrant.

Astringent: Pungent, hard or full-bodied character, creates a drying feeling in the mouth.

Bite: Describes a feeling of astringency that is acidic and strong.

Body: Describes a texture that has presence and coats the mouth.

Bold: Possessing a well-defined, instantly discernible character.

Brisk: Possessing great liveliness with a touch of acidity.

Complex: Very rich in aromas with many subtle qualities.

Delicate: Light, refined.

Fresh: A liquid that gives a feeling of freshness, sometimes a little acidic.

Full: Quality of a liquid that fills the mouth and has persistence.

Fullbodied: Possessing body.

Generous: Supported by a rich, aromatic intensity.

Heady: Rich and complex.

Heavy: Fragrance that is felt in the back of the mouth, dense.

Intense: Strong, powerful presence.

Light: Supple and without body.

Long: With a long finish; the quality of a well-structured liquid.

Mild: Silky, supple, velvety, not astringent, sometimes associated with sweet.

Opulent: Rich, round, heady fragrance.

Persistence: Describes an aroma that is long in the mouth (aftertaste).

Powerful: With a lot of strength, fullbodied.

Pungent: Creating a feeling of astringency that is harsh and coarse.

Raw: A slightly acidic liquid.

Refined: Possessing delicacy and subtlety.

Robust: A strong constitution with a lot of body, powerful.

Rough: A liquid that is too astringent and is unpleasant.

Round: Describes a supple, silky, slightly tannic liquid that fills the mouth.

Runny: A supple, smooth liquid with little body.

Sharp: Brisk, slightly acidic character, narrow and incisive; may be delicate or robust.

Short: Possessing aromas or savors that quickly fade.

Silky: Describes a liquid with a supple texture.

Smooth: Light texture without roughness.

Structured: Well-structured tannic liquid, full and strong, fullbodied but not coarse.

Subtle: Refined and complex.

Sustained: An aroma with a persistent presence.

Tannic: Describes a well-structured liquid that creates a pleasant feeling of astringency.

Unctuous: Thick, mellow, very round texture.

Velvety: With a thickness reminiscent of velvet.

Vigorous: Slightly acidic character without softness.

Warm: Round, comforting liquid with no acidity.

Watery: With a texture like water.

Young: Describes a rather green character, immature, sometimes a little acidic.

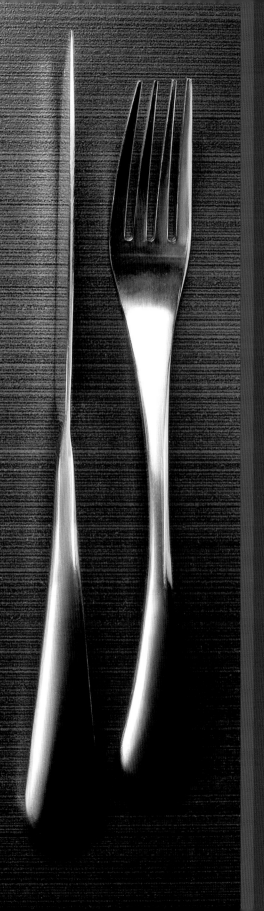

Tea in Gastronomy

IF QUEBEC IN CANADA HAS BECOME A RECOGNIZED
GASTRONOMIC MECCA, IT IS LARGELY DUE TO THE
MANY REMARKABLE CHEFS WHO KNOW HOW TO BRING
OUT THE BEST OF THE LOCAL PRODUCTS AS WELL AS
PRODUCTS FROM AFAR. THAT IS WHY WE DECIDED TO
ASK SOME TALENTED CHEFS AND FOOD LOVERS TO
CREATE RECIPES THAT WOULD COMBINE TEA WITH
OTHER FOODS. WE INVITE YOU TO DISCOVER THIS
NEW ASPECT OF THE FASCINATING WORLD OF TEA!

Bowls of Choco-Chai

SERVES 6 TO 8

1 cup (250 ml) light cream (20%) or whole milk
4 tablespoons (60 ml) *Camellia* chai spice/tea mix
4 tablespoons (60 ml) brown or granulated sugar
6 ounces (180 g) semisweet chocolate
3 eggs

1. Bring the cream and chai to a boil. Add the sugar and stir to dissolve. Remove from the heat and let infuse for 15 minutes.
2. Chop the chocolate using a blender or food processor.
3. Reheat the chai infusion, then strain through a fine sieve.
4. Restart the food processor, pour in the hot infusion and blend until the chocolate is fully melted. Add the eggs one at a time and blend 30 to 60 seconds, until the mixture is very smooth.
5. Fill small tea bowls or glasses, about ⅓ cup (75 ml), with the choco-chai.
6. Refrigerate at least 2 hours then serve with the garnish of your choice.

JOSÉE DI STASIO,
Host of
À la di Stasio

*Suggested garnishes: lightly whipped cream,
cocoa powder or sugar-coated fennel seeds.*

**SUGGESTED
TEA PAIRINGS**

• *Camellia* chai spice/tea mix
• Darjeeling Second Flush
• Assam Banaspaty

Tea-Flavored Panna Cotta BY JOSÉE DI STASIO

SERVES 6

Panna cotta
1 tablespoon (15 ml) gelatin
2 tablespoons (30 ml) cold water
1¼ cups (310 ml) light (20%) or heavy (36%) cream
2 tablespoons (30 ml) jasmine or vanilla tea
½ cup (125 ml) granulated sugar

Tea Jelly
2 cups (500 ml) water
4 teaspoons (20 ml) jasmine or Dong Ding wulong tea
⅔ cup (150 ml) granulated sugar
1 tablespoon (15 ml) gelatin

FOR THE PANNA COTTA
1. Soak the gelatin in the cold water for 5 minutes.
2. Heat the cream and tea. Stir the sugar into the mixture to dissolve. Allow to infuse for 10 minutes.
3. Strain the infusion.
4. Add the prepared gelatin and stir until completely dissolved. Remove from the heat and add the yogurt.
5. Pour into six oiled ramekins or glasses. Refrigerate at least 2 hours, until the preparation has set.
6. If using ramekins, dip them into boiling water for a few seconds to unmold the panna cotta. If serving in glasses, add the garnish of your choice (such as strawberry, raspberry or kiwi coulis; honey-coated orange sections; a *concassé* of tea jelly and small berries).

FOR THE TEA JELLY
A fresh and gentle fragrance to serve with the panna cotta or with seasonal fruit.
1. Bring the water to a boil, then reduce the heat. Once the temperature has dropped to 185°F (85°C), pour the water into a teapot, add the tea and let infuse for 5 minutes.
2. Strain the tea, add the sugar and stir to dissolve.
3. Meanwhile, prepare the gelatin by adding to 3 tablespoons (45 ml) water and setting aside for 5 minutes.
4. Add the prepared gelatin to the hot tea. Pour into a pie plate or round pan and leave to set in the refrigerator for a few hours.
5. Cube the jelly and serve with a citrus salad and light syrup or with honeydew melon and cantaloupe balls or cubes.

The panna cotta and tea jelly can be layered. However, take care to chill the panna cotta in the refrigerator until firm before adding the layer of tea jelly.

SUGGESTED TEA PAIRINGS
- Ali Shan
- Long Jing
- Kamairicha

Creamy Goat Milk, Matcha and White Chocolate Balls with Marjoram Macaroons

SERVES 6 TO 8

4 cups (1 L) whole goat's milk
1/4 cup (60 ml) freshly shaved ginger
2 1/2 cups (625 ml) confectioners' sugar
5 ounces (150 g) ground almonds
2 teaspoons (10 ml) ground marjoram

4 to 5 egg whites
2/3 cup (150 ml) white chocolate
1/2 cup (125 ml) cocoa butter
1 tablespoon (15 ml) Matcha tea

1. To prepare the goat's milk filling, pour the milk into a pan, add the ginger and bring to a boil, stirring constantly. Reduce the heat and reduce the liquid by half over low heat.
2. Place the reduced milk mixture into the blender and blend until very smooth. Pour into 1-inch (2 cm) semicircular molds and chill overnight in the freezer, making sure they are level.
3. To prepare the macaroons, preheat the oven to 350°F (175°C). Sift together the confectioners' sugar, ground almonds and marjoram into a bowl.
4. In a deep bowl, beat the egg whites until stiff, then fold in the sugar-and-almond mixture.
5. Transfer the mixture to a piping bag and form mini macaroons on a baking sheet covered with parchment paper. Let stand 15 minutes at room temperature. Bake for 10 to 12 minutes then leave to cool on a rack.
6. To prepare the Matcha and white chocolate shells, melt the white chocolate in a double boiler and the cocoa butter in a microwave oven. Combine them in a bowl and add the Matcha tea. Set aside.
7. Unmold the frozen semicircular spheres of goat's milk and stick them together in pairs to form balls. Stick a bamboo skewer through the two halves of each ball to hold them together. Place the balls back in the freezer as you work, to keep them from becoming too soft.
8. Dip each ball into the chocolate-Matcha mixture, let excess drain off and place on a tray covered with plastic wrap. Dip each ball a second time. Refrigerate.
9. To serve, top each ball with a marjoram macaroon. Each one must be eaten in a single bite, otherwise the filling will ooze out.

STÉPHANE MODAT,
chef at
L'Utopie restaurant

SUGGESTED TEA PAIRINGS
• Dong Ding
• Aged wulong
• Kabusecha

Pork Flank Braised in Pu er Tea with a Concassé of Jerusalem Artichokes and Cloves, and a Chicory and Star Anise Emulsion

BY STÉPHANE MODAT

SERVES 4 TO 6

1 white onion, coarsely chopped
1 carrot, coarsely chopped
1/2 garlic clove, coarsely chopped
1 leek, ,white part only, coarsely chopped
2 1/4 pounds (1 kg) fresh pork flank
1 teaspoon (5 ml) + 1 tablespoon (15 ml) butter or oil
About 2 cups (500 ml) chicken stock
Salt and pepper, to taste
2 teaspoons (10 ml) Shou Pu er tea

1 cup (250 ml) Jerusalem artichokes, peeled and rinsed in clean water
Salt, to taste
1/4 cup (50 ml) heavy cream (36%)
Pinch ground cloves
1/2 cup (125 ml) chicory
2 star anise
1 teaspoon (5 ml) soy lecithin (available at natural food stores)

SUGGESTED TEA PAIRINGS

- Autumn Flush Darjeeling
- Gabacha
- Hojicha

1. Spread the vegetables in a shallow roasting pan. Set aside.
2. Remove the skin from the pork flank. In a hot skillet, heat 1 teaspoon (5 ml) of butter or oil and brown the meat on all sides. Arrange the meat on top of the vegetables. Add enough chicken stock to almost cover the meat, taking care not to cover it completely. Season with salt and pepper to taste. Cook, uncovered, in a 350°F (180°C) oven for 90 minutes.
3. After 90 minutes, wrap the Pu er tea in cheesecloth. Close tightly with butcher's string and place in the stock. Cover the roasting pan and continue to cook for another 90 minutes. (If cooked uncovered, the crust that forms on the meat will be too hard.)
4. Once the meat is cooked, flatten it between two pie plates so that it looks like a slice of bacon. Refrigerate for at least 2 hours. To serve, cube the meat and reheat it, uncovered, in the cooking stock.
5. Heat a large saucepan of salted water. Plunge the Jerusalem artichokes into simmering water and cook just until a knife sinks easily into them. Jerusalem artichokes need to cook for quite a long time, but at a low boil.
6. Leave the Jerusalem artichokes to cool, and pat dry with a paper towel. Dice them and brown them in 1 tablespoon (15 ml) of butter or oil. Salt to taste. When they are hot, add the cream, to thicken the mixture, and the cloves.
7. To prepare the chicory emulsion, bring a pot of water to a boil. Remove from the heat, add the chicory and star anise and leave to infuse for 15 minutes. Pour the emulsion through a chinois (cone shaped sieve) and blend in the lecithin. Remove the foam that forms on the surface.
8. Arrange pieces of meat and diced Jerusalem artichokes in serving dishes. Add a spoonful of chicory emulsion.

Beef in Wulong Tea

SERVES 4

2 (10-ounce/300 g) pieces of sirloin
Salt and pepper, to taste
2 tablespoons (30 ml) extra virgin olive oil
6 to 7 tablespoons (90 to 105 ml) butter
1 cup (250 ml) water
2 tablespoons (30 ml) wulong tea (such as Shui Xian, Mi Lan Xiang or Qi Lan Xiang)

NORMAND LAPRISE,
Owner and chef of
Toqué! restaurant

1. Season the pieces of beef with salt and pepper to taste. Heat a cast-iron skillet over high heat until it smokes. Add the olive oil and 4 tablespoons (60 ml) of butter.
2. Place the pieces of beef in the skillet and cook until a crust forms, around 3 or 4 minutes on each side, depending on the thickness of the beef. Place the beef in a cold oven for 2 to 3 minutes, depending on the desired degree of doneness. Remove the beef from the skillet. Set aside.
3. Wipe excess fat from the skillet. Melt 2 or 3 tablespoons (30 to 45 ml) of butter and cook until it turns hazelnut brown. Deglaze with water, scraping the bottom of the skillet to recover any browned bits of the meat. Reduce the liquid by half and add the wulong tea. Leave to infuse for 2 to 3 minutes, then pour through a fine strainer. Bring the mixture back to a boil and whisk.
4. Slice the beef and serve with the wulong-flavored drippings.
5. Serve the meat with a vegetable puree and seasonal onions.

SUGGESTED TEA PAIRINGS
• Shui Xian
• Nilgiri Coonoor
• Yunnan

In our grandmothers' time it was customary to deglaze a pan with tea, often a strong black tea, and so this is an affectionate nod to our ancestors and their traditional knowledge.

Strawberries with Jellied Matcha

MAKES 8 APPETIZERS

8 large strawberries
3 sheets gelatin
1 cup (250 ml) cold water, plus extra water for soaking
2 tablespoons (30 ml) powdered Matcha Suisen
Wasabi paste, to taste

CHARLES-ANTOINE CRÊTE,
Head chef at
Toqué! restaurant

1. Slice each strawberry in half and cut a piece off the rounded side of each half so the pieces are flat on both sides. Set aside on a serving dish.
2. Place the sheets of gelatin in cold water to soak. Set aside.
3. Heat the water to 150°F (65°C) and add the powdered Matcha tea. Whisk well. Let stand until the foam subsides.
4. Wring the excess moisture from the gelatin sheets. Place the sheets in the warm tea mixture. Whisk until the gelatin dissolves. Cool in an ice bath until the mixture thickens a little.
5. Place a little wasabi in the center of each strawberry half, then quickly cover with a small spoonful of jellied Matcha. If the Matcha jelly hardens too fast, heat it over a small pan of boiling water to obtain the right consistency.
6. Refrigerate uncovered for 2 or 3 hours before serving.

**SUGGESTED
TEA PAIRINGS**

• Bai Hao Yin Zhen
• Lu An Gua Pian
• Sencha Keikoku

Tomato Coulis with Sencha

YIELDS 1 CUP (250 ML)

10 large ripe plum tomatoes
Ice cubes
4 tablespoons (60 ml) olive oil
10 sprigs thyme
1 head garlic, separated into unpeeled cloves
    cut in half

Salt and pepper, to taste
1 cup (250 ml) water
8 teaspoons (40 ml) Sencha Haruno
1½ teaspoons (7 ml) sugar
1½ teaspoons (7 ml) salt

1. It is important to choose very ripe tomatoes, as they will be easier to peel. Preheat the oven to 300°F (150°C) and bring a large saucepan of water to a boil. Remove the tomato stems and, using a small paring knife, score the base of each tomato in the shape of a cross to facilitate peeling. Fill a large mixing bowl with ice and water.

2. Plunge the tomatoes into the boiling water for about 30 seconds, pull them out then immediately plunge them into the bowl of ice water. Using a paring knife, peel the tomatoes starting at the scored base. They should peel very easily.

3. Line a baking sheet with well-oiled parchment paper. Slice the tomatoes in half lengthwise and place them facedown on the lined baking sheet. Arrange the garlic cloves and the sprigs of thyme on top of the tomatoes. Salt and pepper to taste. Bake in the oven for 3½ hours, until the tomatoes are soft to the touch and slightly dry.

4. Bring 1 cup (250 ml) water to a boil and infuse the tea for 3 minutes, taking care to use the proportions suggested. Do not press the leaves during infusion because the liquid will become too bitter. Remove the leaves and set aside.

5. Blend the still-hot tomatoes in a blender to obtain a smooth puree. With the blender still running, add the tea, sugar and a little salt and combine well.

6. Strain the coulis through a fine strainer. Add pepper to taste. Serve hot or at room temperature with poultry, white meat or lobster.

CLAUDE PELLETIER,
chef at
Le Club Chasse et Pêche
restaurant

SUGGESTED TEA PAIRINGS
• Bocha
• Bai Lin Hong Gong Fu
• Qimen

Cream Pots with Hojicha

SERVES 4

1 1/3 cup (325 ml) cream
2 teaspoons (10 ml) Hojicha tea
5 medium-sized egg yolks
1/2 cup (125 ml) granulated sugar
1 teaspoon (5 ml) vanilla extract

MASAMI WAKI,
Head pastry chef at
Le Club Chasse et Pêche
restaurant

1. Heat the oven to 300°F (150°C).
2. Bring the cream and Hojicha to a boil. Set aside.
3. In a mixing bowl, beat the egg yolks, sugar and vanilla extract until the mixture turns whitish. Slowly pour the tea-flavored cream into the egg mixture, whisking constantly. Pour the mixture into four small glass pots or ramekins.
4. Place the pots in a fairly deep oven dish and add very hot water to the dish. (The water should be hotter than the mixture in the pots.) Cover the dish with aluminum foil. Bake in the oven for 40 minutes, until the mixture is firm.
5. Garnish with pecans and serve warm or chilled with fancy cookies.

SUGGESTED TEA PAIRINGS
• Hojicha
• Rou Gui
• Sun Moon Lake

Scallop Carpaccio with Marinated Celery and Shiitake Mushrooms in a Chinese White Tea Broth

SERVES 6

Carpaccio

1¼ pounds (600 g) fresh size U-10 scallops, sliced

3 tablespoons (45 ml) olive oil

½ lemon, juiced

¼ cup (60 ml) sliced almonds

2 ounces (60 g) shiitake mushrooms, sliced into thin strips (about 1 cup/250 ml)

Fleur de sel, to taste

1. Slice the scallops and place them in a bowl. Add the olive oil, lemon juice, almonds, shiitake mushrooms and fleur de sel.

MARC-ANDRÉ JETTÉ, chef at Newtown restaurant

Marinated Celery

1 cup (250 ml) water

½ cup (125 ml) white wine vinegar

½ cup (125 ml) sugar

2 teaspoons (10 ml) salt

1½ teaspoons (7 ml) cracked black pepper

1½ teaspoons (7 ml) coriander seeds

1½ teaspoons (7 ml) fennel seeds

1 star anise

1½ teaspoons (7 ml) mustard seeds

1 sprig thyme

1 bay leaf

½ pound (220 g) celery, finely sliced (about 2 cups/500 ml)

1. Place all the ingredients except the celery in a small saucepan and bring to a boil. Simmer for 10 minutes.
2. Strain to remove the spices and pour the hot liquid over the raw celery. Allow to cool.

Broth

2 cups (500 ml) water

3½ ounces (100 g) shiitake mushrooms, chopped (about

1²/₃ cups/400 ml)

2 teaspoons (10 ml) Bai Hao Yin Zhen tea

Salt, to taste

SUGGESTED TEA PAIRINGS

- Bai Hao Yin Zhen
- Anji Bai Cha
- Huang Shan Mao Feng

1. Bring the water to a boil in a small saucepan. Place the chopped mushrooms and tea in a bowl and pour the boiling water over. Cover with plastic wrap and leave to infuse for 5 minutes. Strain then salt to taste.

ASSEMBLY

1. Place the marinated celery and a few celery leaves or celery shoots on the scallop carpaccio.
2. Pour a little white tea broth over the entire dish and enjoy.

239

Chocolate–Pu er Set Cream with Kumquats, Hazelnuts, Shortbread and Jelly

SERVES 4

½ cup (125 ml) heavy cream (36%)
½ cup (125 ml) milk
⅛ cup (30 ml) sugar
1½ sheets gelatin, rehydrated
2 tablespoons (30 ml) Pu er tea

4 ounces (120 g) Valrhona brand
Araguani chocolate (72%)

1. In a saucepan, bring the cream, milk and sugar to a boil. Remove from the heat and add the gelatin and tea. Let infuse for 5 minutes.
2. Pour the cream through a chinois then pour it over the chocolate and mix with a hand blender. Coat four small ramekins with vegetable oil then pour the chocolate cream into the greased ramekins. Allow to set in the refrigerator for at least 6 hours.

PATRICE DEMERS,
Head pastry chef at
Newtown
restaurant

Candied Kumquats

12 kumquats
1 cup (250 ml) water
½ cup (125 ml) sugar

1. Cut the ends off the kumquats. Slice each kumquat in half and remove the seeds. Place the kumquats in a small heatproof mixing bowl. In a saucepan, bring the water and sugar to a boil. Pour the boiling syrup over the kumquats. Leave to cool. Refrigerate.

Hazelnut Praline

¼ cup (60 ml) water
½ cup (125 ml) sugar
1⅔ cup (400 ml) roasted hazelnuts

SUGGESTED TEA PAIRINGS

• Pu er
• Assam Khagorijan
• Aged wulong

1. In a saucepan, bring the water and sugar to a boil and cook to 250°F (120°C). Add the hazelnuts and stir with a wooden spoon until the sugar is crystallized.
2. Transfer the mixture to a clean saucepan, reheat over moderate heat and caramelize the hazelnuts, stirring constantly.
3. Place the hazelnuts on a baking sheet covered with parchment paper and let cool. Separate into small pieces while they are still very hot. Set aside in a dry place in a sealed container.

(continued on page 242)

Cardamom-Honey Jelly

1 cup (250 ml) honey
1 cup (250 ml) water
3 tablespoons (45 ml) cardamom pods, crushed
1½ teaspoons (7 ml) agar

1. In a small saucepan, bring the honey, water and cardamom to a boil. Remove from the heat and allow to infuse for 10 minutes. Pour the preparation through a chinois and whisk in the agar. Bring back to a boil and simmer for 1 minute, stirring regularly.
2. Pour into a shallow rectangular mold and allow to set in the refrigerator. Unmold the jelly, dice it finely and blend in a food processor or blender to a smooth puree.

Hazelnut Shortbread

1 cup (250 ml) hazelnuts
1½ cups (375 ml) all-purpose flour
1 cup (250 ml) confectioners' sugar
½ teaspoon (2 ml) salt
¾ cup (175 ml) cold butter, diced

1. Blend the nuts and flour in a food processor and reduce to a powder. Add the confectioners' sugar, salt and butter and process to form a smooth dough. Place the dough on a sheet of parchment paper and cover with a second sheet. With a rolling pin, roll out the dough to a thickness of about ½ inch (1.5 cm). Leave the dough to become firm in a cool place. Bake the shortbread at 350°F (180°C) for 12 minutes, until golden. Leave to cool then cut into cubes.

ASSEMBLY

1. Dip the ramekins in hot water for a few seconds and then, using the tip of a knife, gently detach the set cream from the sides.
2. Unmold the set creams onto serving plates.
3. Garnish each plate with four pieces of candied kumquat, a few hazelnut pralines, a little cardamom-honey jelly and two cubes of hazelnut shortbread.

Ichigo Daifuku BY KAZUYO FUKUNISHI
SERVES 8

8 cups (2 L) water
3 ounces (90 g) mochiko (sweet rice flour)
1 cup (250 ml) granulated sugar
Cornstarch, as needed
8 strawberries
3 ounces (90 g) *anko* or *an* (puree of adzuki beans cooked with sugar)

1. In a microwavable bowl, slowly pour the water over the mochiko, stirring constantly. Add the sugar and combine well. Microwave for 1 minute on high and stir with a wooden spoon.
2. Return to the microwave for 3 to 4 minutes, interrupting once or twice to stir. Continue cooking until the preparation swells. Let the bowl cool for 30 seconds before removing from the microwave and stir again with a wooden spoon.
3. Sprinkle a little cornstarch on a baking sheet. Transfer the mixture to the baking sheet, flatten and cut into eight equal pieces.
4. Coat each strawberry with *anko*, mold into a ball shape and wrap each ball in a piece of rice paste. Pinch the ends to seal the paste and roll again to restore a round shape. Prepare and serve the same day, if possible.

A small Japanese delicacy that is perfect with tea.

SUGGESTED TEA PAIRINGS
- Huiming
- Shan Lin Xi
- Matcha

Indian Chai

YIELDS 4 CUPS (1 L)

2 cinnamon sticks
½ nutmeg seed
12 green cardamom pods
4 whole cloves
2 cups 500 ml) boiling water
½ inch (1.25 cm) piece ginger,
  freshly grated

8 teaspoons (40 ml) dark, full-
  bodied tea (such as Assam)
2 cups (500 ml) milk
8 teaspoons (40 ml) brown or
  granulated sugar

1. Crush the spices (except the ginger) with a mortar and pestle and place them in a saucepan. Heat the spices, then add boiling water and ginger and allow to boil for 15 minutes.
2. Add the tea, milk and brown sugar and bring to a boil. Remove from the heat, cover and allow to infuse for 3 to 5 minutes. Taste and adjust the amount of sugar if desired, or allow to infuse longer for a more full-bodied drink.
3. Strain the mixture and serve.

Note: The main spice used in chai is cardamom. You can substitute the others with pepper, fennel or cloves. There are as many different ways to prepare chai as there are Indians in India!

Iced Tea (Cold Infusion)

YIELDS 4 CUPS (1 L)

1 orange, finely chopped
1 small bunch fresh sweet mint
8 teaspoons (40 ml) Assam or other tea
5 teaspoons (25 ml) raw sugar
20 green cardamom pods
5 star anise
Rose petals (optional)
4 cups (1 L) cold water

1. Place all the ingredients in a large container and add the cold water.
2. Cover and allow to infuse for 10 hours in the refrigerator.
3. Strain then add more sugar, to taste. Serve very cold with pomegranate seeds as a garnish.

Note: Various teas and spices can be used, to suit individual tastes. Cold infusing for a long time allows all the fragrances of a tea to develop without releasing the tannins, creating a very refreshing drink. It is, of course, possible to prepare a hot infusion and dilute it with ice cubes to cool it.

Mint Tea

YIELDS 300 ML (1 ¼ CUPS)

1½ teaspoons (7 ml) organic Chinese gunpowder green tea
1 teaspoon (5 ml) granulated sugar
1 large bunch fresh mint
1 ¼ cups (300 ml) water

1. Heat a teapot.
2. Place the mint in the teapot and add the sugar.
3. Place the tea in a tea strainer and rinse with boiling water.
   Place the strainer in the teapot and add the boiling water.
4. Allow to infuse for 3 minutes, 4 minutes for a more full-bodied tea, then remove the strainer.

Note: As a variation, the leaves can be placed directly in the teapot without the use of a strainer. This method allows the tea to get stronger as it infuses.

PART FOUR

TEA AND HEALTH

The Chemical Components of Tea

"The act of drinking tea must be appreciated for its own sake, without seeking any other justification, for only thus can the tea drinker taste the sunlight, the wind and the clouds."
J. Blofeld, *Thé et tao*

When you pour simmering water over tea leaves and feel transported by the magical aromas they release, the soluble elements that make up the tea leaf are gently transferred to the liquid. During infusion, some chemical elements, such as vitamin C, are destroyed, whereas others are more easily dissolved into the liquid. Roughly speaking, a cup of tea is composed of several hundred active substances. While tea leaves contain the components found in every living organism (proteins, carbohydrates, amino acids and the like) and those characteristic of plant species (such as chlorophyll and cellulose), it is the presence of polyphenols and alkaloids that gives an infusion of tea leaves such astonishing properties.

POLYPHENOLS

Polyphenols, as their name suggests, are a combination of several groups of phenols that make up a family of organic molecules present throughout the plant kingdom. In tea, these phenols are found in the catechins, of which epigallocatechin gallate (EGCG) is the main component. Commonly known as "tannins" and having astringent properties that make living tissues contract, these polyphenols give tea its astringency, strength and thickness.

ALKALOIDS

Alkaloids are naturally occurring heterocyclic organic molecules that contain nitrogen and are found in amino acids. Three kinds of alkaloids are found in tea, the main one being caffeine.

THEINE OR CAFFEINE?

Theine and caffeine are the same alkaloid. Recognized in 1838 as being identical to the caffeine in coffee, the caffeine in tea is, nonetheless, distinguished from the caffeine in coffee because it forms different bonds with other substances, which changes how it affects the body. When tea leaves are infused, the caffeine combines with tannins, which attenuate and stabilize its effect. Tannins prevent caffeine from being released rapidly, so it is absorbed over a longer period of time. The effect, therefore, lasts longer and is more regular.

In tea, caffeine stimulates the central nervous system and the cardiovascular system by enlarging the diameter of the vessels in the cerebral cortex. When ingested in coffee, caffeine has a direct effect on blood circulation through the coronary system, stimulating an acceleration of the heart rate. In other words, tea is a more of a stimulant than an excitant. It sharpens the mind, increases concentration, eliminates fatigue and enhances intellectual acuity.

THE NUTRIENTS PRESENT IN TEA

Tea leaves are 20 percent proteins, but only 4 percent of those proteins, present in the form of albumin, are water soluble. In addition, just like the proteins, only a small percentage of the carbohydrates in tea are soluble in water. Just one carbohydrate, monosaccharide,

is soluble, making tea a low-calorie drink that contains only one or two calories per cup. Tea also contains some 20 amino acids, including theanine, which accounts for 50 to 60 percent of these amino acids. Tea also contains many vitamins (including A, B complex, E, K and flavonoids), about 30 minerals (including potassium, phosphorus, iron, magnesium and calcium), chlorophyll and hundreds of aromatic components.

WATER QUALITY   Since 99 percent of a cup of tea consists of water, the quality of the water used is extremely important. Ancient Chinese masters used to amuse themselves by trying to guess the source of the water used to infuse their tea, and the choice of water is still critically important today. Lu Yu claimed that "the most suitable water is from the same region as the tea," as when in contact with the water that the tree drank all its life, the leaves will reveal their true nature. A rather utopian ideal today, yet the use of high-quality water is strongly advised. Hard, limestone-rich water should be avoided, as should water laden with calcium oxide, magnesium, lead or chlorine (which can cause a bleach aftertaste). The ideal water is pH neutral and contains few minerals.

The Virtues of Tea

"Tea comforts the spirit, banishes passivity, lightens the body and adds sparkle to the eyes."
Shen Nong, *Medicinal Herbs*

Ever since Shen Nong discovered the stimulating and detoxifying properties of tea some 4,000 years ago, humans have been interested in its medicinal properties. It is these properties that first made it popular, at a time when it was considered a medicine. It was thought that its bitter taste stimulated wakefulness, good overall health and the acquisition of great wisdom. In Chinese medicine, during the Tang and Song dynasties, the medicinal effects of tea were recognized more and more. It was recommended to cure and prevent various ills, such as headaches, dark thoughts and bad digestion as well as to dissolve fats. A few centuries later, Li Shizhen (1518–1593), physician and author of *Compendium of Materia Medica*, claimed that tea could regulate the body's internal temperature, calm anxiety, dissolve fats and improve concentration.

Although the stimulating, diuretic and antibacterial properties of tea were recognized by Chinese medicine a very long time ago, it is only recently that modern science has confirmed these benefits. Because of its antioxidant effects, the health benefits of tea are arousing a lot of interest in the medical community, particularly in the areas of cancer prevention and the treatment of degenerative and cardiovascular diseases. Today, we no longer believe that tea is an elixir of immortality or has the mystical powers attributed to it by the Taoists of yore. However, it has virtues that contribute to longevity by stimulating heart function, strengthening the immune system and preventing cellular mutations.

Of course, processing brings out new chemical elements in the leaves, which change their taste as well as their properties, and so each family of tea has its own specific qualities.

THE PROPERTIES OF WHITE TEA

Refreshing and thirst quenching, in China, white tea is consumed mainly in the summer. According to Chinese medicine, it helps to counteract excessive heat and alleviates the symptoms of menopause.

THE PROPERTIES OF GREEN TEA

According to recent studies, green tea appears to contain a higher number of polyphenols than other tea families, making it increasingly popular in the West over the last few years. Thanks to its antioxidant properties, green tea could prevent certain forms of cancer. Also said to enhance intellectual performance, green tea contains more iron, vitamins and catechins

ANTIOXIDANTS   Studied for their antioxidant effects, the polyphenols contained in tea have been the subject of much research in recent years. Research shows that the abundant presence of catechins (molecules belonging to the polyphenols group) in green tea may act as a powerful antioxidant (thereby neutralizing free radicals), which may help prevent the effects of aging and the onset of illnesses such as cancer and cardiovascular disease. Polyphenols protect the body against cell damage, in particular, by fighting the breakdown of cellular membranes caused by various stressors (smoke, pollution, viruses, etc.). They may also prevent the development of the metastases that lead to cancerous tumors.

THE MAJOR PROPERTIES OF TEA

Here are some of the many beneficial properties attributed to tea:

- It supports the heart system.
- It activates circulation.
- It helps detoxification and the elimination of toxins.
- It fights hypertension.
- It reduces fatigue.
- It slows the aging process.

- It helps prevent certain types of cancer.
- It helps digestion.
- It reduces cholesterol.
- It balances body temperature.
- It strengthens the immune system.
- It enhances concentration.

In general, drinking tea regularly reduces the risk of coronary disease and helps strengthen vascular walls while increasing the elasticity of blood vessels. It also slows the absorption of sugars and fats, controls hypertension and helps prevent food poisoning.

than black tea. The dehydration method used in the processing of green tea produces a higher polyphenol content in the leaves.

THE PROPERTIES OF WULONG TEA

Regular consumption of wulong tea (just over ¼ ounce/ 8 grams per day) is said to have a slimming effect by stimulating the metabolizing of lipids. Its relaxing, anti-stress, even euphoric effect is said to be due to the high concentration of aromatic oils, which are drawn out from the leaves during rolling.

THE PROPERTIES OF BLACK TEA

The enzymatic oxidation undergone by the leaves during the processing of black tea converts some of the catechins into theaflavins and thearubigins and destroys some of the vitamins. On the other hand,

the caffeine in black tea is released more rapidly into the bloodstream over a shorter period compared to green tea, as oxidation partially separates it from the tannins. This means that black tea is more effective as a physical stimulant than green tea.

THE PROPERTIES OF PU ER TEA

Because of its specific properties, Pu er tea has long been used as a dietary supplement by many nomadic tribes and ethnic groups living in regions of Asia. As these people ate mostly very fatty yak meat, tea allowed them to balance their diet, counteracting the fat. Today the purging qualities of Pu er teas are recognized as helping specifically to regulate the body and stimulate digestion. Pu er also helps eliminate cholesterol from the body.

IRON ABSORPTION   Tea facilitates digestion by stimulating the elimination of fats. On the other hand, it can inhibit the absorption of iron and calcium from foods. For this reason, drinking tea with meals is not recommended, nor is drinking tea during the half hour before or after a meal.

Biochemical Analyses of 35 Teas

Tea is extremely popular because of its health benefits. Given the number of studies on the multiple virtues of tea that have been published over the last few years, tea enthusiasts have every right to ask what all this really means. Are white teas really lower in caffeine than black teas? Do the different methods of infusion currently used change the concentration of certain components of tea? Do successive infusions of the same leaves produce the same caffeine content as one long infusion?

Until now, most studies only looked at generalities and did not reflect the diversity to be found in the world of tea. In addition, the results obtained by scientists in a laboratory did not necessarily correspond to the results obtained by a tea enthusiast at home, in the context of daily consumption.

And so, wanting to know more about the benefits of certain teas, the team at Camellia Sinensis asked TransBIOTech to measure the concentrations of various components present in an infusion in order to evaluate their attributes.

TransBIOTech is a center for research and biotechnology transfers. The center supports innovation in companies working in the areas of health food products, functional foods, nutraceuticals, cosmeceuticals and life sciences. It provides services in research and development, technical analysis and assistance, especially for clients who want to use the technologies it develops. Thanks to its cutting-edge research facilities, TransBIOTech is able to offer services relating to the characterization and assaying of active ingredients, bioactive molecules and metabolites. In addition, they can provide services relating to animal genotyping, validation of antimicrobial power, cellular biology and microbiology. The various technological platforms that TransBIOTech has developed are linked to the product regulation imposed by Health Canada.

The researchers in immunology and pharmacology at the center participate in preclinical studies. They measure the inflammatory response of different types of human and animal cells when they are brought into contact with a bioactive molecule. They also evaluate the effect of various molecules on the immune system. Their experience in pharmacology also allows them to analyze the power of various molecules to penetrate the intestinal wall as well as their bioavailability and their absorption by the body. In addition, they conduct research into pharmacokinetics, pharmacodynamics and metabolomics.

The team at Camellia Sinensis Tea House asked TransBIOTech to analyze the concentration of certain molecules present in the infusion of the leaves of more than 30 different teas. We should stress that in carrying out their analyses the researchers respected the conditions of preparation we prescribed and also that they analyzed the liquid of infused teas rather than the composition of raw leaves. For each tea the volume of tea to water and the required water temperature were respected. In addition, a teapot suited to each type of tea was used, as well as bottled spring water (pH 7.22). Thus, the results obtained in this scientific context are a true reflection of the tea in the cup of a consumer who follows the same directions.

Of course, these results are not to be considered as absolute but rather on a comparative basis. As with a tea's flavor, the concentration of caffeine and antioxidants can vary depending on where the tea was grown, the climate in which the trees grew, the picking season and the method of processing used. The size and grading of the leaves can also affect the results.

It should also be noted that the infusions studied were prepared in duplicate and analyzed in triplicate. The results presented are the average finding.

Three factors were targeted: caffeine concentration, catechin concentration and the antioxidant power of the tea.

The method chosen for the analysis of caffeine and catechin concentration was liquid chromatography. This technique separates a mixture by forcing it through a solid fixture (separating column) using variable ratios of liquid (mobile phase). Circulating through the solid element at varying speeds according to their affinity with the separating column, the molecules of the mixture emerge separated. Among other things, liquid chromatography can determine the concentrations of the various molecular elements that make up a liquid.

Three techniques were used to analyze the antioxidant power of tea.

First, a large number of teas were sorted using a method (ABTS-TEAC) that provides a rapid comparison of a high number of samples of the same kind.

Later, the ORAC method, recognized in the food sector, was used to quantify the antioxidant power of each tea. The advantage of this method is that it gives a standardized and widely accepted measure of antioxidant power, making it easier to compare different foods.

Finally, a more innovative method, called HORAC, was used to study the antioxidants contained in certain specific teas. By reproducing the defense mechanism against certain free radicals (hydroxyls), this further analysis allowed us to validate the results we obtained previously.

CAFFEINE

The family of xanthines, whose chemical structure is illustrated below, includes a well-known element: caffeine, or 1,3,7-trimethylxanthine. Among the everyday natural products that contain caffeine are coffee, tea, maté, guarana and cocoa.

Theobromine, or 3,7-dimethylxanthine, is the main alkaloid present in cocoa, whereas theophylline, or 1,3-dimethylxanthine, is found in small quantities in tea. These three molecules, which have similar chemical structures, are diuretic and act as psychotropic stimulants.

The table on the following page shows the caffeine content of a 1-cup (250 ml) serving of various teas infused using the method appropriate for each one.

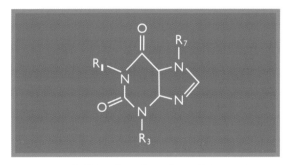

Caffeine: $R_1 = R_3 = R_7 = CH_3$
Theobromine: $R_1 = H, R_3 = R_7 = CH_3$
Theophylline: $R_1 = R_3 = CH_3, R_7 = H$

Source: Merck Index

TABLE 1: Concentration of caffeine in various infusions of tea
(caffeine content by liquid chromatography–UV)

Tea	Family	Producing country	Quantity	Temperature	Length of infusion	Concentration of caffeine
			All teas were infused in a teapot and 2 cups (500 ml) water, except Matcha Sendo, which was whisked in a bowl with a ½ cup (100 ml) water			
Matcha Sendo	Green	Japan	¹/₂₀ oz. (1.5 g)	167°F (75°C)	30 sec.	126 mg
Darj. Sungma First Flush DJ2	Black	India	¹/₆ oz. (5 g)	203°F (95°C)	4.5 min	58 mg
Xue Ya	Green	China	¹/₆ oz. (5 g)	185°F (85°C)	5.5 min	50 mg
Tai Ping Hou Kui	Green	China	¹/₆ oz. (5 g)	185°F (85°C)	6 min	50 mg
Bai Hao	Wulong	Taiwan	¹/₆ oz. (5 g)	203°F (95°C)	6 min	49 mg
Sencha Ashikubo	Green	Japan	¹/₆ oz. (5 g)	167°F (75°C)	4.5 min	48 mg
Long Jing Shi Feng	Green	China	¹/₆ oz. (5 g)	185°F (85°C)	4.5 min	48 mg
Bai Mu Dan Wang	White	China	¹/₆ oz. (5 g)	176°F (80°C)	6 min	39 mg
Hojicha Shizuoka	Green	Japan	¹/₆ oz. (5 g)	203°F (95°C)	4.5 min	27 mg
Sheng Pu er 1997	Pu er	China	¹/₆ oz. (5 g)	203°F (95°C)	6 min	23 mg
Yongming 2006 Shou Pu er	Pu er	China	¹/₆ oz. (5 g)	203°F (95°C)	4.5 min	23 mg
Kamairicha	Green	Japan	¹/₆ oz. (5 g)	176°F (80°C)	3.5 min	23 mg
Xiangming 2006 Sheng Pu er	Pu er	China	¹/₆ oz. (5 g)	203°F (95°C)	4.5 min	22 mg
Assam Banaspaty	Black	India	¹/₆ oz. (5 g)	203°F (95°C)	3.5 min	22 mg
Mr. Chang's Dong Ding	Wulong	Taiwan	¹/₆ oz. (5 g)	203°F (95°C)	4.5 min	20 mg
Yunnan Hong Gong Fu	Black	China	¹/₆ oz. (5 g)	185°F (85°C)	4.5 min	19 mg
Shou Pu er 1995	Pu er shou	China	¹/₆ oz. (5 g)	203°F (95°C)	4.5 min	19 mg
Yerba maté	Yerba mate	Brazil	¹/₆ oz. (5 g)	185°F (85°C)	4.5 min	18 mg
Bancha Shizuoka	Green	Japan	¹/₆ oz. (5 g)	185°F (85°C)	4.5 min	18 mg
Anxi Tie Guan Yin	Wulong	China	¹/₆ oz. (5 g)	203°F (95°C)	4.5 min	17 mg
Bocha	Green	Japan	¹/₆ oz. (5 g)	176°F (80°C)	3.5 min	17 mg
Rou Gui	Wulong	China	¹/₆ oz. (5 g)	203°F (95°C)	6 min	16 mg
Autumn Darj. Sungma DJ480	Black	India	¹/₆ oz. (5 g)	203°F (95°C)	3.5 min	16 mg
Bai Hao Yin Zhen	White	China	¹/₆ oz. (5 g)	167°F (75°C)	6 min	15 mg
Gyokuro Tamahomare	Green	Japan	¹/₆ oz. (5 g)	149°F (65°C)	4.5 min	14 mg
Sencha Fukamushi Aji	Green	Japan	¹/₆ oz. (5 g)	167°F (75°C)	4.5 min	14 mg
Ali Shan 1991 Qingxin	Wulong	Taiwan	¹/₆ oz. (5 g)	203°F (95°C)	4.5 min	13 mg
Organic Huiming	Green	China	¹/₆ oz. (5 g)	185°F (85°C)	4.5 min	13 mg
Dragon Pearls jasmine	Green	China	¹/₆ oz. (5 g)	185°F (85°C)	3.5 min	13 mg
Sencha Isagawa	Green	Japan	¹/₆ oz. (5 g)	167°F (75°C)	3.5 min	12 mg
Mucha Tie Guan Yin	Wulong	Taiwan	¹/₆ oz. (5 g)	203°F (95°C)	4.5 min	12 mg

Among the teas analyzed, it is surprising to find that some black teas (Assam Banaspaty, Yunnan Hong Gong Fu) do not contain a higher concentration of caffeine than many green (and white!) teas, which are usually thought to be less stimulating. This result can perhaps be explained by the fact that the oxidation undergone by black tea helps to reduce the caffeine content. (Note that the Darjeeling Sungma First Flush DJ2 underwent low oxidation.) Given the low number of black teas that were tested for this study, we may conclude that further analysis would be necessary to confirm this supposition.

CAFFEINE CONCENTRATION ACCORDING TO LENGTH OF INFUSION

Wanting to know more about the phenomenon of the dissolution of caffeine in tea, we ordered an analysis of the length of infusion. We chose a tea with a high caffeine content, Long Jing Shi Feng tea, and had it prepared according to a standard method of infusion: 1/6 ounce (5 g) of tea in 2 cups (500 ml) of water at 185°F (85°C).

The graph below shows that a large amount of the caffeine is released during the first three minutes of infusion. It also shows that after six minutes of infusion, even if the curve tends to level off, caffeine is still being released.

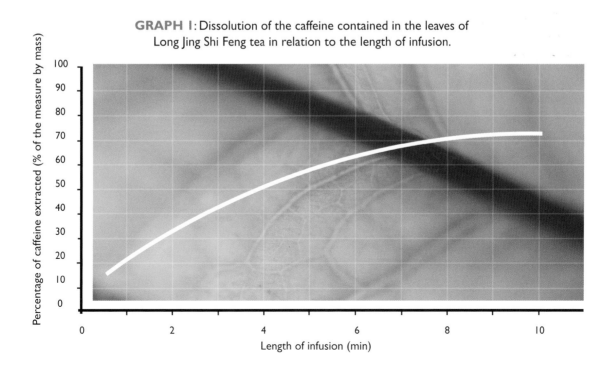

GRAPH 1: Dissolution of the caffeine contained in the leaves of Long Jing Shi Feng tea in relation to the length of infusion.

To better understand the effects of time and temperature on the infusion of tea leaves, we asked for several analyses under varying infusion conditions (see Tables 2 and 3). We then had the caffeine content of a single tea measured according to two different methods of infusion (see Tables 4 and 5). Finally, we measured the caffeine content of a second infusion of the same tea leaves (see Table 6).

TABLE 2: Concentration of caffeine in organic Huiming tea in two infusions of different duration (caffeine content by liquid chromatography — UV)

Tea	Family	Producing country	Infusion	Quantity	Temperature	Length of infusion	Concentration of caffeine in 1 cup (250 ml)
					Both infusions were made in a teapot in 2 cups (500 ml) of water. Fresh leaves were used for each infusion.		
Organic Huiming	Green	China	single	1/6 oz. (5 g)	185°F (85°C)	4.5 min	13 mg
			single	1/6 oz. (5 g)	185°F (85°C)	10 min	21 mg

TABLE 3: Concentration of caffeine in organic Huiming tea using two infusions at different temperatures

Tea	Family	Producing country	Infusion	Quantity	Temperature	Length of infusion	Concentration of caffeine in 1 cup (250 ml)
					Both infusions made in a teapot in 2 cups (500 ml) water. Fresh leaves used for each infusion.		
Organic Huiming	Green	China	single	1/6 oz. (5 g)	185°F (85°C)	4.5 min	13 mg
			single	1/6 oz. (5 g)	203°F (95°C)	4.5 min	19 mg

TABLE 4: Concentration of caffeine in Long Jing Shi Feng infused two different ways

Tea	Family	Producing country	Infusion	Quantity	Temperature	Length of infusion	Concentration of caffeine
					One single infusion made in a teapot using fresh leaves and 2 cups (500 ml) water. Three successive infusions made in a *gaiwan* each using the same leaves and 1/2 cup (100 ml) water.		
Long Jing Shi Feng	Green	China	single	1/6 oz. (5 g)	185°F (85°C)	4.5 min	19 mg (in 2 cups/500 ml)
			first	1/7 oz. (4 g)	185°F (85°C)	45 sec	29 mg (in scant 1/2 cup/100 ml)
			second	same leaves as 1st	185°F (85°C)	45 sec	29 mg (in scant 1/2 cup/100 ml)
			third	same leaves as 1st and 2nd	185°F (85°C)	60 sec	24 mg (in scant 1/2 cup/100 ml)

TABLE 5: Concentration of caffeine in Sencha Ashikubo tea infused using two different techniques

Tea	Family	Producing country	Infusion	One single infusion made in teapot in 2 cups (500 ml) water. Two subsequent infusions each using the same leaves in scant ½ cup (100 ml) water using *senchado* technique.			Concentration of caffeine
				Quantity	Temperature	Length of infusion	
Sencha Ashikubo	Green	China	single	⅙ oz. (5 g)	167°F (75°C)	4.5 min	96 mg (in 2 cups/500 ml)
			first	⅐ oz. (4 g)	167°F (75°C)	45 sec	16 mg (in scant ½ cup/100 ml)
			second	same leaves as 1st	167°F (75°C)	20 sec	16 mg (in scant ½ cup/100 ml)

TABLE 6: Concentration of caffeine in two infusions of Sencha Ashikubo tea

Tea	Family	Producing country	Infusion	Two successive infusions made in a teapot using the same leaves and 2 cups (500 ml) of water.			Concentration of caffeine
				Quantity	Temperature	Length of infusion	
Sencha Ashikubo	Green	Japan	first	⅙ oz. (5 g)	167°F (75°C)	4.5 min	96 mg
			second	same leaves as 1st	167°F (75°C)	3.5 min	83 mg

It is surprising to note that a second infusion of the same leaves of Sencha Ashikubo still contains a lot of caffeine after a first infusion of 4½ minutes. Enthusiasts who try to "decaffeinate" their tea by throwing away the first infusion will be disappointed to see that, as shown by the table above, this practice may be futile. If they wish to avoid the stimulating effect of tea, they would be wiser to choose a less caffeine-rich tea rather than wasting their first infusion.

YERBA MATÉ   If they look at Table 1, on page 254, yerba maté drinkers will no doubt be surprised to learn that this drink is low in caffeine. The explanation probably lies in the customary method of infusion, which is quite different from the one used here. Usually, according to individual taste, a large quantity of yerba maté, about ¾ to 1¾ ounces (20 to 50 g), is infused, whereas only ⅙ ounce (5 g) was used for the purpose of analysis.

ANTIOXIDANT POWER

As we have seen, the antioxidants found naturally in food can help to neutralize some of the free radicals in an organism. These are unstable molecules that try to stabilize by attaching themselves to other molecules in the metabolic system. This damages the healthy molecules and causes them to deteriorate. The body contains a certain stock of antioxidant molecules that counter the effects of free radicals by neutralizing them. Unfortunately, this stock is sometimes insufficient. Therefore, the daily consumption of foods that are high in antioxidants can prevent or delay the damage to human cells and tissues caused by free radicals.[1]

The mechanisms of neutralization of free radicals are so complex that it is difficult to undertake a simple analysis to determine the ability of a particular food to contribute to the process. That is why various complementary tests (ABTS, ORAC, HORAC, NORAC, SORAC and SOAC) have been developed to mimic the trapping mechanisms of radicals. These tests provide an overview of the ability of a food to prevent various diseases associated with the presence of free radicals in the human body. The polyphenolic components of plants are recognized for their antioxidant properties. Many studies recently carried out on tea have shown its strong bioactive and antioxidant potential due to its high polyphenol content. Some studies have shown, for example, that the polyphenols in green tea have a protective effect against the stressors associated with Parkinson's disease.[2]

To determine the antioxidant ability of the teas selected, we first used a rapid screening process (ABTS-TEAC). It is important to note that although this method allows a comparison between samples of a similar type, it doesn't permit a comparison of the results obtained with those from other foods. Another technique that we will see later on does allow this kind of comparison.

TABLE 7: Concentration of antioxidants measured by means of the ABTS-TEAC3 method[3]

Tea	Family	Producing country	Quantity	Temperature	Length of infusion	Concentration of antioxidants in 1 cup (250 ml)
			All teas were infused in a teapot with 2 cups (500 ml) of water, except the Matcha which was whisked in a bowl with 100 ml of water.			
Matcha Sendo	Green	Japan	1/20 oz. (1.5 g)	167°F (75°C)	30 sec	3,775 µmoles
Lu An Gua Pian	Green	China	1/6 oz. (5 g)	185°F (85°C)	4 min	2,500 µmoles
Sencha Keikoku	Green	Japan	1/6 oz. (5 g)	167°F (75°C)	4 min	2,375 µmoles
Long Jing Shi Feng	Green	China	1/6 oz. (5 g)	176°F (80°C)	4.5 min	2,200 µmoles
Anji Bai Cha	Green	China	1/6 oz. (5 g)	185°F (85°C)	6 min	1,800 µmoles

1. CHUNG, H.Y., T. YOKOZAWA, D.Y. SOUNG, I.S. KYE, J. K NO, and B.S. BAEK. "Peroxynitrite -Scavenging Activity of Green Tea Tannin," *J. Agric. Food Chem.*, 46, 4484 (1998).
2. BALUCHNEJADMOJARAD, T. and M. ROGHANI. "Green Tea Polyphenol Epigallocatechin-3-gallate Attenuates Behavioral Abnormality in Hemi-parkinsonian Rat," *Iranian Biomedical Journal*, 10, 203 (2006).
   MANDEL, S.A., Y. AVRAMOVICH-TIROSH, L. REZNICHENKO, H. ZHENG, O. WEINREB, T. AMIT and M.B. YOUDIM. "Multifunctional Activities of Green Tea Catechins in Neuroprotection: Modulation of Cell Survival Genes, Iron-Dependent Oxidative Stress and PKC Signaling Pathway," *Neurosignals*, 14, 46 (2005).
3. ABTS is a chemical compound used to evaluate the antioxidant capacity of a food substance.
   TEAC stands for Trolox equivalent antioxidant capacity, a unit of measurement used to express the results of antioxidant activity caused by the referenced compound, namely Trolox, which is a water-soluble equivalent of vitamin E.

TABLE 7 (continued)

Tea	Family	Producing country	Quantity	Temperature	Length of infusion	Concentration of antioxidants in 1 cup (250 ml)
Tai Ping Hou Kui	Green	China	¹/₆ oz. (5 g)	185°F (85°C)	6 min	1,750 μmoles
Kamairicha	Green	Japan	¹/₆ oz. (5 g)	176°F (80°C)	3.5 min	1,275 μmoles
Darj. Sungma First Flush DJ3	Black	India	¹/₆ oz. (5 g)	203°F (95°C)	3.5 min	1,225 μmoles
Bocha	Green	Japan	¹/₆ oz. (5 g)	176°F (80°C)	3.5 min	1,150 μmoles
Bancha Shizuoka	Green	Japan	¹/₆ oz. (5 g)	185°F (85°C)	4.5 min	1,075 μmoles
Bai Mu Dan Wang	White	China	¹/₆ oz. (5 g)	176°F (80°C)	6 min	1,025 μmoles
Bai Hao	Wulong	Taiwan	¹/₆ oz. (5 g)	203°F (95°C)	6 min	1,025 μmoles
Sheng Pu er Xiangming 2006	Pu er	China	¹/₆ oz. (5 g)	203°F (95°C)	4.5 min	975 μmoles
Xue Ya	Green	China	¹/₆ oz. (5 g)	185°F (85°C)	5.5 min	950 μmoles
Mr. Chang's Dong Ding	Wulong	Taiwan	¹/₆ oz. (5 g)	203°F (95°C)	4.5 min	925 μmoles
Sencha Ashikubo	Green	Japan	¹/₆ oz. (5 g)	167°F (75°C)	3.5 min	900 μmoles
Sencha Isagawa	Green	Japan	¹/₆ oz. (5 g)	167°F (75°C)	3.5 min	875 μmoles
Yunnan Hong Gong Fu	Black	China	¹/₆ oz. (5 g)	185°F (85°C)	4.5 min	875 μmoles
Kabusecha Kawase	Green	Japan	¹/₆ oz. (5 g)	158°F (70°C)	3.5 min	750 μmoles
Shan Lin Xi	Wulong	Taiwan	¹/₆ oz. (5 g)	203°F (95°C)	4 min	750 μmoles
Bai Hao Yin Zhen	White	China	¹/₆ oz. (5 g)	167°F (75°C)	6 min	700 μmoles
Xin Yang Mao Jian	Green	China	¹/₆ oz. (5 g)	176°F (80°C)	3.5 min	700 μmoles
Rou Gui	Wulong	China	¹/₆ oz. (5 g)	203°F (95°C)	6 min	650 μmoles
Assam Banaspaty	Black	India	¹/₆ oz. (5 g)	203°F (95°C)	3.5 min	650 μmoles
Autumn Darj. Sungma DJ480	Black	India	¹/₆ oz. (5 g)	203°F (95°C)	3.5 min	625 μmoles
Organic Nepalese Fikkal	Green	Nepal	¹/₆ oz. (5 g)	185°F (85°C)	3.5 min	575 μmoles
Sencha Tsukigase	Green	China	¹/₆ oz. (5 g)	167°F (75°C)	3.5 min	575 μmoles
Shou Pu er Yongming 2006	Pu er shou	China	¹/₆ oz. (5 g)	203°F (95°C)	4.5 min	575 μmoles
Anxi Tie Guan Yin	Wulong	China	¹/₆ oz. (5 g)	203°F (95°C)	4.5 min	550 μmoles
Organic Huiming	Green	China	¹/₆ oz. (5 g)	185°F (85°C)	4.5 min	500 μmoles
Mucha Tie Guan Yin	Wulong	Taiwan	¹/₆ oz. (5 g)	203°F (95°C)	4.5 min	450 μmoles
Sheng Pu er 1997	Pu er	China	¹/₆ oz. (5 g)	203°F (95°C)	6 min	425 μmoles
Mr. Chen's Ali Shan	Wulong	Taiwan	¹/₆ oz. (5 g)	203°F (95°C)	4.5 min	425 μmoles
Gyokuro Tamahomare	Green	Japan	¹/₆ oz. (5 g)	149°F (65°C)	4.5 min	375 μmoles
Darj. Singell First Flush DJ2	Black	India	¹/₆ oz. (5 g)	203°F (95°C)	4 min	375 μmoles
Shou Pu er 1995	Pu er shou	China	¹/₆ oz. (5 g)	203°F (95°C)	4.5 min	375 μmoles
Sencha Fukamushi Aji	Green	Japan	¹/₆ oz. (5 g)	167°F (75°C)	3.5 min	350 μmoles
Dragon Pearls jasmine	Green	China	¹/₆ oz. (5 g)	185°F (85°C)	3.5 min	175 μmoles

All teas were infused in a teapot with 2 cups (500 ml) of water, except the Matcha which was whisked in a bowl with 100 ml of water.

TABLE 8: Concentration of antioxidants resulting from two successive infusions of four and six minutes compared to the concentration resulting from a single infusion of 10 minutes

Teas	Family	Producing country	Quantity	Temperature	Length of infusion	TEAC concentration in 1 cup (250 ml)
				The four teas were infused in a teapot in 2 cups (500 ml) water. The two successive infusions were made with the same leaves and the single infusion with fresh leaves.		
Lu An Gua Pian	Green	China				
First infusion			1/6 oz. (5 g)	185°F (85°C)	4 min	2,500 µmoles
Second infusion			same leaves	185°F (85°C)	6 min	1,625 µmoles
Single infusion			1/6 oz. (5 g)	185°F (85°C)	10 min	2,925 µmoles
Sencha Asamushi Keikoku	Green	Japan				
First infusion			1/6 oz. (5 g)	167°F (75°C)	4 min	2,375 µmoles
Second infusion			same leaves	167°F (75°C)	6 min	1,025 µmoles
Single infusion			1/6 oz. (5 g)	167°F (75°C)	10 min	2,750 µmoles
Shan Lin Xi	Wulong	Taiwan				
First infusion			1/6 oz. (5 g)	203°F (95°C)	4 min	750 µmoles
Second infusion			same leaves	203°F (95°C)	6 min	1,050 µmoles
Single infusion			1/6 oz. (5 g)	203°F (95°C)	10 min	1,725 µmoles
Darj. Singell First Flush DJ2	Black	India				
First infusion			1/6 oz. (5 g)	203°F (95°C)	4 min	375 µmoles
Second infusion			same leaves	203°F (95°C)	6 min	600 µmoles
Single infusion			1/6 oz. (5 g)	203°F (95°C)	10 min	425 µmoles

TABLE 9: Concentration of antioxidants measured by the ABTS method in Trolox equivalents (TEAC) in two teas infused at various temperatures

Teas	Family	Producing country	Quantity	Temperature	Length of infusion	TEAC concentration in 1 cup (250 ml)
				Both teas were infused in a teapot and 2 cups (500 ml) water. Fresh leaves used for each infusion.		
Organic Huiming	Green	China				
Single infusion			1/6 oz. (5 g)	185°F (85°C)	4.5 min	500 µmoles
Single infusion			1/6 oz. (5 g)	203°F (95°C)	4.5 min	725 µmoles
Gyokuro Tamahomare	Green	Japan				
Single infusion			1/6 oz. (5 g)	149°F (65°C)	4.5 min	375 µmoles
Single infusion			1/6 oz. (5 g)	185°F (85°C)	4.5 min	525 µmoles
Single infusion			1/6 oz. (5 g)	212°F (100°C)	4.5 min	325 µmoles

These analyses lead us to believe that it is usually possible to obtain a higher concentration of antioxidants by increasing the infusion temperature. However, the example of the Gyokuro Tamahomare tea infused at 212°F (100°C) tells us that, in this case, boiling water reduces the concentration of antioxidants.

Following the ABTS-TEAC analyses that allowed us to compare several samples, we pursued our study using two other methods of scientific analysis: the ORAC and HORAC tests. These tests determine whether a food neutralizes the peroxyl and hydroxyl radicals often associated with pathologies of the human body. We should point out that the ORAC test is recognized in the food sector; the HORAC test, because of its innovative character, is less well known.

TABLE 10: Concentration of antioxidants measured by the ORAC method in Trolox equivalents (TEAC)

Teas	Family	Producing country	Quantity	Temperature	Length of infusion	TEAC concentration in 1 cup (250 ml)
			All the teas were infused in a teapot and 2 cups (500 ml) water, except for the Matcha Sendo, which was whisked in a bowl containing a scant ½ cup (100 ml) water.			
Matcha Sendo	Green	Japan	1/20 oz. (1.5 g)	167°F (75°C)	30 sec	3,100 µmoles
Long Jing Shi Feng	Green	China	1/6 oz. (5 g)	185°F (85°C)	6 min	2,425 µmoles
Anji Bai Cha	Green	China	1/6 oz. (5 g)	176°F (80°C)	4.5 min	1,175 µmoles
Kamairicha	Green	Japan	1/6 oz. (5 g)	176°F (80°C)	3.5 min	1,050 µmoles
Darj. Sungma First Flush DJ2	Black	India	1/6 oz. (5 g)	203°F (95°C)	4.5 min	750 µmoles
Mr. Chang's Dong Ding	Wulong	Taiwan	1/6 oz. (5 g)	203°F (95°C)	4.5 min	550 µmoles
Assam Banaspaty	Black	India	1/6 oz. (5 g)	203°F (95°C)	4.5 min	500 µmoles
Sencha Ashikubo	Green	Japan	1/6 oz. (5 g)	167°F (75°C)	3.5 min	425 µmoles
Bai Hao Yin Zhen	White	China	1/6 oz. (5 g)	167°F (75°C)	6 min	300 µmoles
Dragon Pearls jasmine	Green	China	1/6 oz. (5 g)	185°F (85°C)	3.5 min	150 µmoles

As the comparison of these results with those for other foods is not obvious, Graph 2 on the following page presents a comparison of the ORAC antioxidant values of various common beverages. The data used for this table were drawn from the data bank of the United States Department of Agriculture.

GRAPH 2: Comparison of the ORAC values of various common beverages

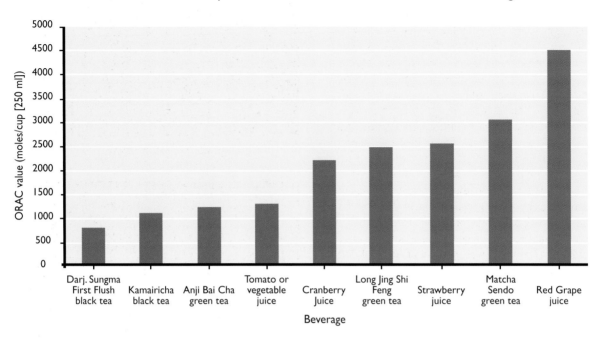

Table 11: Concentration of antioxidants measured by the HORAC method in caffeic acid equivalents (CAE[4])

All teas infused in a teapot and 2 cups (500 ml) water, except for the Matcha, which was whisked in a bowl with a scant ½ cup (100 ml) water.

Tea	Family	Producing country	Quantity	Temperature	Length of infusion	HORAC µmoles CAE/cup 250 ml
Matcha Sendo	Green	Japan	¹/₂₀ oz. (1.5 g)	167°F (75°C)	30 sec	200 µmoles
Long Jing Shi Feng	Green	China	¹/₆ oz. (5 g)	185°F (85°C)	6 min	175 µmoles
Anji Bai Cha	Green	China	¹/₆ oz. (5 g)	176°F (80°C)	4.5 min	175 µmoles
Kamairicha	Green	Japan	¹/₆ oz. (5 g)	176°F (80°C)	3.5 min	150 µmoles
Darj. Sungma First Flush DJ2	Black	India	¹/₆ oz. (5 g)	203°F (95°C)	4.5 min	125 µmoles
Mr Chang's Dong Ding	Wulong	Taiwan	¹/₆ oz. (5 g)	203°F (95°C)	4.5 min	75 µmoles
Assam Banaspaty	Black	India	¹/₆ oz. (5 g)	203°F (95°C)	4.5 min	75 µmoles
Sencha Ashikubo	Green	Japan	¹/₆ oz. (5 g)	167°F (75°C)	3.5 min	25 µmoles
Bai Hao Yin Zhen	White	China	¹/₆ oz. (5 g)	167°F (75°C)	6 min	125 µmoles
Dragon Pearls jasmine	Green	China	¹/₆ oz. (5 g)	185°F (85°C)	3.5 min	0 µmoles

4. CAE (caffeic acid equivalent): A unit of measure that expresses results in relation to the protection offered by the referenced antioxidant, in this case, caffeic acid.

CATECHINS

The protective and anti-cancer powers attributed to tea are mainly due to the presence of a subclass of polyphenic molecules called catechins. These antioxidants come from the metabolism of the tea tree, and they play an important role in the plant's defense. The principal catechins found in tea are catechin (C), epicatechin (EC), epigallocatechin (EGC), epicatechin gallate (ECG) and epigallocatechin gallate (EGCG) (see Figure 1). These elements represent 2 percent to 8 percent of the mass of dried leaves.

The percentage of catechins in tea varies enormously depending on the method of cultivation of the tea trees and the processing of the leaves. As a general rule, black tea contains fewer catechins than green tea because, as green tea does not undergo oxidation, its molecules remain unchanged. That is why we chose to focus our analysis on green teas. For comparison purposes we also analyzed two black teas, a wulong tea and a white tea.

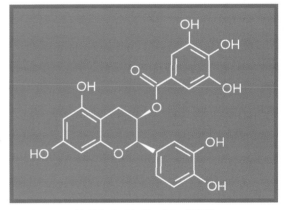

(-)-Epigallocatechin (EGC)

(-)-Epicatechin-3-gallate (ECG)

(-)-Catechin (C)

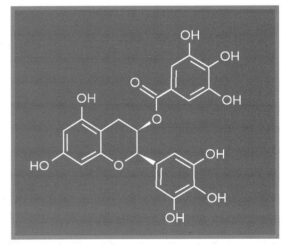

(-)-Epicatechin (EC)

(-)-Epigallocatechin-3-gallate (EGCG)

Figure 1: Principal catechins contained in tea (*Source: Sigma-Aldrich*)

TABLE 12: Concentration of catechins in various infusions

Teas	Family	Infusion conditions	EGCG	EGC	C	EC	ECG
			\multicolumn{5}{c}{Catechins in 1 cup (250 ml) of infusion}
Matcha Sendo	Green	$^1/_{20}$ oz. (1.5 g) in scant $^1/_2$ cup (100 ml) for 30 sec at 167°F (75°C)	98	65	2	21	24
Long Jing Shi Feng	Green	$^1/_6$ oz. (5 g) in 2 cups (500 ml) for 6 min at 185°F (85°C)	60	13	2	8	21
Anji Bai Cha	Green	$^1/_6$ oz. (5 g) in 2 cups (500 ml) for 4.5 min at 176°F (80°C)	47	11	1	4	10
Kamairicha	Green	$^1/_6$ oz. (5 g) in 2 cups (500 ml) for 3.5 min at 176°F (80°C)	33	42	2	10	7
Darjeeling Sungma First Flush	Black	$^1/_6$ oz. (5 g) in 2 cups (500 ml) for 4.5 min at 203°F (95°C)	29	5	1	3	15
Sencha Ashikubo	Green	$^1/_6$ oz. (5 g) in 2 cups (500 ml) for 3.5 min at 167°F (75°C)	18	16	1	6	5
Mr. Chang's Dong Ding	Wulong	$^1/_6$ oz. (5 g) in 2 cups (500 ml) for 4.5 min at 185°F (85°C)	16	18	1	5	5
Dragon Pearls Jasmine	Green	$^1/_6$ oz. (5 g) in 2 cups (500 ml) for 3.5 min at 203°F (95°C)	12	4	1	4	6
Bai Hao Yin Zhen	White	$^1/_6$ oz. (5 g) in 2 cups (500 ml) for 6 min at 167°F (75°C)	3	0	0	1	4
Assam Banaspaty	Black	$^1/_6$ oz. (5 g) in 2 cups (500 ml) for 3.5 min at 203°F (95°C)	2	0	1	1	2

These results confirm the previous findings: teas that showed a high content in the ORAC and HORAC tests are also the highest rated in this analysis.

CONCLUSION

These exploratory tests allowed us to compare different types of teas in order to evaluate their principal virtues. We saw how certain infusion conditions could give rise to significant differences in the concentration of caffeine and antioxidants. The many results obtained for each family of teas showed us, on the one hand, that green teas are not necessarily richer in antioxidants than wulong teas, and on the other hand, that black teas are not necessarily more stimulating than white teas, contrary to certain preconceived ideas in the world of tea.

We also note that Chinese green teas show very good results. Lu An Gua Pian, Long Jing Shi Feng and Anji Bai Cha, three Chinese green teas, demonstrate a high concentration of antioxidants compared to high-quality Japanese Sencha teas.

In the light of all this new data, it appears that tea still has a lot of surprises in store for us and that we are only just beginning to improve our understanding of its beneficial effects. Especially since we know that, from one year to the next, because of varying weather conditions, the regular creation of new cultivars and the constant evolution of growing and processing techniques, the molecular structure of a tea leaf is forever changing. Therefore, we think it wiser to advise the tea enthusiast to choose a tea according to taste and personal preference, giving first priority to sensory pleasure. Therefore, each tea represents a thousand remedies and a thousand pleasures. Remember, it is by savoring various types of tea on a daily basis that we can best profit from the benefits of this mythical drink.

Enjoy!

5. Here is the meaning of the acronyms used to indicate the different types of catechin: EGCG: Epigallocatechin-3-gallate; EGC: Epigallocatechin; C: Catechin; E: Epicatechin; ECG: Epicatechin-3-gallate

BIBLIOGRAPHY FOR THE BIOLOGICAL ANALYSES OF TEA

AGUDO, A., L. CABRERA, P. AMIANO et al. "Fruit and Vegetable Intakes, Dietary Antioxidant Nutrients, and Total Mortality in Spanish Adults: Findings from the Spanish Cohort of the European Prospective Investigation into Cancer and Nutrition" (EPIC-Spain)," *The American Journal of Clinical Nutrition* 85, no. 6 (June 2007): 1634–1642.

BALUCHNEJADMOJARAD, T., and M. ROGHANI. "Green Tea Polyphenol Epigallocatechin-3-gallate Attenuates Behavioral Abnormality in Hemi-parkinsonian Rat," *Iranian Biomedical Journal* 10, no. 4 (2006): 203–207.

CHUNG, H.Y., T. YOKOZAWA, D. SOUNG et al. "Peroxynitrite-Scavenging Activity of Green Tea Tannin," *Journal of Agricultural and Food Chemistry* 46, no. 11 (1998): 4484–4486.

DAI, Q., A.R. BORENSTEIN, Y. WU et al. "Fruit and Vegetable Juices and Alzheimer's Disease: The Kame Project," *American Journal of Medicine* 119, no. 9 (2006): 751–759.

FREI, B., and J.V. HIGDON. "Antioxidant Activity of Tea Polyphenols in Vivo: Evidence from Animal Studies," *Journal of Nutrition* 133, (2003): 3275S–3284S.

GENKINGER, J. M., E. A. Platz, S.C. HOFFMAN et al. "Fruit, Vegetable, and Antioxidant Intake and All-Cause, Cancer, and Cardiovascular Disease Mortality in a Community-Dwelling Population in Washington County, Maryland," *American Journal of Epidemiology* 160, no. 12 (2004): 1223–1233.

JENSEN, G.S., X. WU, K. M. PATTERSON et al. "In Vitro and in Vivo Antioxidant and Anti-inflammatory Capacities of an Antioxidant-Rich Fruit and Berry Juice Blend. Results of a Pilot and Randomized, Doubleblinded, Placebo-Controlled, Crossover Study," *Journal of Agricultural and Food Chemistry* 56, no. 18 (2008): 8326–8333.

MANDEL, S.A., Y. AVRAMOVICH-TIROSH, L. REZNICHENKO et al. "Multifunctional Activities of Green Tea Catechins in Neuroprotection. Modulation of Cell Survival Genes, Iron-Dependent Oxidative Stress and PKC Signaling Pathway," *Neurosignals* 14, no. 1–2 (2005): 46–60.

MARTIN, A., M. SMITH, G. PERRY and J. JOSEPH. "Nutritional Antioxidants, Vitamins, Cognition and Neurodegenerative Disease," *Principles of Gender Specific Medicine*. Edited by Marianne J. Legato, MD. San Diego, CA: Academic Press, 2004: 813–823.

United States Department of Agriculture, Agricultural Research Service, Nov. 2007 http://www.ars.usda.gov/SP2UserFiles/Place/12354500/Data/ORAC/ORAC07.pdf

WEINBERG, B. A and B.K. BEALER. *The World of Caffeine: The Science of the World's Most Popular Drug.* New York, NY: Routledge, 2001.

Index

Acknowledgments

The authors would like to extend their sincere thanks to the following people: Richard Béliveau, François Chartier, Josée di Stasio, Normand Laprise, Christine Lamarche, Charles-Antoine Crête, Stephane Modat, Patrice Demers, Marc-André Jetté, Claude Pelletier, Hubert Marsolais, Masami Waki, Jeff Fuchs, Alexis Bernard, Sébastien Collin, Elsa Marsot, Valérie Roberge, Mathieu Lévesque, Mathieu Dupuis, Kazuyo Fukunishi, Yu Hui Tseng and Fabien Maïolino, Claude Chapdelaine, Ed Behr, James McGuire, Stéphane Erler, Louise Roberge, Mélany Gagnon, Maxime Maheu, Denis Beaumont, Hélène Tremblay, Yolaine Lebeuf, Laurence Cambron Fortin, Julie De Grandmont, as well as all the team at Éditions de l'homme, especially Erwan, Josée, Linda, Céline and Diane. We would also like to warmly thank Marie Henrichon, Annie Tapp, Claudie Pouliot, Marielle Bertin, Nathalie Morrissette and our families. Finally, a very big thank you to the team at Camellia Sinensis, both past and present, to our customers and to our invaluable translators, Yan Xie, Hisako Kobayashi and Pierre Nadeau.

The Camellia Sinensis Team would like to give special thanks to all the craftspeople and the professionals of the tea industry that we have had the pleasure of working with over the years. Their generosity, knowledge and friendship have fueled our passion for tea to this level and without them the whole journey would have been impossible. Thank you!

Special Thanks

Samir Changoiwala and his father, the Mohan family, M. Panjhika, J.P. Gurung, Praveen Periwal, Indi Khanna, Dr. Pathak, Kavi Seth, Krishan Katyal, M. Rai, M. Subba, M. Jah, M. Singh, Sudeep Banherjee, Rajah Banerjhee, M. Bashu and all the generous planters of Darjeeling, Dilan Wijeyesekera, Alexander Kay, Grace Mogambi.

特别感谢
Camellia Sinensis 茶馆的全体成员希望对所有所有茶叶界的手工艺者和专家们致以特别的感谢，在多年的交流中我们乐趣无穷。他们的慷慨，开放，学识和友谊加深了我们对茶的热爱，由于他们，我们的茶业得以昌盛。没有他们，我们的每一步都是不可能的。再次感谢。

郑顺亮・高世和・李传修・林献堂・陈能裕・叶秀资・林贵松・黄正敏・陈世河・徐耀良・
高振盛・张俊宏・陈聪琚・黄正宗・刘天麟・李台强・高肇昀・粘筱燕・彭成国・谢钰臻・
范增平・黄漳沂・张富钦・傅寅斌・谢建华・王喜领・谢曲波・程大福・叶长明・程俊生・
李翠霞・王莉・邓克国・袁辉・黄涛・祝冬娥・李娥媚・张永生・冯艳・吴旺林・刘兵・
林修源・周智修・陈亮・刘栩・傅尚文・彭国定・杨茂旺・黄树炜・陈国义・麦雅琪・
严育梅・王梓光・何卫中・张郑库・胡明・柳荣伟・魏月德・邵胜军・邵建红・唐泽林・
徐云芳・陈长平・王荣欣・张剑

謝辞

カメリアシネンシスチームは、長年にわたり、共に働いてきた、お茶職人の方々、ならびに、茶業界の専門家の方々に対し、心からの感謝の意を表します。一緒に仕事をさせて頂けることを嬉しく思っております。

関係者方々の、寛大さ、知識、そして友情が良い刺激となり、私たちのお茶に対する情熱をこのレベルにまで引き上げてくれました。彼らの協力なしでは、ここまでの道のりを成し遂げることはできなかったことでしょう。ありがとうございました。

谷本 宏太郎・白形 和之・武田 好訓・江塚 恵・小山 直造・小原 志奈子・
小山 俊美・斉藤 克祐・伊澤 勝俊・藤田 和正・杉山 渡・長田 辰美・
福井 伸之・岩田 文明・高柳 直哉・敦賀 弘・吉本 邦弘・中山 雅之

Bibliography

BÉCAUD, Nadia. *Le Tea: la culture chinoise du Tea,* Éditions Stéphane Bachès, 2004.

BLOFELD, John. *Thé et tao: l'art chinois du Tea,* Albin Michel, 1997.

BONHEURE, Denis. *Tea,* Macmillan, The tropical agriculturalist series, Paris, 1990.

BUTEL, Paul, *Histoire du Tea,* Éditions Desjonquères, 2001.

CHAN, Kam Pong. *First Step to Chinese Puerh Tea,* Wushing Books, 2006.

CHOW, Kit, and Ione KRAMER. *All the Tea in China,* China Books, 1990.

COLLECTIF. *China: Homeland of Tea,* 1994.

COLLECTIF. *Tea for two: les rituels du Tea dans le monde,* Crédit Communal, 1999.

MACFARLANE, Alan, and Iris MACFARLANE. *The Empire of Tea,* The Overlook Press, 2003.

DELMAS, François-Xavier, Mathias MINET and Christine BARBASTE. *Le guide de dégustation de l'amateur de Tea,* Chêne, 2007.

FISHER, Aaron. *Tea Wisdom,* Tuttle Publishing, 2009.

GAUTIER, Lydia. *Le Tea: arômes et saveurs du monde,* Aubanel, 2005.

HEISS, Mary Lou, and Robert J. HEISS. *The Story of Tea: A Cultural History and Drinking Guide,* Ten Speed Press, 2007.

HUETS DE LEMPS, Alain. *Boissons et civilisations en Afrique,* Presses Universitaires de Bordeaux, 2001.

KAKUZO, Okakura. *Le livre du Tea,* Éditions Philippe Picquier, 1996.

LU, YU. *Le cha jing ou le classique du Tea,* Jean-Claude Gawsewitch Éditeur, 2004.

MONTSEREN, Jean. *Guide de l'amateur de Tea,* Éditions Solar, Paris, 1999.

SCALA, Olivier, and Marie GRÉZARD. *Teas: cultures, senteurs, saveurs,* Éditions Solar, 2005.

SOSHITSU, Sen. *Vie du Tea, esprit du Tea,* Jean-Cyrille Godefroy, 1998.

UKERS, William H. *All About Tea,* Hyperion Press, 1935 (réédition 1999).

WANG, Ling. *Le Tea et la culture chinoise,* Éditions Langues étrangères, 2006.

Photo Credits

Locations

In Montreal's Latin Quarter
351 Emery
H2X 1J2
Tel.: 514.286.4002

Beside Montreal's Jean-Talon market
7010 Rue Casgrain
H2S 3A4
Tel.: 514.271.4002

In Quebec's Saint-Roch Quarter
624 Rue Saint-Joseph E
G1K 3B9
Tel.: 418.525.0247

www.camellia-sinensis.com